BERTHE MORISOT

Impressionist

BERTHE MORISOT

Impressionist

CHARLES F. STUCKEY *and* WILLIAM P. SCOTT

with the assistance of SUZANNE G. LINDSAY

HUDSON HILLS PRESS, NEW YORK

Mount Holyoke College Art Museum in Association with the National Gallery of Art

This exhibition is supported by a generous contribution from Republic National Bank of New York and Banco Safra, S.A., Brazil.

First Edition

©1987 by the Mount Holyoke College Art Museum and the National Gallery of Art.

Published in the United States by Hudson Hills Press, Inc., Suite 1308, 230 Fifth Avenue, New York, NY 10001-7704.

Distributed in the United States, its territories and possessions, Mexico, and Central and South America by Rizzoli International Publications, Inc.
Distributed in Canada by Irwin Publishing, Inc.
Distributed in Australia by Bookwise International.
Distributed in Japan by Yohan (Western Publications Distribution Agency).

Editor and Publisher: Paul Anbinder
Index: Gisela S. Knight
Designer: Betty Binns Graphics/Martin Lubin
Composition: U.S. Lithograph, typographers
Manufactured in Japan by Toppan Printing Company

Library of Congress Cataloguing-in-Publication Data

Stuckey, Charles F.
    Berthe Morisot, Impressionist.

    Bibliography: p.
    Includes index.
    1. Morisot, Berthe, 1841–1895—Catalogues. 2. Morisot, Berthe, 1841–1895—Influence—Catalogues. 3. Art, French —Catalogues. 4. Art, Modern—19th century—France —Catalogues. 5. Impressionism (Art)—France—Catalogues. I. Scott, William P., 1956–   . II. Lindsay, Suzanne G., 1947–   . III. Mount Holyoke College. Art Museum. IV. Title.
N6853.M64A4   1987   759.4   87-3265

ISBN 0-933920-03-2 (alk. paper)

Berthe Morisot
Impressionist

National Gallery of Art, Washington
6 September–29 November 1987

Kimbell Art Museum
12 December 1987–21 February 1988

Mount Holyoke College Art Museum
14 March–9 May 1988

The exhibition is supported by an indemnity from the Federal Council on the Arts and the Humanities.

Contents

This book is dedicated to the memory of Denis Rouart (1908–1984).

List of Colorplates

Foreword

Since the 1974 centennial of the first Impressionist exhibition, there has been a wealth of new scholarship devoted to nearly every aspect of this movement. To date, however, there still has not been a major retrospective of the work of one of the founders of Impressionism, Berthe Morisot. No other nineteenth-century artist is more deserving of serious reconsideration. Until her untimely death at the age of fifty-four in 1895, Morisot's art was held in the highest regard by her avant-garde colleagues with whom she spearheaded a revolution in taste during the 1870s and 1880s. Nevertheless, her works are often overlooked even today. This retrospective, organized by the Mount Holyoke College Art Museum in association with the National Gallery of Art, Washington, D.C., assesses Morisot's place within Impressionism and establishes her in the vanguard of that movement.

In 1983 Elizabeth Topham Kennan, President of Mount Holyoke College, and C. Douglas Lewis, Curator of Sculpture at the National Gallery of Art and member of the Art Advisory Committee of the Mount Holyoke College Art Museum, greatly admired the painting *Hide and Seek* by Berthe Morisot then hanging in the exhibition *The John Hay Whitney Collection* at the National Gallery of Art. The upcoming sesquicentennial of Mount Holyoke College was uppermost in their minds, and they were struck by the extraordinary achievement of Morisot as they were discussing the legacy of Mary Lyon and her own accomplishment as the founder of this college for women. From that serendipitous event, this superb retrospective of Morisot's works was developed by the Mount Holyoke College Art Museum.

It is fitting that *Berthe Morisot—Impressionist* should open at the National Gallery of Art because four of its greatest patrons, Mr. Whitney, Chester Dale, Ailsa Mellon Bruce, and Paul Mellon, were pioneering collectors of her work. In fact, no other collectors have had a greater commitment to the work of Morisot than Mr. and Mrs. Mellon. Their perspicacity as connoisseurs and generosity as lenders are very evident in this exhibition.

Many other private and institutional lenders, chief among them the Rouart family, have magnanimously lent to this retrospective. Their wonderful cooperation has made it possible for us to assemble Morisot's greatest works, and to all of them we extend our deepest gratitude.

A great many people worked for many years to ensure the success of this exhibition. We wish to thank all those on the staffs of our own institutions who contributed to this effort. Those most responsible for this reassessment of Morisot's work are the authors of this book, William P. Scott, Suzanne G. Lindsay, and most especially Charles F. Stuckey. The entire scholarly community owes them a debt, not only for the important details about Morisot's career that are uncovered here but also for establishing for her a rightful place of leadership within the modern movement. We would also like to thank Paul Anbinder and the staff of Hudson Hills Press for the production of this book. *Berthe Morisot—Impressionist* has received major funding from Republic National Bank of New York and Banco Safra, S.A., Brazil, for which we are extremely grateful. Finally, we wish to acknowledge generous support from the National Endowment for the Arts and from the Federal Council of the Arts and Humanities, which provided an indemnity for the foreign loans.

J. CARTER BROWN
Director
National Gallery of Art

EDMUND P. PILLSBURY
Director
Kimbell Art Museum

T. J. EDELSTEIN
Director
Mount Holyoke College Art Museum

Acknowledgments

Without the good will and in some cases the tireless dedication of many friends and colleagues, the organization of this exhibition and the preparation of its catalogue would hardly have been possible. My friend Teri J. Edelstein, director of the Mount Holyoke College Art Museum, asked me in 1983 if I would organize a retrospective devoted to Berthe Morisot. Too unfamiliar with Morisot's art to feel comfortable about accepting this challenge, I gave her the name of the person who knows the subject best, William P. Scott, a painter who lives in Philadelphia. I knew about him thanks to a mutual friend, Suzanne G. Lindsay, an art historian with a special interest in the American painter Mary Cassatt, Morisot's fellow Impressionist. When Dr. Lindsay and Mr. Scott agreed to take active roles in the project, I decided to make the commitment.

After years of devoted study, encouraged by the late Denis Rouart, William Scott knew where to go to find almost all of Morisot's pictures, and with his own working experience as a painter, he opened our eyes to the finesse and idiosyncrasy of Morisot's techniques and challenged us to take account of questions too often unasked by historians and curators. Suzanne Lindsay took charge of the field research, exhausting both public and private archives to compile the wealth of hitherto unstudied documentary information that became the foundation for my text and the exemplary notes that she supplied to bolster it. The three of us wish to extend deep thanks to the following individuals who helped with documentation, the negotiation of loans, and the realization of this exhibition and catalogue.

Most of all this retrospective required the wholehearted cooperation of the descendants of Morisot and her family, whose wealth of knowledge and hospitality sustained our work from the very beginning. No amount of thanks seems sufficient for Mrs. Denis Rouart, Mr. and Mrs. Clément Rouart, Dr. and Mrs. Julien Rouart, Mr. Jean-Michel Rouart, Ms. Françoise Rouart, Mr. and Mrs. Yves Rouart, Mrs. Agathe Rouart-Valéry, Mr. and Mrs. Jacques Fischer, and Mr. Jean-Dominique Rey.

We are, moreover, deeply indebted to individuals on the staffs of the three participating museums. At the Mount Holyoke College Art Museum: Teri J. Edelstein, Director;

Sean B. Tarpey, Registrar; Wendy M. Watson, Curator; Amy M. Wehle, Business Manager; and Anne Rogers, Curatorial Assistant. At the Kimbell Art Museum: Edmund P. Pillsbury, Director; William B. Jordon, Deputy Director; and Peggy Buchanan, Registrar. And at the National Gallery of Art, Washington, D.C.: J. Carter Brown, Director; John Wilmerding, Deputy Director; Sydney Freedberg, Chief Curator; Andrew Robison, Senior Curator and Curator of Graphic Arts; Daniel Herrick, Treasurer; D. Dodge Thompson, Chief of Exhibition Programs; Ann M. Bigley, Cameron Castiel, and Cheryl Hauser, Exhibition Officers; Gaillard Ravenel, Chief of Installation and Design; Mary Suzor, Registrar; Anne Halpern, Associate Registrar; Ira Bartfield, Chief, Photographic Services; Richard Amt, Head of Photography Laboratory, Rae Bayer, and the staff of the Photography Laboratory; Anne von Rebhan, Slide Librarian, and the staff of the Slide Library; Elizabeth A. Croog, Associate General Counsel; Elizabeth A. C. Weil and Al Viebranz, Corporate Relations; Neil T. Turtell, Acting Chief Librarian; Ted Dalziel and Thomas F. J. McGill, Jr., Librarians; David Brown, Curator of Southern Renaissance Painting; Nicolai Cikovsky, Jr., Curator of American Painting; Jack Cowart, Curator of Twentieth-Century Painting; Franklin W. Kelly, Assistant Curator of American Art; Nan Rosenthal, Curator of Twentieth-Century Painting; Annette Schlagenhauff, Research Assistant, Twentieth-Century Painting; David Bull, Head of Painting Conservation; Ann Hoenigswald, Conservator; J. Russell Sale, Head of Education; Eric Denker and Wilford W. Scott, Staff Lecturers; and Laura Smith, Development Office. Special thanks are extended to the staff of the Department of Modern Painting: Florence E. Coman, Assistant Curator; David Cateforis, Summer Intern, 1986; Darcy Gallucio, Secretary, and Amy Mizrahi, Research Assistant, both of whom contributed greatly to the research and editing of the catalogue; and Nancy J. Iacomini, Exhibitions Assistant, who devoted long hours to the orchestration of every phase of this enterprise.

We also wish to single out the talented professionals associated with Hudson Hills Press, thanks to whom the exhibition catalogue has become a beautiful book that will delight Morisot's admirers for years to come: Paul Anbinder, President; Jane Fluegel, editor; and Betty Binns and Martin Lubin, designers. The following archivists, art dealers, and scholars, whose efforts on our behalf went way beyond routine professional courtesies, also deserve to be singled out here: Caroline Godfroy and France Daguet, Durand-Ruel & Cie, Paris; Guy and Michel Dauberville, Galerie Bernheim-Jeune, Paris; Waring Hopkins, Galerie Hopkins-Thomas, Paris, along with Delphine Montalant, Alain Clairet, and Yves Rouart, who are preparing a new catalogue raisonné of Morisot's works in every medium; Chittima Amornpichetkul and Anne Higonnet, both preparing doctoral dissertations on Morisot; Kathleen Adler and Tamar Garb, who have just prepared a new English edition of Morisot's correspondence and a new monograph on her art; Jane Roberts, who has prepared an English edition of Julie Manet's *Diary*; Janine Bailly-Herzberg; Juliet Bareau; John Rewald; and Frances Weitzenhoffer.

Finally, Suzanne Lindsay, William Scott, and I take pleasure in acknowledging the invaluable help of these colleagues: William Acquavella, Acquavella Galleries, New York; Louise d'Argencourt; Martha Armstrong; E. Digby Baltzell; Jan C. Baltzell; Rutgers Barclay, Barclay Fine Art, Inc., New York; His Grace, the Duke of Beaufort, Marlborough Fine Art Ltd., London; Sylvie Béguin, former Chief Curator, Department of Paintings, Louvre, Paris; Marie Theres Berger; Ruth Berson, Associate Curator, The Fine Arts Museums of San Francisco; Philippe Brame, Galerie Brame-Lorenceau, Paris; Richard R. Brettell, Searle Curator of Paintings, The Art Institute of Chicago; Harry Brooks, Wildenstein & Co., New York; Françoise Cachin, Director, Musée d'Orsay; Victor Carlson, Senior Curator of Prints and Drawings, Los Angeles County Museum of Art; Beverly Carter; Michael Clarke, Assistant Keeper, National Gallery of Scotland, Edinburgh; Sylvie Clément; Micheline Colin; Aline Dardel; François Daulte, President, Hermitage Foundation, Lausanne; Philip Diotallevi, Wildenstein & Co., New York; W. Daniel Donahue; Douglas Druick, Prince Trust Curator of the Department of Prints and Drawings, The Art Institute of Chicago; Anne Dumas, Assistant Curator, Department of European Paintings and Sculpture, The Brooklyn Museum; Jack Eckert; Mark L. Evans, Assistant Keeper, National Museum of Wales, Cardiff; Arlene Feaster; Richard Feigen, Richard L. Feigen and Co., New York; David Fertig; Michael Findlay, Christie's, New York; Jay McKean Fisher, Curator of Prints, Drawings, and Photographs, The Baltimore Museum of Art; Iona Fromboluti; Marc Gerstein, Co-Chairman, Art Education Program, Toledo Museum of Art; Dennis Gillespie; Eileen Goodman; Paul Grimes; Margrit Hahnloser-Ingold; Lynn W. Hanke, Acquavella Galleries, New York; Michel Hoog, Chief Curator, Musée de l'Orangerie, Paris; Melissa Hough; John House, Courtauld Institute (University of London); Ay-Whang Hsia, Wildenstein & Co., New York; Paul Josefowitz; Samuel Josefowitz; Beverly Keefer; Ellen Melas Kyriazi; Leanna Lee-Whitman; Olivier Legrand; Timothy Lennon, Conservator, The Art Institute of Chicago; Nancy Little, Librarian, M. Knoedler & Co., New York; Barbara Lyons, Harry N. Abrams, Inc.; Mary McClean; Suzanne Folds McCullagh, Associate Curator of Prints and Drawings, The Art Institute of Chicago; Gayle McDaniel; Alexandra McLean; Nancy M. Mathews, Associate Professor of Art History, Randolph Macon Woman's College, Lynchburg, Virginia; Roger Marcel Mayou, Adjunct Curator, Musée d'Art et d'Histoire, Fribourg; Achim Moeller, Achim Moeller Fine Art Ltd., New York; Charles S. Moffett, Curator-in-Charge, Department of European Paintings, The Fine Arts Museums of San Francisco; Alexandra R. Murphy, Curator of Paintings, Sterling and Francine Clark Art Institute, Williamstown; Rose Naftulin; Travers Newton, Conservator, Williamstown Regional Art Conservation Laboratory, Inc., Williamstown; Adolfo Nanclares, Minister of Cultural Affairs, Embassy of Argentina, Washington, D.C.; Mary Nomecos; Michael Olszewski; Mrs. Jean Paysant; Ivan Phillips; Jane Piper; Joseph Rishel, Curator, Philadelphia Museum of Art and the John G. Johnson Collection, Philadelphia; Robert Schmit, Paris; Susan Schussler; George Shackelford, Associate Curator, European Painting, Museum of Fine Arts, Houston; Mrs. Charles Slatkin; Katherine Solander, Assistant Curator, Department of Education, The Cleveland Museum of Art; Susan A. Stein, Exhibitions Coordinator, Department of European Paintings, Metropolitan Museum of Art, New York; N. Lee Stevens; Michel Strauss, Sotheby's, London; John L. Tancock, Sotheby's, New York; Bruce Thompson; Brad Thorstensen; Dean Walker, Curator, Ackland Art Museum, Chapel Hill; Richard J. Wattenmaker, Director, Flint Institute of Arts, Michigan; Shirley Watts; Gabriel and Yvonne Weisberg; Rolf Westad; Angela Westwater; Nancy Whyte, Christie's, New York; Heidi Williams; Fronia E. Wissman; Peter Zegers, Visiting Curator, Department of Prints and Drawings, The Art Institute of Chicago.

CHARLES F. STUCKEY

BERTHE MORISOT

Impressionist

Berthe Morisot

Monday, March 2, 1896, was the first anniversary of the death of Berthe Morisot, the doyenne of avant-garde French art, who had been among the founders of the revolutionary Impressionist movement. The artist's only child, seventeen-year-old Julie Manet, visited the family tomb at the Passy cemetery, where the fragility and delicate tones of some early blossoming white azaleas seemed —according to her diary—to symbolize the essentials of Morisot's brushwork and color harmonies. "My ambition is limited to the desire to capture something transient, and yet, this ambition is excessive," the painter had written in one of her sketchbooks.[1] Leaving the cemetery, Julie crossed Paris to the Durand-Ruel gallery on the rue Laffitte. More than four hundred paintings, pastels, watercolors, drawings, and sculptures by Morisot were arranged around the gallery floor, propped against deep-red velvet walls, in preparation for a memorial retrospective exhibition.[2] Four old friends were there to supervise the installation: the artists Claude Monet (1840–1926), Pierre-Auguste Renoir (1841–1919), and Edgar Degas (1834–1917); and poet Stéphane Mallarmé (1842–1898), who had written the preface to the catalogue. No exhibition in the history of art has ever had a more distinguished installation committee.

For three consecutive days they debated what to include and how best to arrange the pictures; whether the works on paper should be integrated with the oils or presented as a separate group in a back room. Degas favored integration and urged the others to place the works on paper on a large portable panel that could be moved into the main exhibition room. "These drawings are superb," Degas argued, "I value them on a par with all these paintings."[3] Morisot, for whom conventional distinctions between different mediums were largely irrelevant, might well have sided with the contentious Degas had she been there. In the end, however, the panel was removed, because the others wanted to insure ample room for spectators to stand back from the paintings. When scrutinized at close range, Morisot's feathery brushstrokes often appear arbitrary, even disjointed; but observed from a few feet away, they coalesce as if by magic and describe light-saturated atmospheres with brisk accuracy. Of course, Morisot's best pictures are remarkable descriptions of far more than superficial appearances, since they suggest the enveloping experience of space and the feeling of reverie sustained by color and light. Renoir advocated placing an ottoman in the middle of the room to encourage visitors to savor the works at leisure.

It was Julie's job to label the pictures with the numbers assigned to them in the exhibition catalogue. As she did so, she made notes about dates, sitters, and owners; most of the works had been made well before she was aware of her mother's genius, many before she was born.[4] Transcribed into her diary, these notes would eventually become the basis for a fully illustrated catalogue of Morisot's paintings, pastels, and watercolors (but not, *pace* Degas, the drawings, prints, and sculptures), a project undertaken twenty-odd years later with the celebrated dealer Ambroise Vollard (1868–1939).[5] Stalled for long intervals, the project was finally realized in 1961, thanks to the ef-

FIGURE 1

Photograph of Julie Manet at age sixteen, 1894. Private collection, France.

forts of Marie-Louise Bataille and Georges Wildenstein, only five years before Julie's death. Along with the edition of correspondence between Morisot and her family and friends, which was published by Julie's youngest son, Denis Rouart (1908–1984), in 1950, this catalogue begun in 1896 is an invaluable contribution to the history of Impressionism. Neither publication, however, does much to explain the development of Morisot's approach to art or to the place of her pictures within the history of Impressionism as a whole. These subjects provide the rationale for this catalogue and exhibition, which reassemble a considerable number of the works first exhibited in Morisot's honor in 1896.

There are many reasons for the relative neglect of Morisot by collectors and historians since 1896, what we now call sexist attitudes chief among them. But simple chauvinism aside, insufficient and sometimes incorrect in-

formation about her career and her works and infrequent opportunities to see them have diminished curiosity for nearly a century. Like most modern biographies, Morisot's is shaped largely by what the subject herself concealed from posterity. Since she apparently destroyed all but about two dozen of the works she executed before reaching the age of thirty, her crucial formative years can only be reconstructed in a vague way—and with considerable guesswork.

Berthe Morisot was born in Bourges on January 14, 1841.[6] She had two older sisters, Yves (1838–1893) and Edma (1839–1921), and a younger brother, Tiburce (born c. 1848).[7] Her father was a high-ranking civil servant who moved his family from one provincial capital to another as he changed posts. Then, around 1852, they finally settled in Passy, on the western outskirts of Paris.[8] At the end of this very year Louis-Napoleon Bonaparte (1808–1873), who had been elected to a four-year term as President in 1848, was proclaimed Emperor Napoleon III, thus inaugurating eighteen years of unprecedented economic expansion for France and its capital city. Berthe Morisot grew up watching the dramatic transformation of Paris in the hands of the Emperor's chief regional administrator, Georges Haussmann (1809–1891).[9] Haussmann had a mandate to make the French capital a new imperial Rome, the most spectacular city in the world, with a network of grand boulevards radiating outward from its center, connecting its modern railroad stations, imposing municipal buildings, and stylish squares and parks. It was thanks to Haussmann that the unspoiled landscape of the ancient Bois de Boulogne (figure 2), just beyond Passy, became an enormous park for Parisians. Beginning in the 1870s this romantic natural interlude in the urban fabric was one of Morisot's favorite spots in which to paint and draw.

As a rejoinder to the Great Exhibition of 1851 in London, Napoleon III began to organize an even more ambitious World's Fair that would be held in Paris with elaborate pomp in 1855 as a symbol of France's new prosperity, progressivism, and international political power. The vast exhibition complex commissioned for the Champs Elysées included the imposing iron and glass Palais des Beaux-Arts by Hector-Martin Lefuel (1810–1880). The centerpiece of the World's Fair, this magnificent building housed the large, prestigious survey of contemporary art sponsored by the government's Fine Arts Ministry and known as the Salon.

It is likely that the Morisots would have been among the more than nine hundred thousand visitors to this exhibition, which included several major retrospectives, one of them honoring France's leading Neoclassical painter,

Jean-Dominique Ingres (1780–1867), and another, his lifelong rival, Eugène Delacroix (1798–1863), the leader of the Romantic school. To further stress state support for artists of all ideologies, the Emperor personally awarded decorations, medals, and honorable mentions to nearly five hundred artists. A first-class medal was bestowed on Rosa Bonheur (1822–1899), the celebrated woman painter, whose *Hay Making in Auvergne* was bought from the exhibition by the state for its museum of contemporary art at the Palais du Luxembourg. Moreover, after decades of struggle for acceptance by Salon officials, Camille Corot (1796–1875), the veteran landscape painter who would later agree to supervise the artistic development of the Morisot sisters, received a second-class medal, and the Emperor acquired for his private collection Corot's *Souvenir of Marcoussis*.

FIGURE 2

Felix Bracquemond, *The Bois de Boulogne*
Etching. 24.3 x 18.4 cm (9⁹⁄₁₆ x 7¼ in.). The George A. Lucas
Collection of the Maryland Institute, College of Art, on
indefinite loan to The Baltimore Museum of Art, BMA
1933.53.4632.

From a later vantage point, it is no less noteworthy that a controversial younger painter named Gustave Courbet (1819–1877) staged his own independent exhibition in competition with the official Salon of 1855 after the unusually nonpartisan admissions jury had rejected the largest two of his submitted paintings. Advocating Realism in art in the spirit of Honoré de Balzac (1799–1850) and Charles Baudelaire (1821–1867), Courbet based his art on familiar scenes from modern life. A bold challenge to the prevailing traditions of idealistic classicism and exotic romanticism, Courbet's modern-life paintings rallied the support of a new generation of maverick artists, including Edouard Manet (1832–1883), Degas, and Monet, all of whom took Realism as a guiding principle in the following decade. The Impressionist movement, which in the 1870s Morisot would be instrumental in shaping by her participation in a series of independent exhibitions outside of the official Salon, was in effect the direct outgrowth of Courbet's rebellious enterprise in 1855.

That same year Morisot's father, who had studied to become an architect as a young man, took a new position as senior counsel at the national accounting office.[10] Not long afterward, Mme Morisot decided as a surprise for her husband on his birthday to have their young daughters study painting with a private master. The scant information about Morisot's art and music lessons is based on recollections recorded nearly seventy years later by her brother, Tiburce, who would have been no more than nine years old when the birthday surprise was engineered.[11] According to Tiburce, their teacher, Geoffroy-Alphonse Chocarne (b. 1797), an advocate of the Neoclassical style of Ingres, rued the growing popularity of Delacroix, whose lively, boldly colored brushwork was heretical to the sort of disciplined drawing Chocarne stressed to his new students.[12]

Their teacher's lessons quickly seemed dull to the Morisots, and Yves lost interest altogether. Since the venerable state-sponsored Ecole des Beaux-Arts was closed to women altogether until 1897, a different private teacher remained the only recourse.[13] The Morisots now turned to Joseph Guichard (1806–1880), who lived nearby in Passy; Edma and Berthe found him inspirational.

Guichard had also studied with Ingres at the Ecole des Beaux-Arts but subsequently renounced the Italianate classical heritage for the bravura romanticism of Delacroix.[14] By the early 1840s Guichard had received commissions for several large projects for public buildings and churches, including Notre-Dame-de-Grâce, Passy, in the Morisots' parish. He had shown portraits and history paintings at the Salons on a regular basis since the early 1830s, but for

FIGURE 3

FIGURE 3

Paule Gobillard Painting [BW 208], 1887
Oil on canvas. 86 x 94 cm (33⅞ x 37 in.). Private collection.

unknown reasons he stopped showing there altogether after 1853. In general, little is known about Guichard, except that he told amusing stories and took special interest in beginning artists.[15] If it were not for Guichard, the engraver Félix Bracquemond (1833–1914), who like Morisot would take part in the independent Impressionist exhibitions from the outset in 1874, might never have taught himself to become an artist. After Guichard left Paris in 1862 to join the faculty of the municipal art school in his native Lyons, he made several modern-life paintings, and in 1868 he initiated a drawing school for women there.

According to Tiburce, his sisters' first sessions with Guichard were limited to riveting lectures about art, followed by visits to the Louvre to instill reverence for masterpieces and the ambition to excel. Guichard then taught them the basics in the traditional manner by having them draw after plaster casts of celebrated classical statues. Just this sort of classroom accessory appears in a nostalgic series of oils and pastels that Berthe Morisot made thirty-odd years later, showing her nieces, Paule and Jeanne Gobillard, and her daughter, Julie, at easels in their apartment (e.g., figure 3).

Tiburce recalled Guichard's fervor as a teacher, describing with considerable drama the artist's admonition to the girls' mother once he had gauged their potential:

Given your daughters' natural gifts, it will not be petty drawing-room talents that my instruction will achieve; they will become

painters. Are you fully aware of what that means? It will be revolutionary—I would almost say catastrophic—in your high bourgeois milieu. Are you sure you will never one day curse the art, once allowed into this household, now so respectably peaceful, that will become the sole master of the fate of two of your children?[16]

Undeterred by this warning, Mme Morisot allowed her daughters to continue, and by March 19, 1858, they were evidently working in oils, for they were granted permission to copy old-master paintings at the Louvre.[17]

Scores of students and independent artists registered to make such copies as a way of understanding the compositional and technical subtleties of celebrated masters of the past (figure 4). There is no way to know how often Berthe went there, since the Louvre's records of copyists' admission cards, valid for a full year, are incomplete. Two are recorded under her name, one for 1858 and another for 1865.[18] But Morisot's first biographer, Armand Fourreau, without citing his evidence, dates the only two surviving early copies, both after large, complex religious pictures by Veronese, as 1860 (*The Crucifixion*, BW 2) and 1861 (*Christ in the House of Simon*, BW 3).[19]

Why she selected these particular works for study or why of all her early museum copies she eventually decided to preserve these alone is unclear. Nor is it known why in 1884, as a fully developed painter, Morisot returned to the Louvre to make a copy after a work by François Boucher, which she hung in a prominent position above the mantelpiece of her own living room (see colorplate 62).

FIGURE 4

Winslow Homer, *Art Students and Copyists in the Louvre Gallery*, 1867
Wood engraving, published in *Harper's Weekly*, Jan. 11, 1868.

Copyists at the Louvre often introduced themselves to one another, and according to Fourreau, in 1859 Morisot not only met Bracquemond there, but his colleague Henri Fantin-Latour (1836–1904) as well.[20] A self-taught artist like Bracquemond, Fantin disavowed the regimenting principles taught at the Ecole des Beaux-Arts. Although this was several years before he became a regular member of the Morisot family's social circle, Fantin may have explained his individualistic ideas to Edma and Berthe upon meeting them.

The jury for the Salon of 1859 rejected the works of so many artists, including Edouard Manet, that police had to disperse a demonstration by the angry painters. Fantin, who was among those spurned by the Salon jury, exhibited his works in protest at the studio of François Bonvin (1817–1887) in April, along with rejected works by his still unacclaimed colleague James McNeill Whistler (1834–1903).[21]

Fantin's enthusiasm for the controversial teaching methods of Horace Lecoq de Boisbaudran (1802–1897) may be what led Edma and Berthe to request lessons in plein-air (outdoor) painting from Guichard.[22] Unprepared to give such instruction himself, Guichard introduced the Morisots to Achille Oudinot (1820–1891), a disciple and friend of the famous landscape painters Camille Corot and Charles Daubigny (1817–1878). Oudinot, in turn, presented the sisters to Corot.[23]

No living French artist was better known around 1860–61, when this introduction was made, than the peripatetic "Papa" Corot, whose works ranged from decorative Arcadian landscapes staged with all the artifice of a ballet performance to informal topographical "portraits" of the Italian and French countryside. His works had been presented at the Salons since the heyday of Romanticism in 1827. Too informal by Ecole des Beaux-Arts standards, his art was above all predicated on capturing impressions, the initial awareness of light-triggered sensory stimuli prior to mental categorization of any sort.

As early as 1849 Corot began to exhibit unpretentious "studies" executed in one quick session before the impression of his subject had lost any freshness. For most critics, such pictures were no better than the undistinguished exercises of a beginner still incapable of modulating adjacent patches of color or smoothing away traces left by the brush. For Corot's partisans, however, his studies were little miracles of truth, as bright as the outdoors, thanks to just a few simple colors, heightened or subdued in value by mixing them with more or less white pigment. Morisot inherited directly from Corot not only her blond palette and her delight in undisguised brushwork, but also a predi-

lection for small landscape studies with simply rendered little figures and, most important, an aspiration to observe the world with utter innocence. "Every day I pray that the Good Lord will make me like a child," Corot said. "That is to say, that He will make me see nature and render it the way a child would, without preconceptions."[24] Morisot would express this same hope quite literally by painting little children who are awestruck by the colors and shapes around them.

Still, although Corot sometimes dined at the Morisots' home, how often or where he instructed them is unrecorded.[25] He reputedly was opposed to teaching in any formal sense and seldom allowed admirers and collectors to see him at work in his studio.[26] All that is recorded in Morisot family legend is that Corot lent Edma and Berthe several of his own paintings to copy.[27]

With Corot in the picture, Morisot family summer vacations often became expeditions to informal artists' colonies where plein-air painting was the first order of business. For example, in 1861 the girls evidently went to Ville d'Avray, the town where Corot's family had its country house, located on the Seine about eight miles west of Paris, and the following summer they toured the Pyrenees along the Spanish border.[28]

Although the studies Corot submitted to the Salon of 1863 were accepted by the jury, vehement controversy arose because about three-fifths of the works submitted by some five thousand artists were rejected. To quell the outrage, the Emperor proclaimed an unprecedented alternative Salon des Refusés for artists at odds with official taste. Bracquemond and Fantin were among the refused artists, as was the future Impressionist Camille Pissarro (1830–1903); but it was Whistler, with his *Woman in White*, and Manet, with his shocking *Déjeuner sur l'herbe*, who were singled out for derision.

A few months after this landmark event in the history of modern art, the Morisots went off to a rented farmhouse at Le Chou, a picturesque village on the Oise River, and there the sisters began paintings for their Salon debut the following year.[29] Oudinot was a neighbor, as was the celebrated painter Charles Daubigny. Evidently the Morisots were especially impressed with the studio boat from which Daubigny painted riverside motifs (figure 5).[30] In subsequent years, both sisters would follow his example and paint in small boats, despite the fact that sudden movements from swells could and sometimes did jar their painting hands.

Sadly, it seems that at most only one of the landscapes submitted by the Morisots to the Salon of 1864 and accepted by the jury may have survived, a competent river

FIGURE 5

Jean-Baptiste-Camille Corot, *Daubigny Working on His "Botin" near Auvers-sur-Oise*, 1860
Oil on canvas. 24.5 x 34 cm (9⅝ x 13⅜ in.). Formerly Knoedler Galleries, New York.

FIGURE 6

Jean-Baptiste-Camille Corot, *Souvenir of Mortefontaine*, 1864
Oil on canvas. 64.8 x 88.9 cm (25½ x 35 in.). Musée d'Orsay, Paris.

scene by Edma in the manner of Corot. Even though the Morisots, unlike Pissarro, did not describe themselves as students of Corot in the Salon catalogue (instead they listed Guichard and Oudinot as their teachers), the title listed for one of Berthe's works—*Souvenir*, or "memory"—is likewise in his manner, suggesting reverie or poetic license more than Realist description.[31] Corot himself, who was an elected member of the jury that year, exhibited *Souvenir of Mortefontaine* (figure 6), which was bought by the state for the Palais du Fontainebleau.

At least two newspaper art columnists covering the Salon mentioned the sisters' works briefly, noting the obvious influence of Corot.[32] A letter written to Edma and Berthe later that year by the sculptor Aimé Millet (1819–1891) reveals that, given their earnest commitment to absolute originality, they were far more upset than pleased by such comments. He had seen several of their works at Oudinot's studio, as the sisters did not yet have one of their own:

Oudinot talked about the so-called reproach against you for making Corots. First of all, that is not entirely true; furthermore what seems like a reproach is praise as we see it . . . how and why at their age do [the Morisot sisters] hope not to be anyone's "daughters." Was not Raphael the "son" of Perugino? Distinguished men have always been the children of their masters until years of work and experience allow them to blossom in turn and become themselves.[33]

This brief excerpt from Millet's letter, the earliest indication of Morisot's self-critical mentality, may help to explain why most of her works from the 1860s were destroyed.

To be fair, given Corot's protean innovations in composition and color, his influence was nearly impossible to avoid in the 1860s, and Morisot was not the only beginning landscape painter to despair.[34] In 1864, for example, both Pissarro and Monet, Morisot's future Impressionist colleagues, were also faced with the predicament posed by the Corot heritage. Writing from Normandy in October 1864 to his fellow student Frédéric Bazille (1841–1870), Monet, who would exhibit at the Salon for the first time in 1865, described three recent paintings, commenting: "You may perhaps find a certain connection with Corot, but if so it is entirely without imitation of any sort." He noted that "the motif and above all the calm hazy effect" are the only similarities, but added that he had worked "as conscientiously as possible, without thinking of any [other] painting. Moreover, you know that that is not my way of doing things."[35]

The year 1864 was important for more than the Morisot Salon debut. That year Berthe's father was promoted to chief counsel at the state accounting office, and the family moved to the opposite side of the rue Franklin, still in Passy. Although they were simply renting the property, they began construction of a studio in the garden for Edma and Berthe, whose professional ambitions by now justified this considerable expense.[36]

When Mme Morisot responded to a rental advertisement for a summer house in the Normandy beach village of Beuzeval, she initiated a close friendship with a veteran figure painter, Léon Riesener (1808–1878).[37] He was a grandson of the master cabinetmaker Jean-Henri Riesener (1734–1806) and first cousin to Delacroix, whose towering achievements were widely discussed in Paris in 1864, following the auction of his estate in February and a large memorial exhibition in August.

One of Riesener's daughters, Rosalie (b. 1860), following family tradition, was getting ready for her own debut at the Salon of 1865. Early that year Morisot and Rosalie Riesener registered with the Louvre for permission to copy large allegorical paintings by Peter Paul Rubens, the artist most admired by the latter's father.[38] Moreover, Morisot now copied several chapters of Riesener's unpublished writings on a wide variety of historical, stylistic, and technical topics: "Drawing with color," "The theory of the influence of physical nuances arising from the effect of daylight on the chemical colors of objects," "The importance of color," and so on.[39] As for Riesener's own works, his landscapes and portraits in pastel may perhaps have stimulated Morisot to try that medium.

Thanks to the Rieseners, the Morisots met Adèle d'Affry (1836–1879), the young Swiss widow of the Duke of Castiglione Colonna; her debut under the pseudonym Marcello at the Salon of 1863 marked her as one of the most promising sculptors of the new generation.[40] Caught in Marcello's spell, Morisot took lessons in sculpture for a few months from Millet.[41] As might be expected, no early work in this new medium has survived either. In turn, Morisot posed for Millet, who had been commissioned to execute architectural decorations for an apartment house on the Seine at 14, quai de le Mégisserie. Her profile was incorporated in one of the Muse medallions on the cornice.[42] Like Marcello, Millet received an important commission in connection with the construction of the new Paris Opéra designed by Jean-Louis-Charles Garnier (1825–1898) in 1860 and finally completed fifteen years later. It was Millet who introduced the Morisots to the celebrated composer Gioacchino Rossini (1792–1868), who was enough taken with Berthe's musical talents to choose a piano for her—and even to autograph it.[43]

Morisot's earliest exhibited figure painting, included in the Salon of 1865, was called *Etude* ("Study"; colorplate 1) in the catalogue. As one critic implied, this modest title, which Corot often used to describe landscape impressions, is not especially appropriate for a painting of a young reclining woman, dressed in classical fashion in a loose white robe, who pensively regards her own reflected image in a quiet stream.[44] Accented by an intense red ribbon, Morisot's figure contrasts sharply with the deep-green setting, suggesting that she may have painted them independently of one another. Many artists did so out of expediency, to avoid the costs of transporting a model from Paris to the countryside and lodging her for the several weeks necessary to finish the painting. Referring to Manet, Emile Zola (1840–1902) remarked in 1867 that the challenge of painting figures in an outdoor setting was every painter's "dream," but the Morisot sisters found it no less difficult to fulfill than did their male colleagues.[45] Later, in 1869, when Berthe admired Bazille's *Village View* at the Salon, she wrote to Edma: "He has tried to do what we have so often attempted—a figure in the outdoor light —and this time he seems to have been successful."[46] *Etude*, however, is the only known example of the sisters' efforts in this vein before 1869.

As a newcomer to figure painting, Morisot kept the pose and gestures as simple as possible, but several details in *Etude* foreshadow characteristics of her later works: the pinpoints of color in the foreground to suggest flowers, the careful attention to the distant view, and, most of all, the delicate interplay of white on white, here between fabric and flesh. The somewhat clumsy handling of the bodice is clearly the result of repainting, perhaps by Morisot herself but possibly by a later, more prudish hand. According to Morisot's mother, although the painting was well lighted at the Salon, it lacked its numbered label and so viewers could not identify the artist or the title by consulting the catalogue.[47]

Given Morisot's strong reaction the previous year to the suggestion that she painted like Corot, it comes as a surprise that she would undertake a subject so nearly identical to several works by him[48] and that newspaper critics did not again refer to his influence. Since the only comparable dated pictures with reclining figures by Corot are both inscribed 1865, it is altogether possible that Corot now decided to show his admiration for Morisot by developing her compositional idea (figure 7). An undated etching by Bracquemond (figure 8) is likewise so close in concept to Morisot's *Etude* that it can be understood either as an inspiration for it or as an *hommage* after it.

Morisot also exhibited a still life at this Salon. Now lost, it showed the corner of a table with a cauldron, a candlestick, and a box of radishes, according to a description in a review of the exhibition.[49] Edma, who exhibited a still life and a Normandy landscape at the Salon of 1865, also began to attempt figures around this time. Presumably Edma's sober portrait of Berthe (figure 9), a red ribbon in her hair, standing before her easel with brushes

FIGURE 7

Jean-Baptiste-Camille Corot, *The Secret of Love*, 1865
Oil on canvas. 50 x 68 cm (19¾ x 33¾ in.).

FIGURE 8

Felix Bracquemond, *Nymph Reclining at the Edge of the Water*, c. 1864
Etching. 19.5 x 18.9 cm (7¹¹⁄₁₆ x 7⁷⁄₁₆ in.). The George A. Lucas Collection of the Maryland Institute, College of Art, on indefinite loan to The Baltimore Museum of Art, BMA 1933.53.4636.

and palette, should be dated around 1865, when the sisters were working in their own newly completed studio.

The most hotly debated figure painting of 1865 was, of course, Manet's shocking nude *Olympia*, a parodistic modern-life version of Titian's venerated *Venus of Urbino*. "Abuses rain upon me like hail," Manet wrote to Baudelaire, and indeed guards were needed to protect the painting from vandals at the Salon before officials decided to move it to an obscure position high on the wall of the same *M* room where Morisot's *Etude* was hanging.[50] Since the *Olympia* controversy goes unmentioned in what survives of the Morisot family correspondence from this year, however, claims that Manet had by now already made their acquaintance seem unlikely.[51]

The Morisot family summered on the Normandy coast at the Petites Dalles in 1865, not too far from the Rieseners in Beuzeval. They evidently also visited the northern coast of Brittany around Dinard, for at the Salon of 1866 Edma exhibited a view of the Rance estuary there at low tide. Both titles listed under Berthe's name in the catalogue for that Salon indicate Normandy subjects. One of these, *La Bermondière (Orne)*, now lost, was a small painting of a stream.[52] The other, *Thatched Cottage in Normandy* (colorplate 2), is Morisot's first masterpiece, one of the very earliest harbingers by any painter of the Impressionist style of the 1870s.

Striped nearly from top to bottom by nine or ten slender tree trunks that form a screen between the immediate foreground and the ostensible subject, the farmyard in the distance, this abstract modern composition is in no way indebted to the example of her teachers or colleagues.[53] Seeking to evoke the experience of being immersed in space, Morisot accented the foreground with calligraphic

FIGURE 9

Edma Pontillon, *Berthe Morisot Painting*, c. 1865
Oil on canvas. 100 x 71 cm (39⅜ x 27¹⁵⁄₁₆ in.). Private collection.

COLORPLATE 1

Study, 1864
Oil on canvas. 60.3 x 73 cm (23¾ x 28¾ in.). Mr. and Mrs. Fred
Schoneman.

wisps of white paint to indicate uncut grass so near at
hand that the eyes cannot focus on it sharply. And higher
up, at both the left and right, jabs of dark paint indicate
the leaves of trees and brush intruding from just behind
or beyond her visual field.

Although some biographers claim that the Morisot sisters went back to Brittany in the summer of 1866, no surviving painting by either Edma or Berthe documents such
a trip.[54] Instead, one of Edma's two paintings in the Salon
of 1867 showed a view of the Channel coast at Houlgate,
suggesting that she may have spent the previous summer

in Normandy; Berthe's only picture in the Salon depicted
moored barges on the Seine below the Pont d'Iéna with a
bit of the skyline of Paris in the background (figure 10).[55]
Since she usually had two paintings ready for each Salon,
it may be that she suffered her first jury rejection that year.

Although the tower visible in the background to the
left of center in this picture represents the French light-
house erected as an attraction for the 1867 World's Fair,
Morisot's cityscape is hardly a celebration of this topical
event. There was in fact an impressive view of the festive
fairground architecture much closer to home, and just such
a "guidebook" view was painted in June by Manet (figure
11).[56] By now the Morisots knew this most controversial of

COLORPLATE 2

Thatched Cottage in Normandy, 1865
Oil on canvas. 46 x 55 cm (18⅛ x 21⅝ in.). Private collection.

contemporary French artists, for a letter from Mme Morisot to Edma refers to the independent exhibition of Manet's works staged at his own expense beginning in late May on the place de l'Alma, a relatively short distance from the fair and the Morisot residence.[57] This letter, full of art-world gossip, particularly reveals the extent to which the Morisots had become part of the avant-garde milieu: Mme Loubens, whose portrait Degas would paint, had overheard Fantin admit that he had once been enamored of Edma, whom he understood to be disinterested in marriage; and Mme Loubens overheard Manet express admiration for Edma's work, which he had seen at an art-dealer's shop. Unfortunately there is no record of the specific pic-

tures Edma and Berthe had begun to place on consignment with the dealer Alfred Cadart (1828–1875), who had already shown works by Bracquemond and Manet.[58]

Mme Morisot, to judge from her letters, was constantly concerned about Edma's and Berthe's marriage plans—or rather the lack of them. Their sister, Yves, had finally wed on December 1, 1866. Her husband, Théodore Gobillard (1833–1879?), a tax collector in Quimper, had lost an arm serving in the army in the controversial Mexican campaign.[59] Just such current political issues were debated at the Morisots' Tuesday soirées, which were attended by an increasing number of eminent bachelors, including the lawyer Jules Ferry (1832–1893), who would become mayor

FIGURE 10

The Seine below the Pont d'Iéna [BW 11], 1866
Oil on canvas. 51 x 73 cm (20 x 31 in.). Private collection.

FIGURE 11

Edouard Manet, *The World's Fair of 1867*, 1867
Oil on canvas. 108 x 196.5 cm (42½ x 11⅛ in.). Nasjonalgalleriet, Oslo.

of Paris in 1870, then minister of public instruction and fine arts in 1879, and premier in the early 1880s. According to the recollections of Tiburce Morisot, his father provided Ferry with accounting-office statistics to help expose the danger posed by the municipal debt brought about by Haussmann's grandiose urban-renewal projects.[60] Published as the *Comptes fantastiques de Haussmann* in 1867–68, this blatant attack on the government enhanced Ferry's growing political reputation.[61]

Art was no less an issue than politics at these dinners, and Morisot developed a romantic attachment to one of the painters who frequented them, Pierre Puvis de Chavannes (1824–1898), a veteran Salon artist, who since 1861 had received widespread praise and important commissions for public murals.[62] She may even have first met her future husband, Manet's younger brother Eugène (1834–1892), at one of these soirées. It was Edma, however, who now became engaged: to Adolphe Pontillon (1832–1894), a naval officer who had known Manet since they served together as cadets in 1848.[63]

As a result, the sisters took their last joint summer painting expedition in 1867, visiting Yves and Théodore in Brittany, where Berthe painted a view of Roz-Bras (figure 12), her single entry at the Salon of 1868 but not necessarily the only work she submitted to the jury. Although this scene was painted from the bank of the Pont-Aven River, letters sent to Roz-Bras from Mme Morisot indicate that the sisters were also working in Daubigny's manner from a boat, one that rocked too much. "Imagination is all very well," was her advice, "but not when it makes things more difficult," adding: "I can see Berthe's sneering and annoyed expression as she says to me: 'Why don't you take the brush yourself?'"[64]

Mme Morisot took advantage of her daughters' absence from Passy to houseclean their studio:

I am frightened by what I have done. I have hung the canvases in the studio. Your father says that you will undo my work the moment you come back, and your brother says that you will be justified in doing so, because I ought not to meddle in other people's business. For my part I think that it is even less the proper business of Louis [family butler?] to pile up helter-skelter all those luckless canvases, some of which are torn, and to efface drawings by crowding them in among the paintings; yet he has to clean the place, and it is somebody's business to put a little order into this grand mess.[65]

FIGURE 12

The Pont-Aven River at Roz-Bras [BW 12], 1867
Oil on canvas. 55 x 73 cm (21⅜ x 28⅞ in.). Mr. and Mrs. Joseph Regenstein, Jr., Chicago, Illinois.

This letter is the only sure indication that Berthe worked on drawings during these years, since few if any surviving works on paper date from before 1870.

Although most critics ignored the Morisots in their reviews of the Salon of 1868, one who at least mentioned them was Emile Zola, the brilliant and controversial novelist who had become Manet's staunchest advocate. Possibly it was Manet who drew Zola's attention to the Morisots' works, for by now the sisters were regulars at the Manets' Thursday soirées, where they met, among others, Zacharie Astruc (1835–1907), the Hispanophile writer and critic; Alfred Stevens (1828–1906), the Belgian genre painter of domestic modern-life scenes, whose enormous popular success contrasted sharply with Manet's failure to win general acceptance; and Edgar Degas, who abandoned his early ambitions to become a celebrated history painter when he was seduced by Manet's modern ideas around 1865.[66] Despite the fact that Morisot, as a woman, was unable to participate in the polemical debates about modern art that took place at the Café Guerbois, she would quickly become altogether familiar with the major issues from conversations with Manet and the others, whether at her own family's soirées on Tuesdays, the Stevenses' on Wednesdays, or the Manets' on Thursdays.

To be sure, the sisters' professional ambitions at first met with sexist skepticism, exemplified by comments in a letter from Manet to Fantin in August 1868: "I quite agree with you, the Mlles Morisot are charming. Too bad they're not men. All the same, women as they are, they could serve the cause of painting by each marrying an academician, and bringing discord into the camp of the enemy."[67] At first the men were more interested in Morisot as a potential model than as a colleague. For example, she evidently sat for Stevens, whose informal bust-length portrait (figure 13), broadly rendered in the manner of Frans Hals, was inscribed in 1868 as a gift to Manet, for whom she also agreed to pose in the fall of this same year.[68] Although modeling was a good way for her to learn firsthand about the studio methods of both Stevens and Manet, it took a great deal of time, which may help to explain why Morisot herself made no submission to the Salon of 1869.

Ironically, Manet, whose foremost goal was to work spontaneously, without preliminary drawings and oil studies, was notorious for making endless revisions as he developed his figure paintings. Morisot and her fellow volunteers, the landscape painter Antoine Guillemet (1842–1918) and the violinist Fanny Claus (1846–1877), learned for themselves how well deserved Manet's reputation was when they agreed to pose for his painting *The Balcony* (figure 14), a parodistic version, set in Haussmann's

Paris, of a genre painting by Goya. Describing Manet's progress, Mme Morisot wrote: "Antoine says [that Manet] has made him pose fifteen times, with no likeness to show for it, that Mlle Claus looks terrible, but that both, exhausted from standing in the pose, declare, 'It's perfect, no improvement needed!'... Manet appears quite mad, he is confident of a great success, then suddenly doubts assail him and he turns moody."[69] In Manet's completed picture, the models all appear to be bored from the ordeal of posing. Yet, precisely because the figures ignore one another, *The Balcony* captures a true-to-life moment in an unprecedented way, with the humorous suggestion that an awkward pause may be an especially accurate document of any everyday event.

While posing at Manet's studio, Morisot would have observed the evolution of his brilliant portrait of his wife, a shimmering study in whites (figure 15).[70] Since Morisot's own portrait of Marguerite Carré in pinks (BW 31) so closely follows Manet's example, it probably should be

FIGURE 13

Alfred Stevens, *A Portrait of a Young Lady*, 1868
Oil on canvas. 55 x 39 cm (21⅝ x 15⅜ in.). National Gallery of Ireland, Dublin.

considered a simple exercise and dated late 1868. Marguerite Carré and her sister Valentine, who lived down the street from the Morisots, were friendly with the noted Dr. Blanche, whose seven-year-old son Jacques-Emile (1861–1942) visited them while this portrait was in progress. He recalled later how in true Manet fashion Berthe wiped out each day's efforts in dissatisfaction, and thus the portrait took months to finish.[71]

Morisot was no less aware of Puvis's hopes and self-doubts as he prepared for the Salon of 1869. Visiting his studio with her mother, she would have seen *Marseilles: Gateway to the Orient* in progress (figure 16).[72] Asked later about the genesis of this mural, commissioned for the new municipal museum in Marseilles, Puvis explained the false starts that preceded his final composition, with its view of the busy port from the deck of a ship "cut in half by the frame [that] forms the foreground." Morisot's own special enthusiasm for depicting port scenes was very likely stimulated by listening to Puvis's deliberations.

FIGURE 15

Edouard Manet, *Reading*, 1868
Oil on canvas. 61 x 74 cm (24 x 29¼ in.). Musée d'Orsay, Paris.

FIGURE 14

Edouard Manet, *The Balcony*, 1868
Oil on canvas. 169 x 125 cm (66½ x 49¼ in.). Musée d'Orsay, Paris.

FIGURE 16

Pierre Puvis de Chavannes, *Marseilles: Gateway to the Orient*, 1868
Oil on canvas. 98.1 x 146.3 cm (38⅝ x 57⅝ in.). The Phillips Collection, Washington, D.C.

In the weeks preceding the Salon opening, the Morisots prepared for Edma's marriage on March 8, 1869.[73] Yves, who had just moved from Quimper to Mirande in the southwest of France, would presumably have returned to Paris for the wedding. In any case, she was in Passy that spring, after Edma's departure for the Brittany port of Lorient, where her naval-officer husband was stationed. Without Edma, her closest friend and professional confidante, Berthe turned increasingly to such new colleagues as Manet, Degas, Puvis, and Stevens for support.

When the Salon of 1869 opened at the beginning of May, Puvis's painting, displayed at the top of the entrance staircase, was generally disliked.[74] Manet's *The Balcony* was, of course, on display in the *M* room: "I am more strange than ugly," Berthe reported to Edma, adding that to many viewers Manet's portrait of her suggested a "femme fatale."[75]

As for the works by Corot and Daubigny at the Salon, she admitted to Edma, "the landscapes bore me."[76] Determined for the present to develop her skills as a figure painter, Morisot now planned to do a portrait of her mother and Yves in their garden, but this project never came to fruition. Family letters indicate that still-life painting also intrigued Morisot during the next months.[77] The only early still life to survive, however, is a broadly rendered, unfinished study of peonies (figure 17), closely related to a group of pictures that Manet painted in 1865.[78]

FIGURE 18

Edgar Degas, *Portrait of Yves Gobillard*, 1868
Pastel on paper. 48 x 30 cm (19 x 11¹³⁄₁₆ in.). The Metropolitan Museum of Art, Bequest of Joan Whitney Payson, 1975.

FIGURE 17

Peonies, c. 1869
Oil on canvas. 32.9 x 15.2 cm (12¹⁵⁄₁₆ x 6 in.). From the Collection of Mr. and Mrs. Paul Mellon, Upperville, Virginia.

Edma envied Berthe's intimacy with these modern masters: "Your life must be charming at this moment, to talk with M. Degas while watching him draw, to laugh with Manet, to philosophize with Puvis."[79] Degas, who dedicated himself to painting portraits of women during the latter 1860s, persuaded Yves to pose for him at the rue Franklin, and the Morisots all watched as, disregarding Manet's dogma of spontaneity, he made a preliminary pencil study and then a pastel sketch of Yves's head alone (figure 18) in order to guide his work on a larger oil version developed later in his own studio. When Degas showed his pastel study of Yves at the Salon of 1870, Morisot called it a masterpiece.[80] Curiously, neither Degas nor Morisot posed with Manet's other friends early in

COLORPLATE 3

The Harbor at Lorient, 1869
Oil on canvas. 43.5 x 73 cm (17⅛ x 28¾ in.). National Gallery of
Art, Washington, D.C., Ailsa Mellon Bruce Collection, 1970.

1869 for the large group portrait in homage to Manet that Fantin was already preparing with the Salon of 1870 in mind.

Morisot visited her sister Edma in Lorient from early June until no later than early August (see figure 19), returning with two small oil paintings that were very well received by her new associates. In *The Harbor at Lorient* (colorplate 3), Edma is seated on a stone parapet, shading herself with a parasol and looking down into the water. When Puvis commented that Morisot had accurately rendered the details of the nautical architecture in this picture, she admitted that her brother-in-law had helped with advice. Manet so admired the painting that Morisot immediately gave it to him.[81] Later that same summer, when Manet and his family took a vacation in Boulogne, he himself painted a group of port pictures, quite probably in response to Morisot's present.

Many of Morisot's most successful pictures, as here, would record both the pleasure of scrupulous observation and the very different pleasure of reverie. Described in

minute detail, with the boats that satisfied Puvis's need for exactitude and the milling townspeople on the far bank, the port scene in the middle distance is suspended between two interactive fluid fields of light blue rippled with white: the bright, cloud-streaked sky and the calm, reflecting water. The water's dappled surface is what holds Edma's attention as she rests on the parapet, removed from the bustling activity in the distance, a counterpart to the painter herself observing the enthralling fabric of colors mirrored in the water. The figure of Edma is a tour de force of brushwork, her long white dress modeled with broad, dissolving strokes of pale pink and pale violet, dotted with purple at the hem and collar. Although the parapet is the most proximate object in Morisot's composition and ought logically to have been described with precision, she rendered it most freely of all, scumbling and smudging grays and browns. It is in this nearly incoherent flurry of paint that Morisot decided to place her signature.

29

Meanwhile Morisot set to work on a portrait of "the little Delaroches," about whom nothing is known, save their reluctance to pose outdoors in the garden.[84] Whether or not Morisot ever completed this project is open to debate. Although a curious painting called *Two Seated Women* (colorplate 5) has often been associated with the Delaroche double portrait, the women depicted are hardly "little." Furthermore, the two figures are dressed in identical fashion and have virtually identical and inert features. Yet nothing suggests that the Delaroches were twins. Even if they were, would Morisot have stressed their resemblance to the point of caricature? Or should this picture, closely related to the portrait of his wife that Manet painted in 1868 (figure 15), be understood as a sort of parody, with the same model posed twice in defiance of common sense?

The second painting that Berthe brought back from Lorient, *Young Woman at a Window* (colorplate 4), is hardly less remarkable. Alone with her thoughts, Edma sits in an easy chair that has been rolled up to a French window, opened to a view across the street. There, with tiny strokes of paint, Morisot indicates green awnings and figures at their windows. Since Edma ignores the view to regard a painted fan in her lap, however, her presence near the window seems merely to be for the benefit of the painter, intent on recording the play of daylight on a long white dress. Although Morisot's little picture contains narrative genre-scene elements arranged in the manner of Stevens, it is painted far more loosely than Stevens's works, and the peculiar lack of gesture, facial expression, and significant props creates a mood that recalls the awkward silence in Manet's *Balcony*.

By coincidence, Manet had begun a similar, albeit much larger, painting of a seated woman in a long white dress (figure 20) while Morisot was at Lorient. His enthusiasm for his model, a young painter named Eva Gonzalès (1849–1883), clearly annoyed both Morisot and her mother, who were amused if not pleased by Manet's inability to get his new sitter's face right, even after forty attempts.[82] Projecting his own frustrations, Manet even urged Morisot to rework the face and the hem of the dress in her little picture of Edma.[83]

COLORPLATE 5

Two Seated Women, c. 1869–75
Oil on canvas. 52.1 x 81.3 cm (20½ x 32 in.). National Gallery of
Art, Washington, D.C., Gift of Mrs. Charles S. Carstairs, 1952.

The striking, superficial similarities between the figures notwithstanding, they are painted in two quite different manners, the figure on the left in thin paints, that on the right with loaded brushes. Could Morisot have done the first and some other artist the second? Moreover, the right-hand figure sits on a chair that is placed incongruously where it could not fit, given the presence of the sofa upon which her counterpart sits. Such a bizarre detail suggests the influence of Manet, who humorously sprinkled his works with analogous illogical details to debunk the ideal of strict Realism.[85] The back of this chair, highlighted behind the figure where a shadow should be and darkened

COLORPLATE 4

Young Woman at a Window (The Artist's Sister at a Window), 1869
Oil on canvas. 54.8 x 46.3 cm (21⅜ x 18¼ in.). National Gallery
of Art, Washington, D.C., Ailsa Mellon Bruce Collection, 1970.

at the right where light should strike it, is no less irrational. Even so, the carefully orchestrated sequence of tones from dark to light, modulated by an olive scarf draped over the chairback, is hardly accidental.

Unfortunately, the framed fan represented on the background wall, a present to Morisot from Degas, cannot be dated and thus establish a *terminus ante quem* with which to date this "double portrait."[86] The fan's presence here, however, documents an intriguing rapport between Degas and Morisot about which little is known. Another example of this rapport is the striking similarity between some of the panoramic coastal landscapes that Degas made, presumably around 1869, and a no less Whistlerian pastel by Morisot, *Boats at Dawn* (colorplate 6), which is generally dated 1864, evidently on stylistic grounds, although a later date seems more likely. There is no written document to suggest, however, that Degas and Morisot ever worked together in Normandy.

COLORPLATE 6

Boats at Dawn, c. 1869
Pastel on paper. 19.7 x 26.7 cm (7¾ x 10½ in.). Mr. and Mrs.
Richard A. Hess.

For the Salon of 1870, Morisot undertook a large double portrait of her mother and Edma. Consciously or unconsciously, she relied for the general composition of *Mme Morisot and Her Daughter Mme Pontillon* (colorplate 7) on works by Fantin-Latour, perhaps because Edma, to whom Morisot apparently gave the painting, deeply admired him.[87] Among the pictures that Fantin was preparing for the same Salon was a double portrait of his future wife and sister-in-law, which he called *Reading* (figure 21), as if to stress its genre overtones. Yet despite the similarities between these two artists' paintings, including the subdued facial expressions, Morisot's is flooded with light from a window, the reflection of which appears in a mirror visible behind Edma's head, while Fantin's records a dim

filtered light, slightly reminiscent of old-master paintings with darkened coats of varnish.

Just prior to sending her paintings to the Salon admissions jury in March 1870, Berthe allowed Manet to critique them, and her irrepressible colleague got carried away as he tried to improve her large double portrait. Morisot reported the incident in a letter to Edma:

COLORPLATE 7

*Mme Morisot and Her Daughter Mme Pontillon
(The Mother and Sister of the Artist),* 1869–70
Oil on canvas. 101 x 81.8 cm (39½ x 32¼ in.). National Gallery
of Art, Washington, D.C., Chester Dale Collection, 1963.

FIGURE 21

Henri Fantin-Latour, *Reading*, 1870
Oil on canvas. 97 x 127 cm (38³⁄₁₆ x 50 in.). Calouste Gulbenkian
Foundation, Lisbon.

He found it very good, except for the lower part of the dress.
He took the brushes and put in a few accents that looked very
well; mother was in ecstasies. That is where my misfortunes
began. Once started, nothing could stop him; from the skirt he
went to the bust, from the bust to the head, from the head to
the background. He cracked a thousand jokes, laughed like a
madman, handed me the palette, took it back; finally by five
o'clock in the afternoon we had made the prettiest caricature
that was ever seen. The carter was waiting to take it away [to
the Salon admissions jury]; he made me put it into the hand-
cart, willy-nilly. And now I am left confounded. My only hope
is that I shall be rejected. My mother thinks this episode funny,
but I find it agonizing.[88]

In trying to help, Mme Morisot aggravated the situation,
as she in turn explained to Edma:

[Berthe] grieves and worries me; . . . and it seems that I made
matters worse by telling her that the improvements Manet
made on my head seemed to me atrocious. When I saw her in
this state, and when she kept telling me that she would rather
be at the bottom of the river than learn that her picture had
been accepted, I thought I was doing the right thing to ask
for its return. I have got it back, but now we are in a new
predicament: won't Manet be offended? He spent all Sunday
afternoon making this pretty mess, and took charge himself of
consigning it to the carter. It is impossible to tell him that the
entry did not get there in time, since your little sketch from
Lorient went with it. It would be puerile to tell this to anyone

but you; but you know how the smallest thing here takes on the
proportions of a tragedy because of our nervous and febrile
dispositions, and God knows I have endured the consequences.[89]

In the end they decided to resubmit the picture,[90] but
art critics, even those well disposed to Morisot, such as
Manet's supporter Théodore Duret (1838–1927), paid it no
heed in their Salon reviews. This odd oversight suggests
that the journalists were aware of Manet's contribution to
Morisot's painting and wished to avoid a sensitive issue.
Manet had gained a reputation for overreacting to negative comments after he challenged the supportive critic
Edmond Duranty (1833–1880) to a duel in February 1870.[91]
In any event, Manet's unsolicited collaborator's role is
clearly visible in the painting as it appears today. The bold

FIGURE 22

Photograph of Berthe Morisot. Private collection.

FIGURE 23

FIGURE 23

Edouard Manet, *Repose*, 1870
Oil on canvas. 148 x 113 cm (58¼ x 43¾ in.). Museum of Art,
Rhode Island School of Design, Providence, Bequest of Mrs.
Edith Stuyvesant Vanderbilt Gerry.

FIGURE 24

Caricatures of Manet's portrait of Berthe Morisot at the Salon
of 1873 by, left to right, Bertall, "Revue comique du Salon,"
Illustration, 24 May 1873; Cham, "Le Salon pour rire," *Charivari*,
23 May 1873; and Cham, "Promenade au Salon des Réfusés,"
Charivari, 8 June 1873.

Goya-like treatment of Mme Morisot's face, her long, sum-marily defined fingers, and the broadly painted expanse of her black dress are all far closer in style to other works of Manet than to Morisot's own.

Fortunately, this incident in no way ruptured their friendship. In early May 1870, Manet pressed Morisot to act as go-between in persuading her Passy neighbor Valentine Carré to pose for him;[92] it has been presumed that he set to work that summer on a painting of Valentine called *In the Garden* (see figure 26), the composition of which in turn is assumed to have influenced Morisot's subsequent work. Since the identification of the sitter for Manet's painting is a matter of some debate, however, and since it was not among the works that Manet sent to Duret for safekeeping in September 1870, *In the Garden* may actually have been done the following summer instead, after Morisot had already developed the same pictorial idea.[93] A large painting that Manet did send to Duret in September was a portrait of Morisot seated casually on a dark red sofa (figure 23).[94] Called *Repose* when it was finally exhibited at the Salon of 1873 (figure 24), this picture, with its sweeping brushwork, especially in the long white dress, may have been painted in reaction to Duret's review of the Salon of 1870 in which he praised Stevens for popularizing a new type of genre painting based on solitary female figures with as little personality as dolls.[95] Predicated for the most part on an obsession with the visual splendors of billowy Second Empire dresses, explained Duret, Stevens's genre pictures never included male figures with their relatively conservative haberdashery. Whether or not Manet sought to rival Stevens at his own game, *Repose* must have taken most of Manet's time from May to September of 1870—and a good deal of Morisot's as well.

It is unknown whether either Manet or Morisot left Paris to vacation that summer. Presumably many vacation plans were postponed, for on July 19 France declared war on Prussia over an insignificant diplomatic slight. Dispatched with the Imperial army to Metz, Tiburce Morisot was taken prisoner by the Prussians (although he escaped in January).[96] On September 2 the French forces were humiliated near Sedan, and the Emperor was captured. Scornful of his defeat at the hands of the Germans, a mob of Parisians voted Napoleon III out of office and established a republic committed to mobilizing the National Guard to defend their city. Art stopped suddenly, as Parisian families fled the quickly advancing enemy troops for safety outside the capital. Manet, for example, sent his mother, wife, and stepson away to Bordeaux, and it was then that he asked Duret to store his paintings.

Disregarding advice from her parents and from Manet to escape before the Prussians encircled Paris and laid siege, Morisot wrote to Edma in September:

I have made up my mind to stay, because neither father nor mother told me firmly to leave; they want me to leave in the way anyone here wants anything—weakly, and by fits and starts. For my own part I would much rather not leave them, not because I believe that there is any real danger, but because my place is with them, and if by ill luck anything did happen, I should have eternal remorse. I will not presume to say that they take great pleasure in my presence; I feel very sad, and am completely silent. . . . The house is dreary, empty, stripped bare; and as a finishing touch father makes inexplicable and interminable removals. He seems to be very much occupied with the preservation of some old pieces of furniture of the First Empire. . . . The militia are quartered in the studio, hence there is no way of using it.[97]

Communication with family members outside Paris was difficult. Mail service functioned irregularly, relying upon the help of courageous balloon aviators and pigeons, which Puvis would memorialize in allegorical paintings (figure 25). Puvis immediately joined the National Guard, as did Bracquemond, Stevens, Manet, and Degas, who found himself under the command of his former schoolmate, Henri Rouart, thus renewing a friendship that would directly affect Morisot after the war.

Located relatively close to the German lines outside the perimeter of Paris, Passy was an especially frightening place to stay. The constant noise of the bombardments overwhelmed Morisot, as did the hunger and cold when rations ran out and when, with the onset of a particularly severe winter, there was no fuel for heat. Her health never fully recovered from these privations.[98]

FIGURE 25

Pierre Puvis de Chavannes, *The Carrier Pigeon*, 1871
Oil on canvas. 136.5 x 84 cm (53¾ x 33 in.). Musée d'Orsay, Paris.

The new year, celebrated by a visit of the Manet brothers to the rue Franklin, brought no respite.[99] "The bombardment never stops," wrote Mme Morisot on January 8, 1871. "It is a sound that reverberates in your head night and day; it would make you feverish if you were not already in that state. This is not my complaint, but Berthe's."[100] Paris surrendered on January 28, and German occupational forces soon bivouacked in the Bois de Boulogne to oversee controversial national elections to establish a legal government with which to negotiate a treaty. Anticipating the possibility of more fighting in Paris, the Morisot family left Passy for the western suburb of Saint-Germain-en-Laye. The new regime seated at Versailles, with Adolphe Thiers (1797–1877) as its chief executive, immediately sought to reorganize the French army and suppress the autonomy of the municipal National Guard in Paris. Hardly less opposed to the policies of Thiers than they had been to the German occupation, the citizens of Paris boldly elected their own Socialist-oriented government on May 26, calling it the Commune. Civil war ensued.

Loyal to Thiers's national government,[101] the Morisots in Saint-Germain could hear his forces shelling the Commune's battery on the Trocadéro, just below Passy. Unprepared to endure the interminable waiting, Berthe wrote to Edma that she planned to join her in Cherbourg: "I tried to do a watercolor after nature: impossible. I feel like a child who will never be able to do anything; the landscape here is magnificent, even exceptional, but it always seems to me that seascapes are more comprehensible."[102] She further confided: "I hope that you can put yourself in my position, and understand that work is the sole purpose of my existence, and that indefinitely prolonged idleness would be fatal to me from every point of view. . . . I do not know whether I am indulging in illusions, but it seems to me that a painting like the one I gave Manet could perhaps sell, and that is all I care about."[103] In early May Morisot left her parents for the coast to begin to fulfill this aspiration. The picture in Manet's collection to which Morisot referred was her *Harbor at Lorient* (colorplate 3), painted in Edma's company during the summer of 1869, and Morisot would indeed do a similar picture for the art market after she joined her sister on the coast in June.

Edma brought Morisot confidence, but many other factors suddenly contributed to an outburst of work, including a deeply felt need for financial independence from her parents and a need to develop ideas that had accumulated over more than a year of unavoidable inactivity. Morisot's inclination to work in watercolors would transform the way she worked in oil, lightening her palette still more and expanding her repertoire of brushstrokes with calligraphic flourishes.[104] Even if the war experience weakened her health, somehow Morisot emerged from the interruption of her career as a fully mature artist.

The change is already apparent in the watercolor and oil versions of *The Harbor at Cherbourg* (colorplates 8 and 9). Whereas in her 1869 Lorient oil she feathered her strokes to describe a seamless and fluid continuum of sea water, at Cherbourg she left each short stroke intact, without concern for covering every bit of the canvas, defining physical appearances such as the roll of the water's surface with groups of blue and gray dashes. She also limited her description of figures and boats in her oil to a minimum number of essential undisguised strokes, as if she were working as loosely as she would in watercolor. Although she still preferred a palette of closely related tones without the sudden, sharply contrasting highlights that Renoir and Monet began to favor around 1870–71, her stenographic way of translating forms and light into atomic units of brushed color analogous to raw retinal stimuli is fully Impressionist.

Moreover, observed from an elevated window, as scenes in Japanese prints sometimes are, the composition of her oil is a drastic departure from the ground-level idiom of Corot's art. Literally overlooking what is close up (the foreground), such an elevated vantage point can present everything at a distance from the artist and is consequently a rationale for an unconventionally simplified rendering of forms, which, of course, lose detail the farther they are removed from a spectator. The elevated vantage point also brings attention to the fact that *The Harbor at Cherbourg*, or any picture for that matter, is of necessity only a fragment of a larger spatial continuum: a viewer not only sees the scene depicted but inevitably imagines the artist's viewpoint in a different, albeit connected, space outside the picture. The implication that pictorial space is in essence fragmentary is sustained in Morisot's *Harbor at Cherbourg* by details along the right margin, such as the tip of a stafflike object (a raised traffic barrier, a mast, a flagpole?), the precise identity of which cannot be ascertained from this particular viewpoint. Manet had begun to represent such mysterious fragments along the edges of his pictures in the early 1860s to stress how his compositions were utterly true to life, unedited and unposed.

Of course, Morisot's informal view of Cherbourg from a window overlooking the harbor is a humorous little portrait: the tiny figures of mother and child strolling, just three or four tiny marks of paint too bright for the rest of the scene, represent Edma and her daughter Jeanne, now some eighteen months old. Nothing here suggests war. Around Paris, however, the fighting intensified, and the elder Morisots feared that their home had been destroyed, along with the garden studio.[105] Even though no letters document the Morisots' personal losses in detail, the ravages of war may also help to explain the scarcity of early works by either Edma or Berthe.[106] On May 21, 1871, Thiers's army assaulted Paris, setting up its staff headquarters on the rue Franklin. During the infamous "Bloody Week" that followed, more than twenty thousand Communards were killed, and central Paris, including the government accounting office and the city hall, was wasted by fire.

The Harbor at Cherbourg, 1871
Watercolor and pencil on paper.
15.6 x 20.3 cm (6¼ x 8 in.).
From the Collection of Mr. and
Mrs. Paul Mellon, Upperville,
Virginia.

When the fighting ended, Morisot's parents hurried back to Passy to estimate damages, see how friends had fared, and start a return to normal life. They worried more than ever about Berthe's security, given her disinterest in marriage; they had discouraged the romance with Puvis,[107] and they wondered whether Manet's brother Eugène might try to win her now. After Morisot's return from Cherbourg in late July, her mother wrote to Edma to express concern about Berthe's future as a professional artist:

She has perhaps the necessary talent—I shall be delighted if such is the case—but she has not the kind of talent that has commercial value or wins public recognition; she will never sell anything done in her present manner, and she is incapable of painting differently. Manet himself, even while heaping compliments on her, said: "Mlle B. has not wanted to do anything up to now. She has not really tried; when she wants to, she will succeed."

But we know that she wants to, and that when she does something, she sets about it with the greatest ardour. But all she accomplishes is to make herself sick. If one must do bad work in order to please the public—for, really, you have made me feel that all my ideas of painting are wrong—she will never do the kind of work that dealers buy in the hope of reselling it. When a few artists compliment her, it goes to her head. Are they really

sincere? Puvis has told her that her work has such subtlety and distinction that it makes others miserable, and that he was returning home disgusted with himself. Frankly, is it as good as all that? Would anyone give even twenty francs for these ravishing things?

I have become sceptical—that's possible. . . . I am therefore a bit disappointed to see that Berthe won't settle down like everybody else. It is like her painting—she will get compliments since she seems to be eager to receive them, but she will be held at arm's length when it comes to a serious commitment.[108]

Such discouraging comments only added to Morisot's determination to achieve professional success, if need be in London, where friends such as Fantin had found collectors for their works. In a letter to Edma, Morisot reported how she had immediately taken one of her Cherbourg watercolors to a dealer, "one of the most important in Paris" (possibly Durand-Ruel), for framing.[109] The same letter reveals that Morisot had developed some of her most important compositional ideas during her recent stay in Cherbourg: "It seems that the watercolor of you in gray is my masterpiece—not the other." Two known watercolors, both relatively stiff as far as the drawing of the figures is concerned, portray Edma in gray: *At the Edge of the Forest* (colorplate 10) and *Woman and Child in*

COLORPLATE 9

The Harbor at Cherbourg, 1871
Oil on canvas. 41.9 x 55.9 cm (16½ x 22 in.). From the Collection
of Mr. and Mrs. Paul Mellon, Upperville, Virginia.

a Meadow (colorplate 11). In the second, the harbor at
Cherbourg is visible in the background. In both, Edma
reclines on the ground tending little Jeanne, who is barely
able to stand. Jeanne faces the artist in one; in the other,
she has turned her back. This figure of a distracted child
would become a favorite motif for Morisot, as would that
of a woman in a long dress seated on the grass.

These watercolors raise crucial questions about
Morisot's relationship to Manet, because similar motifs
occur in many of his works from the early 1870s (e.g.,
In the Garden, figure 26), and it remains unclear who
influenced whom. Since Morisot experimented with
Manet's innovative pictorial ideas in the late 1860s, establishing a sort of student-teacher dependency, it would seem
that where her later works closely resemble Manet's, his
preceded hers. However, whereas Morisot chided herself

on several occasions when she felt that her own works too
closely resembled pictures by colleagues, Manet, for his
part, openly plagiarized salient features from other artists
(Raphael, Titian, Velázquez, and Goya, to name only a
few). Considering their contrasting notions of originality
in art, one cannot ignore the possibility that in the early
1870s Manet began to appropriate from Morisot, too.

In the same letter to Edma written after Morisot returned from Cherbourg, she noted: "I am doing Yves with
Bichette," referring to their sister and her three- or four-
year-old daughter, Paule, who were evidently visiting Passy.
"I am having great difficulty with them. The work is losing all its freshness. Moreover as a composition it resembles a Manet. I realize this and am annoyed."[110] She may
have been describing any of three undated pictures, all
with counterparts in Manet's work.

41

COLORPLATE 10

At the Edge of the Forest, 1871
Watercolor on paper. 19.1 x 22 cm (7½ x 8⅝ in.). From the
Collection of Mr. and Mrs. Paul Mellon, Upperville, Virginia.

COLORPLATE 11

Woman and Child in a Meadow, 1871
Watercolor on paper. 21 x 24 cm (8¼ x 9⁷⁄₁₆ in.). Courtesy of
Galerie Hopkins and Thomas, Paris.

FIGURE 26

Prunaire, engraving after Edouard Manet's *In the Garden,* c. 1873–74.

FIGURE 27

Edouard Manet, *Gare Saint-Lazare,* 1872–73
Oil on canvas. 93 x 114 cm (36½ x 45 in.). National Gallery of
Art, Washington, D.C., Gift of Horace Havemeyer in memory
of his mother, Louisine W. Havemeyer, 1956.

First, there is Morisot's panoramic landscape *View of Paris from the Trocadéro* (colorplate 12), similar to the one painted by Manet during the World's Fair of 1867 (see figure 11). A view of the capital with peace restored would have been an appealing subject to paint in 1871, and the tiny figures in the foreground are closely related in concept to the miniature portraits of Edma and Jeanne in *The Harbor at Cherbourg,* which is known to have been painted that year. But since Morisot did not sell her view of Paris to Durand-Ruel until 1873, an earlier date is open to question. Besides, there are three small figures in Morisot's *View of Paris from the Trocadéro,* whereas her letter suggests a picture with just two.[111]

The painting of "Yves with Bichette" might refer to any of the several variations by Morisot on the motif of a mother seated in the grass overseeing a child, except that the child in these works is too small to represent Yves's daughter. These compositions all resemble Manet's *In the Garden* (figure 26). But, as we know, Manet may not have begun *In the Garden* in 1870 as has generally been assumed. If Morisot was annoyed that one of her works resembled this particular painting by Manet, why would she then go on to repeat the same basic motif several times over? All things considered, Morisot's Cherbourg watercolors may have preceded Manet's Impressionist canvas.

It is most likely that "Yves with Bichette" refers to Morisot's *On the Balcony* (colorplate 13), with its background view of the Parisian skyline observed from the Trocadéro. Although the models for this painting have often been identified as Edma Pontillon and her three-year-old niece, Paule (Bichette) Gobillard, there is no evidence that the two were in Paris at the same time during the early 1870s. Rather, it is likely that Morisot painted Yves Gobillard with her daughter Bichette, who in 1871 would indeed have been the size of the child in *On the Balcony*; furthermore, the railing along the foreground of this painting calls to mind the similar detail in Manet's *Balcony* (see figure 14), for which Morisot had posed in late 1868. The figure of the little girl, her back turned as she looks out toward Paris, repeats an idea formulated in one of the 1871 Cherbourg watercolors of Edma dressed in gray (colorplates 10 and 11). If indeed *On the Balcony* is to be identified as the "Yves with Bichette" that Morisot fretted about in the late summer of 1871, it is ironic that Manet in turn would soon draw upon this variation on his own earlier work. His *Gare Saint-Lazare* (figure 27), begun by the autumn of 1872, also includes a little girl viewed from the back, turned to look off through an iron railing to observe the arrival or departure of a train at the Saint-Lazare station.[112] (Morisot regarded *On the Balcony* so highly that she executed a small copy of it in watercolor [colorplate

COLORPLATE 12

View of Paris from the Trocadéro, c. 1871–72
Oil on canvas. 46.1 x 81.5 cm (18⅟₁₆ x 32⅟₁₆ in.). Collection of the
Santa Barbara Museum of Art, California, Gift of Mrs. Hugh N.
Kirkland.

14]. Whereas, given her strict commitment to spontaneity, she made a watercolor copy of an oil only this one time, Manet for his part frequently copied his important works in watercolor, a preliminary step toward producing etchings to record them.)

Since the same turned-away figure appears in so many of Morisot's pictures, its special rationale deserves further consideration. Although turning a figure away seems fundamentally opposed to the goals of portraiture, which normally places emphasis on frontality, doing so solves the perennial problem faced by artists obliged to depict restless children who pose badly. But more than mere expediency was involved. With these turned-away figures, Morisot's family portraits become unposed modern genre paintings. The turned-away figures also add a strong spatial suggestion to her compositions, since viewers must try to imagine what has caught the child's attention, and why. Wondering what the child sees inevitably leads to wondering how it sees, and whether it sees without adult prejudices and presumptions. Like Corot and her Impressionist colleagues, Morisot sought to observe the world with child-

like innocence as sparkling flakes of color, and her figures of distracted children are ultimately a rationale for the bold, whimsical style that prevailed in her work throughout the remainder of her career.[113] But she alone attempted, beginning in 1871 with such paintings as *On the Balcony,* to contrast completely different modes of visual experience—the child's and the adult's—in one and the same picture.

The most extraordinary of Morisot's complex early pictures with a turned-away child is *Interior* (figure 28). Although the models may again be Yves and Bichette, Edma and her daughter Jeanne have also been suggested;[114] in any case, this painting has no overtones of Manet. Here the carefully observed woman, presented in profile as if seated for a formal portrait, seems oblivious to the far less formal world experienced by her child. Tended by an adult, the girl in the background has spread the window curtain just wide enough to look out, but the bright daylight has so dissolved forms that what the child sees is indistinguishable in Morisot's picture. As for the seated woman, the empty chair next to her suggests she is awaiting some-

COLORPLATE 14

On the Balcony, c. 1871–72
Watercolor on paper. 20.5 x 16.4 cm (8⅛ x 6⅞ in.). The Art
Institute of Chicago, Gift of Mrs. Charles Netcher in Memory
of Charles Netcher II.

COLORPLATE 13

On the Balcony, c. 1871–72
Oil on canvas. 60 x 50 cm (23⅝ x 19⅝ in.). Private collection.

FIGURE 28

Interior [BW 26], c. 1871
Oil on canvas. 60 x 73 cm (23⅝ x 28¾ in.). Private collection.

FIGURE 29

Portrait of Mme Pontillon [BW 419], 1871
Pastel on paper. 81 x 65 cm (31⅞ x 25⅝ in.). Musée du Louvre,
Cabinet des dessins, Paris.

FIGURE 30

Edouard Manet, *Berthe Morisot with a Fan,* 1874
Oil on canvas. 61 x 50 cm (24 x 19¹¹⁄₁₆ in.). Musée d'Orsay, Paris.

one or that someone has recently left her. Behind her is a large planter, and partly visible on the floor below the planter, propped against it, is a framed still-life painting of a vase of flowers. This picture within a picture (which has never been identified and may represent a lost work by Morisot) is a sort of counterpart to the seated woman, who could be described as a fragment of a conventional portrait within the context of a domestic genre painting. The disparate yet beautifully integrated details in this painting, part living room, part artist's studio, evoke a complex mood of reverie that will become an essential characteristic of Morisot's mature works.

The artist seems never to have exhibited this important picture, although it may perhaps have been the light-flooded painting refused by the jury for the Salon of 1872. A sympathetic letter to Morisot from Puvis in the wake of this refusal gives the only meager clue to which of Morisot's

FIGURE 31

Photograph of Berthe Morisot. Private collection.

FIGURE 32

Edouard Manet, *Berthe Morisot with a Bunch of Violets,* 1872
Oil on canvas. 22 x 27 cm (8¾ x 10¾ in.). Private collection.

works was found unacceptable: "How long is needed for old-fashioned conventional eyes to bear frank, innocent natural light?"[115] The same jury did, however, accept Morisot's forceful pastel *Portrait of Mme Pontillon* (figure 29). The lack of contrast between the black lap, arms, and bodice virtually obscures the anatomy of the pregnant sitter.[116] But Morisot compensates for the resulting flat silhouette with elegant economy by merely positioning Edma's white hands on her enlarged abdomen. The remarkable finesse of this pastel, the first that Morisot is known to have exhibited, suggests that many earlier less masterful works in this medium may have been destroyed.[117]

The apparent paucity of works by Morisot from the period immediately following her return from Cherbourg in the summer of 1871 can be explained by the probability that her Passy studio was undergoing repair. Although Aimé Millet apparently put his working quarters at her

disposal, she evidently preferred to accept Manet's invitation to model for him.[118] The latter had heretofore been unable to work productively because of postwar nervous depression.[119] Not counting the two Salon paintings for which Morisot posed in 1868 and 1870, there are nine smaller, less formal, sometimes humorous pictures of Morisot by Manet, such as *Berthe Morisot with a Fan* (figure 30). Only two are dated, *Berthe Morisot with a Bunch of Violets* from 1872 (figure 32) and another from 1873.[120] This ongoing series continued at intervals (it is curious that Morisot never did Manet's portrait) until Berthe's marriage to Eugène Manet at the end of 1874.

Manet's career reached a milestone in early 1872 when, thanks to the intervention of Stevens, the dealer Paul Durand-Ruel came to Manet's studio and bought twenty-two paintings all at once, thus initiating an ongoing market for his work with the same gallery that had begun, in a

FIGURE 33

Harbor Scene [BW 42], 1871
Oil on canvas. 33 x 41 cm (13 x 16⅛ in.). Musée Léon-Alègre,
Bagnols-sur-Céze; painting currently missing.

more modest way, to support Pissarro, Monet, and Degas. In early July, Morisot asked Manet to show a seascape that she had done at Cherbourg (figure 33) to his new dealer, who bought it on July 10, along with three watercolors, including one of Edma, *Young Woman on a Bench* (color-plate 15).[121] Curiously, Durand-Ruel chose not to buy an unidentified portrait of a woman and a pastel portrait of Morisot's cousin, Madeleine Thomas, seated next to a pet parrot (BW 426);[122] the pastel is relatively conventional in subject, composition, and style, as if Morisot had designed it specifically to appeal to the art market.

The Cradle (colorplate 16), a portrait of Edma gazing at her infant daughter Blanche, born late in 1871, falls into the latter category. Her right hand on the cradle, her left to her chin, Edma seems unconsciously to echo the pose of little Blanche, whose features, visible beneath a gauzy canopy, are softly blurred. Morisot's rendering of the sleeping infant's cocoonlike world with washes of white and gray scumbling, dotted with pink on the canopy's border, is a tour de force of free brushwork designed to contrast with the carefully detailed features of the mother. Whether taken as a double portrait or a genre scene, *The Cradle* is most explicitly a picture about looking, Morisot's subject of preference for the next few years.

It was probably while Edma was in Paris for the birth of her second daughter that Morisot painted *Mme Pontillon and Her Daughter, Jeanne* (colorplate 17), a small double-portrait watercolor of Edma looking at her first child. Both are seated on an Empire-style chaise longue, surely one of the "old pieces of furniture" that M. Morisot had taken pains to place in safekeeping during the recent war. The variety of the pale lavender touches forming the floral pattern of Edma's dress indicates a considerable mastery of watercolor techniques. Yet the motley strokes at the upper and right borders—apparently a loose rendition of a curtain—give this particular picture a special character. A flurry of suspended strokes of different shapes and sizes, these marks could just as easily be understood as test patches to help the artist choose her palette. Whatever the case, the freedom of handling heralds the sort of rapid brushwork that would characterize Morisot's style in all mediums for the rest of her career. *Mme Gobillard and Her Daughter, Paule* (colorplate 18), a luminous, delicate watercolor double portrait of Yves reclining on another Empire-style sofa with her daughter standing nearby, is so closely related that it should probably also be dated mid-1871—a supposition supported by the apparent age of the child.

When plans for a joint Morisot-Manet family seaside vacation failed to develop in 1872, Morisot took a working vacation on the southern coast of France with Yves. Bad weather and pestering children curious to watch her painting outdoors made work difficult, however, and from Saint-Jean-de-Luz, the sisters ventured on to Madrid in September to see the great works by Manet's favorites, Velázquez and Goya, with Manet's old friend Astruc for a guide.[123]

Around this time the Morisot family moved to a new home in Passy at 7, rue Guichard, only a few blocks from where they had been living. In March 1873 Morisot put her *View of Paris from the Trocadéro* (colorplate 12) on consignment with Durand-Ruel, who sold it the following month for the respectable price of 750 francs to Ernest Hoschedé (1837–1891), the reckless department-store magnate, who bought on speculation Impressionist paintings by the dozen in the early 1870s.[124] A small beach landscape by Morisot (BW 55), similar in treatment to Corot's famous studies, was included in a benefit sale held in April for refugees from Alsace seeking to escape the newly im-

COLORPLATE 15

***Young Woman on a Bench
(Edma Pontillon),*** 1872
Watercolor on paper. 24.9 x
15.1 cm (9¹³⁄₁₆ x 5¹⁵⁄₁₆ in.). National
Gallery of Art, Washington,
D.C., Ailsa Mellon Bruce
Collection, 1970.

COLORPLATE 17

Mme Pontillon and Her Daughter, Jeanne, 1871
Watercolor on paper. 25.1 x 25.9 cm (9⅞ x 10¹³⁄₁₆ in.). National
Gallery of Art, Washington, D.C., Ailsa Mellon Bruce Collection,
1970.

COLORPLATE 16

The Cradle, 1872
Oil on canvas. 56 x 46 cm (22¹⁄₁₆ x 18⅛ in.). Musée d'Orsay, Paris.

posed German regime there. Durand-Ruel bought it out of this sale for his gallery stock.[125]

Only a single Morisot pastel was accepted for the Salon of 1873, titled *Blanche* (BW 420) in the catalogue, as if it were a portrait.[126] But the little girl who posed for this picture, perhaps Morisot's most conventional figure painting, cannot yet be identified. Since Morisot usually submitted two works, it is possible that the jury refused an oil this year, as it had the previous year. The ultraconservative taste of the jury unleashed a storm of protest from rejected artists in 1873; and, as had happened a decade before, the government organized a simultaneous alternative Salon.[127] Even before the opening of the official Salon on May 15, some newspapers reported that a group of artists dissatisfied with the Salon system, including Monet, Pissarro, and Alfred Sisley (1839–1899), were planning to create a cooperative society to mount their own independent group exhibitions.[128]

Although Manet, who was awarded a medal at the Salon of 1873, was unwilling to join this group, several of its organizers were associated with his dealer, Durand-Ruel, who had already begun to present group shows of what he called "The Society of French Artists" at a gallery in London with which he had been collaborating since 1870. According to the Durand-Ruel gallery records, he sent one of Morisot's works to London at the end of May, and the catalogue of the Society's winter 1873 exhibition, which listed Corot and Daubigny as members of the steering committee, included *The Young Mother* under her name. Although this title could refer to *On the Balcony* (colorplate 13), it best describes *The Cradle* (colorplate 16).[129] Since her fellow exhibitors in London included Degas, Monet, Pissarro, and Sisley, Durand-Ruel's Society of French Artists could perhaps be considered a sort of prototype for the artists' cooperative these same individuals were organizing in Paris.

By December the renegades had agreed to a charter, calling themselves, without any art polemics, the "Société Anonyme Coopérative d'artistes-peintres, sculpteurs, etc.," which translates as the Artists' Cooperative Society, Inc. Dues for annual membership were kept to a low sixty francs, and the charter named Pissarro, Monet, and Degas's friend Rouart as members of the administrative board. Renoir was listed as a member of its steering committee.[130] As far as is known, neither the date nor the location for the initial exhibition had yet been determined.

Although Morisot has always been identified as a charter member, it seems doubtful that propriety would have allowed her as a single woman to attend the early organizational meetings during the winter of 1873–74, when her father was gravely ill (he died of heart disease on January 24, 1874). Moreover, an undated letter to Morisot's mother from Degas (whose own father died on February 23) indicates that Morisot probably joined the group at a slightly later stage.[131] By the time of Degas's letter, the Société had rented the studio-gallery of the celebrated photographer Nadar (Gaspard-Félix Tournachon, 1820–1910) on the busy boulevard des Capucines in central Paris not far from the Opéra, and the painter asked Mme Morisot whether her daughters might be willing to consider participating in its first exhibition. Manet advised against it.[132]

A letter from Puvis to Morisot, dated April 7, only a week before the opening of the first Impressionist exhibition at Nadar's on April 15, indicates that Morisot had again submitted works to the Salon that spring.[133] Puvis's comments suggest that the jury had already refused some of her works, although no decision had yet been reached with regard to the watercolors she had submitted. Since her name is missing from the Salon catalogue, these must ultimately have been refused as well, as were two of the three oils that Manet had submitted and works by Eva Gonzalès and Marcello. Puvis's letter indicates that by now Morisot had agreed to exhibit at Nadar's, and he warned that the enterprise was liable to be a fiasco.

Puvis's fears were justified, but only in a limited way. Most newspaper accounts of this historic exhibition referred to only a small number of the twenty-nine participating artists. Morisot, the only woman, was included in this core group, dubbed "impressionists" by the critics, who characterized the works of the group in ideological terms, concluding that their bright, broadly handled style was an act of defiance against Salon taste. In general, however, excepting the outlandish, negative remarks published in a humor magazine, the reviews were passably favorable for all the artists except Monet and Cézanne. However, Morisot's decision to exhibit horrified her former teacher Guichard, who wrote to Mme Morisot: "As painter, friend, and physician, this is my prescription: [Berthe] is to go to the Louvre twice a week, stand before Correggio for three hours, and ask his forgiveness for having attempted to say in oil what can only be said in watercolor."[134]

According to the exhibition catalogue, Morisot showed four oils, two pastels, and three watercolors.[135] The works refused by the jury only days before were probably among them. The catalogue is not a perfect guide, however, since an unlisted work was described in a newspaper review of

COLORPLATE 18

Mme Gobillard and Her Daughter, Paule, 1871
Watercolor on paper. 15 x 20 cm (5⅞ x 7⅞ in.). Private
collection.

the show: the pastel portrait of Edma (figure 29) already
exhibited at the Salon of 1872.[136]

The four oils by Morisot were *The Harbor at Cherbourg*
(colorplate 9) and *The Cradle* (colorplate 16) from 1871 and
1872 and two more recent works. The third, *Hide and
Seek* (colorplate 19), painted the previous year at Maurecourt, the country estate of Edma's father-in-law, already
belonged to Manet according to the catalogue. Looking is
the general theme of *Hide and Seek*; it depicts Edma with
three-year-old Jeanne as they pause to play near a little
cherry tree during a summer's stroll. Although Morisot's

"touch," the way she indicated the grass and leaves with
rough stabs and dashes of green, accented here and there
in white, impressed several critics as fresh and graceful,
none referred to the tiny branch visible at the far right.[137]
This whimsical fragment suggests that Morisot's composition as a whole is but a part of the spatial continuum
extending in every direction, most of it hidden from the
viewer in the spirit of hide and seek.

The fourth oil, listed as *Reading*, can be identified as a
painting in the Cleveland Museum of Art (colorplate 20),
thanks to details in a review by Jean Prouvaire: "In her

COLORPLATE 19

Hide and Seek, 1873
Oil on canvas. 45.1 x 54.9 cm (17 ¾ x 21⅝ in.). Collection of
Mrs. John Hay Whitney.

watercolors as in her oils, [Morisot] likes grassy fields where some young woman holds a book [or sits] near a child. She juxtaposes the charming artifice of a young woman from Paris with the charm of nature. This is one of the tendencies of this emerging school [of artists], to mix Worth [the haute-couture fashion designer, 1825–1895] with the Good Lord."[138] He especially admired Morisot's treatment of detail, how she arranged a pink-bordered muslin scarf next to a green umbrella. Yet, referring to this same picture, for which Edma had posed the previous summer while the sisters vacationed on the Normandy coast, the satirist Louis Leroy (1812–1885) complained that the freely rendered hands looked like little animals.[139] More than any other painting by Morisot in the first Impressionist exhibition, this one exemplifies the special pictorial problems that would remain her obsession in years to come: seeking decorative harmonies by stressing similar shapes (here, an umbrella and a fan) and textures (the flower-dotted field and the floral-print dress) and by overlapping objects with similar colors (the blue-green umbrella, hat ribbon, and grass; the white dress with its violet shadows and the book with its white pages and lavender cover). Although *Reading* is ostensibly a genre painting of modern life, including such deftly rendered vignettes as the farmer's cart in the background on the right, Morisot carefully selected and orchestrated every detail for abstract art-for-art's-sake goals.

The pastels and watercolors by Morisot in the first Impressionist exhibition cannot all be identified. Those that can, however, justify Guichard's objection that she treated form with the same delicate stroking touches regardless of medium. The landscape in her pastel *A Village (Maurecourt)* (colorplate 21), for example, is handled in much the same way as the background of *Hide and Seek*. Yet the seemingly casual marks of color here record a wealth of detail: the little sandy path that disappears as it recedes into fields and orchards, the complicated skyline of the village, the screen of trees lining an invisible road running along the horizon.

Although none of Morisot's works in the first Impressionist show extended the tendencies of free brushwork so far as Monet's *Impression, Sunrise*, probably 1873, for which the new movement was named, *On the Beach* (figure 34), the painting by Morisot that Durand-Ruel apparently included in his 1874 group show in London only a few weeks later, was hardly less bold. Made in Normandy the previous summer, *On the Beach*, with its simple zones of sky, sea, sand, and shadow, punctuated by little figures, lampposts, and ships, all observed from afar, epitomizes Morisot's extreme commitment to simplicity and infor-

mality in the name of pure painting. Although unsigned, and thus presumably not a work that Morisot chose to exhibit, her pastel, *Corner of Paris, Seen from Passy* (colorplate 22), which seems to date from around 1872–73, judging from its style, is no less extraordinary as a precursor of the unorthodox modes of calligraphic drawing and asymmetrical composition associated with the first phase of Impressionism.

On the Beach notwithstanding, at first Durand-Ruel usually handled Morisot's more conventional works, such as the double portrait of Mme Lucien Boursier and her daughter (figure 35), relatives of Morisot's father. Stevens bought it in June 1873 for eight hundred francs.[140] Since he could presumably have acquired it directly from the artist, this purchase from Durand-Ruel may have been intended as a sign of support to counter Mme Morisot's perennial scepticism about her daughter's art career. But Stevens's purchase could just as well be understood as an indication that Morisot was often too modest to let friends have examples of her work. Jacques-Emile Blanche's account of a visit to her studio in the rue Guichard around this time suggests such a reluctance, and it also gives an idea of the props she was collecting for her pictures:

A middle-class apartment, but in that apartment the bedroom of a young girl is the studio of a great artist. Antimacassars, white curtains, portfolios, rustic straw hats, a green gauze bag for gathering butterflies, a cage with parakeets, a litter of fragile accessories; no bric-a-brac, no art objects, except some studies, [and] in a splendid location on the wall, hung with a striped gray moiré paper, a silver-flecked landscape by Corot.

She has nothing of her own to show me; she destroys everything that she makes at this time; "oil painting is too difficult." This morning, once again, in desperation she threw into the lake of the Bois de Boulogne a study of swans that she was following in a boat; wanting to give me a small gift, she searches in vain for a watercolor. In vain.[141]

Of course, Morisot's surviving watercolors of swans on the lake of the Bois de Boulogne all date from more than ten years later, so the accuracy of Blanche's account is open to question. The green butterfly net, however, appears in two pictures of Edma and her children in their Maurecourt garden, both painted during the spring of 1874, just after the Impressionist show.

One of these, *Butterfly Hunt* (figure 36), is a variation in composition and mood of *Hide and Seek* (colorplate 19), although now the landscape setting is more dense, and in order to capture the flickering light in the leaves, the brushwork is freer. If it is finally impossible to tell whether the yellow or white dots of paint sprinkled in the

COLORPLATE 20

Reading, 1873
Oil on canvas. 45.1 x 72.4 cm (17¾ x 28½ in.). The Cleveland
Museum of Art, Gift of the Hanna Fund.

foreground are meant to indicate flowers or butterflies, the lack of precision enhances Morisot's general theme of looking. Viewers of this picture look at Edma looking for a butterfly to catch, just as little Jeanne, a few feet back, looks at her mother with the enviable intensity of a child at play. *On the Grass* (figure 37) is an informal group portrait of Edma, her children, and their dog at rest in a different part of the same garden; the butterfly net has been put down into the grass, rendered in pastels with hundreds of little lines in various values of green to capture the shifting outdoor light that was the ultimate challenge for all the Impressionists.

Edma, her children, and family friends also posed for Morisot during a vacation in Fécamp on the Normandy coast later that summer; she painted two important compositions of figures on the terrace of a villa overlooking the ocean, one called *On the Terrace* (figure 38) and the other *Villa at the Seaside* (BW 38). Rendered in a simplified style, freely brushed without apparent regard for de-

tail, both compositions are predicated, as her *On the Balcony* (colorplate 13) had been, on the abrupt juxtaposition of foreground and background, without a gradual transition between the two. Boats out on the Channel or vacationers strolling along the cliffs are indicated by spontaneous but deft strokes that give the essential shapes and colors with the conciseness of Gustave Flaubert's prose. Gesture and expression play virtually no role at all in these pictures, which might otherwise be categorized as genre portraits. Little Jeanne Pontillon, her back turned, can be seen looking at the tiny distant shapes in *Villa at the Seaside,* but Mme Lucien Boursier, the model for *On the Terrace,* appears oblivious to her surroundings, as if Morisot had tried to capture the model's fatigue with her role. The utter absence of narrative seems calculated to draw atten-

COLORPLATE 20A

Reading [detail]

58

FIGURE 34

On the Beach [BW 28], 1873
Oil on canvas. 24.1 x 50.2 cm (9½ x 19¾ in.). Virginia Museum
of Fine Arts, Richmond, Collection of Mr. and Mrs. Paul Mellon.

FIGURE 35

Mme Boursier and Her Daughter [BW 34], c. 1873
Oil on canvas. 74 x 52 cm (28¾ x 22⁵⁄₁₆ in.). The Brooklyn
Museum, 29.30, Museum Collection Fund.

FIGURE 36

Butterfly Hunt [BW 36], 1874
Oil on canvas. 47 x 56 cm (18½ x 22¹⁄₁₆ in.). Musée d'Orsay, Paris.

FIGURE 37

On the Grass [BW 427], 1874
Pastel. 73 x 92 cm (28¾ x 36³⁄₁₆ in.). Musée Petit Palais, Ville de Paris.

COLORPLATE 21

A Village (Maurecourt), 1873
Pastel on paper. 47 x 71.8 cm (18½ x 28¼ in.). Private collection.

tion to the entirely pictorial aspects of these works—their eccentric geometric compositions and strange color harmonies in greens, blues, and silver grays.

Vacationing nearby this summer, forty-one-year-old Eugène Manet paid court to Morisot, painting alongside her on at least one occasion.[142] Oddly, almost nothing at all is known about Eugène. Like his celebrated brother, Edouard, he painted and mingled in literary and political circles. Although later in his life he took civil-service posts and even wrote a novel (published in 1889), the certificate registered when he married Morisot on December 22, 1874, describes his occupation simply as "landowner."[143] His appearance at this time is recorded in a portrait painted by Degas as a wedding present (figure 39). Family legend has it that Degas posed Eugène in Morisot's studio in the fall of 1874 and then decided to add a Normandy landscape background from imagination to evoke the locale of the courtship.[144] In composition and palette, this somewhat

atypical portrait by Degas—depicting a figure seated on the grass—seems to have been designed as an *hommage* to Morisot's *Reading* (colorplate 20). As his wedding present, Edouard Manet painted *Berthe Morisot with a Fan* (figure 30), his last and most graceful portrait of her, a gold ring on her hand. And Marcello, who moved in 1872 to 47, rue Saint Petersburg, just down the street from Manet, also started a portrait of Morisot (figure 40) around the time she became engaged.

Edouard Manet, despite his unswerving opposition on principle to the Impressionist exhibitions outside of the Salons, had decided to devote himself to adopting the fundamental innovations of Impressionist brushwork and composition. Undoubtedly Morisot, who saw him more often than the other painters did, was the most important catalyst. But Manet spent the summer of 1874 on the Seine near Argenteuil, where he benefited from the presence of Monet and Renoir, who were working outdoors in the area.

FIGURE 38

On the Terrace [BW 37], 1874
Oil on canvas. 45 x 54 cm (17¹¹⁄₁₆ x 21¼ in.). Private collection.

FIGURE 39

Edgar Degas, *Portrait of Eugène Manet*, 1874
Oil on canvas. 81 x 65 cm (31⅞ x 25⁹⁄₁₆ in.). Private collection.

It was probably during the course of her sittings for Manet in the fall of 1874 that Morisot met the most gifted poet of his generation, Stéphane Mallarmé. Having met Manet in 1873, the poet stopped almost daily at the painter's studio on his way home from the school where he taught English.[145] Mallarmé shared Morisot's whimsical sensitivity to visual nuances in the frivolous trappings and moods characteristic of modern life. In September 1874, Mallarmé went so far as to bring out an ephemeral little periodical, *La Dernière mode* (The Latest Fashion), devoted to society gossip, apparel, and the arts.

Paintings by Morisot that show women in the privacy of their dressing rooms from this time share the innocent spirit of Mallarmé's enthusiastic accounts of ribbons, belts, and jewels. The apparently unfinished "portrait" of her friend Mme Hubbard (colorplate 23), who reclines informally on a daybed in a white muslin summer dress and yellow slippers, may be the first of these.[146] That Morisot neglected to resolve part of the background and the right edge of this her first "symphony" (to use Whistler's term for his white-on-white figure compositions) is especially noteworthy, since before this she seems to have destroyed

FIGURE 40

Marcello, *Portrait of Berthe Morisot*, c. 1874
Oil on canvas. 168 x 115 cm (66⅛ x 45¼ in.). Musée d'Art et d'Histoire, Fribourg, Switzerland.

COLORPLATE 22

Corner of Paris, Seen from Passy, c. 1872–73
Pastel on paper. 27 x 34.9 cm (10⅝ x 13¾ in.). Private collection, New York.

all her unresolved works out of dissatisfaction. Starting now she preserved and sometimes exhibited or sold works that were less than fully developed by conventional commercial standards, apparently because she valued these evocative "fragments" as highly as the so-called finished works.

Her new status as a married woman in no way tempered Morisot's commitment to the avant-garde. On the contrary, she presented herself as one of its standard-bearers when in March 1875, along with Monet, Renoir, and Sisley, she organized a public auction of recent works, something living artists had seldom before dared to do. It was a scandal. Renoir later recalled that when a detractor referred to Morisot as a whore, Pissarro punched him in the face, setting off a brawl;[147] and according to Durand-Ruel, who

acted as one of the auctioneers, police had to be called in to keep peace between the adherents of the new art and its opponents, some of whom disrupted the sale by screaming derisively.[148] Despite Manet's efforts to encourage support for this auction from newspaper critics, what were perceived as dangerous revolutionary tendencies in the new style of painting were condemned and ridiculed. Accordingly, *Le Figaro*'s influential critic Albert Wolff (1835–1891) declared: "The impression which the impressionists achieve is that of a cat walking on the keyboard of a piano or of a monkey who might have got hold of a box of paints."[149]

The bids for the pictures in this auction were disastrously low. Morisot's associates were obliged to buy back many of their own works, and Durand-Ruel was likewise

COLORPLATE 23

Portrait of Mme Marie Hubbard, 1874
Oil on canvas. 50.5 x 81 cm (19⅞ x 31⅞ in.). The Ordrupgaard
Collection, Copenhagen.

put in a difficult situation, because the prices he set on his
own stock of works by these artists were jeopardized by
the far lower prices at the sale. Morisot fared best of all,
but her oils sold for less than half of what Durand-Ruel
had recently charged clients such as Stevens for her work.

Unfortunately, it is impossible to identify all of the
dozen items by Morisot in the sale: five oils, three pastels,
and four watercolors. A work called *Interior* (figure 41,
now called *Young Woman with a Mirror*), which brought
the highest price, selling to Hoschedé for 480 francs, was a
recent painting of a seated woman in a white dressing
gown looking at herself in a hand mirror as light floods
into her room from a large window in the background.[150]
Henri Rouart bought Morisot's *Villa at the Seaside* (BW
38). Since this picture eventually passed from Rouart to
Degas, it may have been the latter who urged his friend to
make this acquisition.[151] Rouart kept a second work by
Morisot that he bought at this sale, however: *By the
Seashore* (colorplate 24), a translucent little watercolor of
Edma and her children on the beach. Morisot's brother-in-

law Gustave Manet (1835–1884), also bought two of her
pictures, and her cousin Gabriel Thomas (1854–1932)
bought a pastel along with a landscape painting by Renoir.[152]

It has often been implied that whereas Monet, Renoir,
and Sisley badly needed to sell paintings in order to survive, Morisot was under less financial pressure. But her
family's correspondence throughout 1875, concerned as it
is with whether and where Eugène Manet could find a job
of some sort, with positions in Constantinople, Beirut,
Grenoble, and London all discussed as possibilities, suggests that Morisot's determination to sell may likewise
have been motivated by economics.[153] And the same letters indicate that Morisot, who spent the spring of this year
at one of the Manet country properties in Gennevilliers,
was immediately sending new works to Paris for sale.[154]

These works tended to be relatively small in scale and
to depict the same Zolaesque working-class subjects
—shipping, farming, the commercial-laundry business
—that Monet, Pissarro, and Degas began to paint during
the mid-1870s. Rather than creating idyllic souvenirs of

COLORPLATE 24

By the Seashore, 1874
Watercolor on paper. 16 x 21.3 cm (6 ⁵⁄₁₆ x 8 ³⁄₈ in.). Private
collection.

the unspoiled Seine Valley countryside in the spirit of
Corot, Morisot portrayed the new farming and cottage
industries that had recently been developed in rural areas,
thanks to controversial irrigation projects using sewage
water from Paris.[155] Even so, Morisot stressed the striking
patterns of color and light in these landscapes, without
in any way commenting on political issues. In the most
successful of them, *Laundresses Hanging Out the Wash*
(colorplate 25), the lines of white sheets observed from a
slightly elevated vantage point shine as brightly as the
clouds in the sky and are rendered with the same loose
brushwork.

If one were to judge from Morisot's letters home, her
summer vacation with Eugène on the Isle of Wight ("the
prettiest place for painting—if one had any talent") later
in 1875 was a disappointment as far as her work was
concerned.[156] Rain, wind, and rambunctious children presented insurmountable problems, at least for painting in
oils. "My work is going badly," she reported to Edma,
"and this is no consolation. It is always the same story. I
don't know where to start.... On a boat ... everything
sways.... The view from my window is pretty to look at,

but not to paint. Views from above are always incomprehensible ... the little I am doing seems dreadful to me....
I miss the babies as models."[157] Yet Morisot's paintings of
the Isle of Wight altogether contradict this overly modest
letter. Her pictures of the tourists and the yacht-filled riverside observed from their window at Globe Cottage (e.g.,
Harbor Scene, Isle of Wight [figure 42]) or from a rented
boat (BW 49 and 56) are exceptionally vibrant, kaleidoscopic impressions captured with a spontaneity unprecedented in her work.[158] With disregard for conventions of
compositional balance and clarity of outline, she developed a daring visual shorthand. In her paintings of the
harbor (colorplates 26 and 27), just a few flourishes of her
brush were sufficient to record the strollers who crossed
her field of vision or to capture the boats and ships aflutter
with sails and flags. This exciting, abbreviated style, designed to suggest the appearance of movement no less
than of objects, incorporates fat, choppy dashes with the
face of her brush, quick wobbly lines with its tip, scratches
with the end of its handle, and scumbles applied by wiping the brush dry. None of her Impressionist colleagues
had yet worked in such an experimental vein. Despite

COLORPLATE 25

Laundresses Hanging Out the Wash, 1875
Oil on canvas. 33 x 40.6 cm (13 x 16 in.). National Gallery of
Art, Washington, D.C., Collection of Mr. and Mrs. Paul
Mellon, 1985.

FIGURE 41

Young Woman with a Mirror (Interior) [BW 61], c. 1875
Oil on canvas. 54 x 45 cm (21¼ x 17¾ in.). Private collection.

FIGURE 42

Harbor Scene, Isle of Wight [BW 52], 1875
Oil on canvas. 48 x 36 cm (18⅞ x 14³⁄₁₆ in.). Private collection.

FIGURE 43

Eugène Manet on the Isle of Wight [BW 51], 1875
Oil on canvas. 38 x 46 cm (14¹⁵⁄₁₆ x 18⅛ in.). Private collection.

Morisot's complaints about swaying too much, *Bow of a Yacht* (colorplate 28) and other watercolors painted in a little boat rowed among the towering hulls of anchored ships are as sure-handed in execution as they are daring in composition.

Although Eugène was an uncooperative model, Morisot got him to straddle a chair for as long as she needed to paint *Eugène Manet on the Isle of Wight* (figure 43), a bizarre, asymmetrical portrait. Turned to look out the raised window of their room, its sill lined with flower-pots, Eugène regards figures on the riverside, themselves turned to look at the yachts. These figures are little patches of color visible through the interstices of the windowpaning and picket fence. Indeed, almost everything in this complicated little masterpiece is fragmented: light entering through the window dissolves the curtain into squiggles of white, and the garden and boats glimpsed through this same curtain are incoherent marks that would be impossible to identify were it not for the context of the scene as a whole.

COLORPLATE 26

Harbor Scene, Isle of Wight, 1875
Oil on canvas. 38 x 46 cm (14¹⁵⁄₁₆ x 18¼ in.). Private collection.

From this resort island the newlyweds went on to London, where riverside shipping motifs continued to fascinate Morisot. Family correspondence suggests that she sought out dealers and artists, including Whistler and James Tissot (1836–1902), a French expatriate whose photographically detailed modern-life paintings reputedly sold for around 300,000 francs.[159] After Morisot's return to France in the autumn, Eugène and Edouard Manet both encouraged her to send some recent works to a show at the Dudley Gallery in London.[160] If she did so, however, the

works were evidently unacceptable, for the gallery's catalogues do not list anything by Morisot.

Living on the rue Guichard in the apartment of her mother, who had become seriously ill, Morisot concentrated on figure painting, evidently using the same model who had posed for *Interior* (figure 41) the year before.[161] In January 1876, Hoschedé, who already owned *Interior*, bought *Woman at Her Toilette* (figure 44), another of the broadly rendered, light-flooded dressing-room scenes, from Durand-Ruel, who included three paintings by Morisot in

COLORPLATE 27

Harbor Scene, Isle of Wight, 1875
Oil on canvas. 43 x 64 cm (16⅞ x 25¼ in.). Collection of The
Newark Museum.

a group show that he organized for a London gallery in April.[162] That same month the stalwart dealer placed his Paris gallery on the rue le Peletier at the disposal of the Impressionists for their second group exhibition, which included about two hundred and fifty works by nineteen artists. Morisot, again the only woman exhibitor, showed fourteen oils, three watercolors, and three pastels. Wolff wrote in *Le Figaro*:

At Durand-Ruel's there has just opened an exhibition of so-called painting. The inoffensive passer-by, attracted by the flags that decorate the façade, goes in, and a ruthless spectacle is offered to his dismayed eyes: five or six lunatics—among them a woman—a group of unfortunate creatures stricken with the mania of ambition have met there to exhibit their works. Some people burst out laughing in front of these things—my heart is oppressed by them. Those self-styled artists give themselves the title of non-compromisers, impressionists; they take up

canvas, paint, and brush, throw a few tones haphazardly and sign the whole thing.[163]

Eugène Manet wanted to challenge the writer to a duel.[164]

It was a nude by Renoir, listed in the catalogue as *Study*, that received the most abuse from critics. Presented in an unresolved state, Renoir's painting gives viewers a behind-the-scenes account of the creative act in progress, initiating a cult of the unfinished fragment as a powerful expressive mode. But for many critics, Morisot's works —none of them categorized as "studies" in the catalogue —epitomized "slapdash" Impressionism. One reviewer compared the boats in her Isle of Wight paintings to a schoolboy's inept doodles,[165] and another suggested that to make these same pictures she had merely rubbed her canvas with her palette.[166] Such ill-informed comments notwithstanding, Morisot's innate sensitivity as a colorist was

FIGURE 44

Woman at Her Toilette [BW 73], c. 1875
Oil on canvas. 46 x 38 cm (18⅛ x 14¹⁵⁄₁₆ in.). Formerly
private collection, France; painting currently missing.

apparent to virtually every reviewer. Wrote Paul Mantz
(1821–1895):

The truth is that there is only one Impressionist in the group at
rue le Peletier: it is Berthe Morisot. She has already been
acclaimed and should continue to be so. She will never finish a
painting, a pastel, a watercolor; she produces prefaces for books
that she will never write, but when she plays with a range of
light tones, she finds grays of an extreme finesse and pinks of
the most delicate pallor.[167]

There were even several critics, such as Arthur
Baignières (d. 1913), who understood that Morisot was seeking something new in art, to capture the commonplace
experience of glancing, how the eye is dazzled before it
can adjust to details:

She carries the [Impressionist] system to an extreme, and we
are all the sorrier as she has rare qualities as a colorist. Several of
her canvases represent views of the Isle of Wight and it is

impossible not to recognize it; when you look at them quickly,
blinking your eyes, the greenery, sky, the houses of England are
there before us. You should not, for example, come closer [to
the paintings] nor look at details; [do so and] the illusion
disappears and you find yourself in the presence of monstrous
beings, incoherent dabs and crazy perspectives. Mlle Morisot is
such a dedicated Impressionist that she wishes to paint even the
motion of inanimate things.[168]

No one, however, was particularly struck by the fact
that her five paintings from England (among them
colorplate 26 and perhaps colorplate 27) were variations
on a single motif, yet this group anticipated the controversial series of related views of train stations and dancers
that Monet and Degas exhibited at the following show.
To a more limited extent, Morisot's figure paintings in
the 1876 exhibition were also serial in concept, since the
same model had posed for four different pictures.[169] Her
appearance in the two white-on-white dressing-room
scenes that soon belonged to Hoschedé,[170] *Interior* (figure

FIGURE 45

Young Woman in a Ball Gown [BW 81], c. 1876
Oil on canvas. 86 x 53 cm (33⅞ x 20⅞ in.). Musée d'Orsay,
Paris.

COLORPLATE 28

Bow of a Yacht, 1875
Watercolor on paper. 20.6 x 26.7 cm (8⅛ x 10½ in.). Sterling
and Francine Clark Art Institute, Williamstown, Massachusetts.

41) and *Woman at Her Toilette* (figure 44), could be seen to represent preliminary activities in the day of a fashionable woman who emerges in full evening dress—"finished," so to speak—in *Young Woman in a Ball Gown* (figure 45) and *Figure of a Woman (Before the Theater)* (colorplate 29). Whereas the two dressing-room pictures are conventional genre scenes, including settings, props, and gestures, the others, lacking such details, are for the most part portraits. In *Figure of a Woman (Before the Theater)*, a tiny, dark canvas that reminded at least two critics of a Goya, Morisot's model holds opera glasses; this is a token reminder that the theme of Morisot's art as a whole is looking.[171]

Like Eugène Manet, whose portrait by Degas (figure 39) was included in the second Impressionist exhibition, Morisot may have encountered a likeness of herself there; the etchings contributed by the bohemian artist Marcellin Desboutins (1823–1902) could have included a representation of Morisot (figure 46).[172] Desboutins had himself posed for a large figure painting that Manet exhibited this same spring in his studio after it was refused by the Salon jury.

As Zola had taken up his pen to defend Manet's honor a decade earlier, now Mallarmé composed an essay to protest this most recent jury refusal, articulating Manet's ideas about art and stressing his leader's role in the development of Impressionism. Appearing in the first issue of an

FIGURE 46

Marcellin Desboutins, *Portrait of Berthe Morisot,* 1876
Etching. 26 x 17.5 cm (10¼ x 6⅞ in.). Bibliothèque Nationale,
Paris.

FIGURE 47

Luncheon on the Grass [BW 47], 1875
Oil on canvas. 60 x 74 cm (23⅝ x 29⅛ in.). Private collection.

ephemeral English art journal, rather than a French periodical where it would have reached an audience more familiar with the debate about Manet, Mallarmé's account
includes perceptive remarks about Morisot's art, which
the poet characterized as especially feminine, albeit without defining what he meant by that designation. Referring to a picture by Morisot in the 1876 Impressionist
exhibition, *Luncheon on the Grass* (figure 47), one of her
few images to show a man together with a woman,
Mallarmé stressed Morisot's novel, understated approach
to genre painting:

That couple yonder, the least details of whose pose is so well
painted that one could recognize them by that alone, even if
their faces, seen under the shady straw hats, did not prove them
to be portrait sketches, give their own characteristics to the
place they enliven by their visit. The air of preoccupation, of
mundane care or secret sorrows, so generally characteristic of
the modern artist's sketches from contemporary life, were never
more notably absent than here.[173]

Mallarmé's insider's awareness that the figures here are
portraits of specific individuals suggests that he had discussed his observations with the artist herself. A letter
from Mallarmé to Morisot, dated December 23, 1876, although formal in tone, further documents the beginning
of a special rapport between poet and painter, who now
exchanged visits.[174] This same letter was foremost one of
condolence, for Mme Morisot had died a week earlier.[175]

Mourning did not, however, prevent Morisot from participating in the third Impressionist exhibition, which
opened in April 1877 in rented rooms across the street
from Durand-Ruel's gallery. Eugène decided not to accept
Degas's invitation to exhibit with the group.[176] Whereas
this year Monet, Renoir, and Gustave Caillebotte (1848–
1894) all showed large new works, Morisot's less grandiose
pictures, which were displayed in the same room as
Renoir's *Dance at the Moulin de la Galette*, were mostly ignored by the press, except for several comments made
about their exquisite white and silver-gray harmonies.[177] A
pastel (figure 48) of a woman seated informally with her
legs extended on a little couch in a shadowy room epitomized this new tendency. In sharp contrast to Morisot's
lively English pictures of the previous year, here the only
movement is the rapidity of the strokes of white that render
light from a window as it dances across the model's white
bodice and skirt. Trying to evoke Morisot's unique style

COLORPLATE 29

Figure of a Woman (Before the Theater),
1875–76
Oil on canvas. 57 x 31 cm (22½ x 12³⁄₁₆ in.).
Courtesy of Galerie Schröder und Leisewitz,
Kunsthandel, Bremen, Federal Republic of
Germany.

FIGURE 48

Daydreaming [BW 434], 1877
Pastel on canvas. 50.2 x 61 cm (19¾ x 24 in.). The Nelson-Atkins Museum of Art, Kansas City, Missouri (Acquired through the Anonymous Fund).

FIGURE 49

The Cheval Glass [BW 64], 1876
Oil on canvas. 65 x 54 cm (25⁹⁄₁₆ x 21¼ in.). Thyssen-Bornemisza Collection, Lugano, Switzerland.

for the very first book devoted to the Impressionists, published in 1878, Théodore Duret wrote: "The artist completes her canvases with light strokes of the brush here and there over the background; it's as if she is scattering flower petals."[178]

Unfortunately, it is impossible to identify most of the works listed by title under Morisot's name in the catalogue. She may have decided to destroy the one referred to as *Horsewoman*, for there is no extant painting by her of a figure in fashionable riding apparel, which would have been similar in theme to recent works by Manet and Renoir.[179] *The Black Bodice* (colorplate 30), a "portrait" of a pensive, seated model in a black evening dress, is perhaps the *Head of a Girl* named in the catalogue. But only one of the two dressing-room paintings listed can be identified, *The Cheval Glass* (figure 49), a picture of a young woman in a slip who looks at her reflected image in a full-length mirror.[180] The quiet, private meditations of this figure contrast sharply with the saucy pride of a related figure in Manet's *Nana* (figure 50), the large dressing-room scene that was removed from the Salon of 1877.

FIGURE 50

Edouard Manet, *Nana,* 1876–77
Oil on canvas. 154 x 115 cm (60¾ x 45¼ in.). Hamburger Kunsthalle, Hamburg, Germany.

COLORPLATE 30

The Black Bodice, 1876
Oil on canvas. 73 x 59.8 cm (28¾ x 23½ in.). The National
Gallery of Ireland, Dublin.

COLORPLATE 31

At the Water's Edge, 1879
Watercolor on paper. 21 x 28 cm (8¼ x 11 in.). From the
Collection of Joan Whitney Payson.

Around this time, Morisot and Eugène left the rue Guichard to take an apartment nearby on what is now the avenue Victor Hugo.[181] Most of the Impressionists and some of their earliest supporters suffered financial hardships thanks to the badly depressed art market throughout 1877 and 1878. Monet had to sell his new paintings for only 100 francs each. Hoschedé, the most active collector of his works, went bankrupt and was forced to sell. The dressing-room scene by Morisot that he had acquired in 1875 (figure 41) brought only 260 francs when part of his collection was put up for auction on February 18, 1878. It was bought by Victor Chocquet (1821–1891), the pioneering collector of works by Cézanne.[182] At a later auction, in June, *Woman at Her Toilette* (figure 44), Hoschedé's other dressing-room

picture by Morisot, was sold to Mary Cassatt (1844–1926) for only 95 francs.[183]

Cassatt, an American painter, had settled in Paris in 1874 to pursue an art career. A passionate promoter of her new colleagues' pictures, she seems to have begun her own remarkable collection of Impressionist paintings at the Hoschedé sale, when she also acquired her first work by Monet. Encouraged by Degas, Cassatt began to participate in the Impressionist group exhibitions in 1879, showing figure paintings that are closely related in spirit to works by Morisot, who was not a participant that year.

Evidently Morisot at first expressed a willingness to exhibit some fans decorated in watercolors (now lost) in the 1879 exhibition, as Degas and Pissarro did, but at the

COLORPLATE 32

Luncheon in the Country, 1879
Watercolor on paper. 14 x 22 cm (5½ x 8¹¹⁄₁₆ in.). Courtesy of
Galerie Hopkins and Thomas, Paris.

last moment she decided against taking part at all.[184] The fact that Morisot gave birth to her only child, Julie, on November 14, 1878, probably played an important part in this decision not to exhibit.[185] Almost at once, Julie and the wonder with which the child encountered the world around her became Morisot's favorite themes. "She is like a kitten," Morisot wrote to Edma's daughter Jeanne, "always happy; she is round as a ball; she has sparkling eyes and a large grinning mouth."[186]

Perhaps because maternal duties interfered with her established routine for painting in oils, around 1879–80 Morisot began to paint in watercolor more than she ever had before, and her new works in this portable, less time-consuming medium tend to be freer and livelier than any

of her earlier work on paper. In the most complex of these new watercolors, *At the Water's Edge* (colorplate 31), a well-dressed young couple lounges by the lake in the Bois de Boulogne. Sketching the figures' outlines with her active brush, Morisot varied the thickness and character of the line to the point where the dots and skeins of color that ostensibly describe a lap or a skirt become intricate, abstract patterns in their own right.

In other signed watercolors from this period, Morisot used color sparingly, letting the paper's whiteness and a sparse web of lines define figures and objects. In one of her most accomplished exercises in white tones, *Luncheon in the Country* (colorplate 32), a white tablecloth littered with empty glasses and a nurse in white uniform holding

COLORPLATE 33

Cows, 1880
Watercolor on paper. 20 x 26 cm (7⅞ x 10¼ in.). Mount
Holyoke College Art Museum, South Hadley, Massachusetts,
Museum Purchase: Gift of Alice Hench Fiske in memory of
Paula Radway Utell and the Warbeke Art Museum Fund, 1985.

little Julie are depicted with an economy of means that is truly extraordinary. Similarly, in *Cows* (colorplate 33), from a series of views that Morisot painted in Normandy in 1880, she demonstrated her delicacy of touch and remarkable sensitivity to tonal nuance.

As for Morisot's oil paintings, it is difficult to determine those to be dated 1878–79, just prior to the fourth Impressionist exhibition, but the balcony setting with venetian blinds that appears in two closely related works may correspond to her avenue Victor Hugo apartment. Morisot's lively brushwork notwithstanding, both *Seated Woman* (figure 51) and *Behind the Blinds* (colorplate 34) are close in spirit to *Hearts Are Trumps* (figure 52) by the

English painter John Everett Millais (1829–1896), whose canvas was very highly regarded when it was exhibited at the Paris World's Fair in 1878. Whether or not Millais's picture influenced Morisot, *Behind the Blinds* is a remarkable variation on her own *Woman at Her Toilette* (figure 44), the dressing-room subject done a few years earlier, in which the model wears the same costume and sits on the same black side chair. These details seem odd, however, in the context of the new balcony setting for *Behind the Blinds*, which is hardly a standard genre picture. Still more peculiar is the large cushion lodged awkwardly between the chair back and the balcony railing, evidently for the comfort of the model, whose pensive demeanor is in fact

COLORPLATE 34

Behind the Blinds, 1878–79
Oil on canvas. 73.5 x 59.5 cm (29 x 23 ⅜ in.). Mr. and Mrs.
Moreton Binn.

Seated Woman [BW 78], 1878–79
Oil on canvas. 80 x 100 cm (31½ x 39⅜ in.). Private collection,
New York.

John Everett Millais, *Hearts Are Trumps*, 1872
Oil on canvas. 165.7 x 219.7 cm (65¼ x 86½ in.). Tate Gallery,
London.

designed to show with humor the trials of posing. Oddest
of all, perhaps, is that Morisot never exhibited this won-
derfully offbeat picture.

By the fall of 1879, Cassatt and Morisot were discussing advance arrangements for the fifth Impressionist
exhibition.[187] Morisot's abstention from the fourth group
show in no way lessened the impact of her work, for as far
as most critics were concerned, she dominated the fifth
Impressionist exhibition in 1880, presented in a noisy, badly
lit building on the rue des Pyramides. As the journalists
realized, she was the only real Impressionist in this show,
since Monet, Renoir, and Sisley had decided not to participate. Degas's stricture obliging members of the group to
boycott the official Salon was at issue.[188] Degas, who had
never adopted the free brushwork that characterized the
work of these painters, replaced them with, among others, Jean-François Raffaëlli (1850–1924) and Federico
Zandomeneghi (1841–1917), whose works were hardly more
Impressionist than his own.

The visionary printmaker Odilon Redon (1840–1916)
expressed dismay in his diary at a decline in Morisot's
talents, as far as oil painting was concerned.[189] But in a
long, thoughtful review of this 1880 exhibition, Paul Mantz,
struck by her commitment to virtuoso brushwork and pale
color harmonies, tried to explain why many viewers tended
to regard her sketchlike oils as unfulfilled promises and
thus missed their inherent poetic qualities: "It's like looking at beautiful apple trees covered with pink and white
flowers sparkling in April frosts. Taking a dim view, the

Edouard Manet, *Before the Mirror*, 1876
Oil on canvas. 93.4 x 71.4 cm (36¼ x 28⅛ in.). The Justin K.
Thannhauser Collection, Solomon R. Guggenheim Museum,
New York.

COLORPLATE 35

Woman at Her Toilette, c. 1879
Oil on canvas. 60.3 x 80.4 cm (23¾ x 31⅝ in.). The Art Institute
of Chicago, The Stickney Fund.

cider manufacturer anticipates a bad apple crop, but the colorist delights in the spectacle's delicacies as images of hope."[190] Like Mantz, who imagined that Jean-Antoine Watteau would have appreciated Morisot's light-handed genius, Charles Ephrussi (1849–1905) pointed out that her opalescent works celebrated the quintessentially French Rococo tradition of Jean-Honoré Fragonard: "She grinds flower petals onto her palette, in order to spread them later on her canvas with airy, witty touches, thrown down a little haphazardly. These harmonize, blend, and finish by producing something vital, fine, and charming that you do not see so much as intuit."[191] The spiritual kinship of Morisot's art to that of eighteenth-century masters so impressed some later writers that many biographers now claim, perhaps incorrectly, that Fragonard was in fact her great-great-uncle on her father's side.[192]

Many of the works that Morisot exhibited with the Impressionists in April 1880 suggest an ongoing dialogue with Manet, who at the same time held a one-artist exhibition of recent works in the gallery space of *La Vie moderne,* a popular arts, fashion, and society periodical. Like Morisot's, his works were described by critics as unfinished and "embryonic" and his free brushwork as spotty and incoherent. Evidently taking their cue from Degas's advocate Duranty, who in 1876 had dared artists to describe the essence of modern life with no more than a figure's back to go by,[193] both Manet and Morisot showed pictures of women who have turned to observe themselves in bedroom mirrors. Rendered with long, rustling brushstrokes in pinks, blues, and whites, Morisot's *Woman at Her Toilette* (colorplate 35) and Manet's *Before the Mirror* (figure 53) are like visual poems, with orchestrated details

81

COLORPLATE 36

The Lake in the Bois de Boulogne (Summer Day), 1879
Oil on canvas. 45.7 x 75.3 cm (18 x 29 ⅝ in.). The Trustees of the
National Gallery, London.

worthy of their friend Mallarmé: brushed blond hair, sat-
ins, powder puffs, and flower petals. Morisot went so far
as to sign her name along the bottom of the mirror, as if
to stress that the image in her painting is as fragile, ephemeral, and incomplete as a silvery reflection.

Not only did Morisot and Manet use the same sort of
flourished, overlapping brushstroke, they evidently used
the same model. The unidentified woman who posed for
Manet's *The Plum* (c. 1877–78), for example, apparently
also posed for Morisot's *The Lake in the Bois de Boulogne*
(colorplate 36). This last work, in which a woman in blue
and another in white ride in a boat accompanied by swans,
is of course Morisot's reprise of Manet's *Boating* (figure
54), begun in 1874 but not exhibited until the Salon of
1879. Like Manet, Morisot presents the figures in close-up,
as if she were with them on the boat; yet such proximity
seems not to have obliged her to render observations in
detail. On the contrary, she defined her figures with the
same rippled brushwork that she used for the lake's sur-

face in the background. Given this suffused texture,
Morisot's painting has a decorative unity that in turn seems
to have appealed to Manet. The figures in *The Lake in
the Bois de Boulogne* reappear in the same costumes in
Morisot's *In the Garden* (colorplate 37), quite probably the
boldest work of all in the 1880 Impressionist exhibition.
Here Morisot's free brushwork obliterates the face of the
leaning figure into a comma of red and her gesture into a
white blur, thus sacrificing the last vestige of conventional
genre painting for an utterly abstract texture. The boldly
flickered paint, at odds with the calm subject matter, expresses instead the speed of Morisot's own visual act.

Manet, who would give Morisot a special easel as a
New Year's gift,[194] must have been particularly impressed
by a pair of paintings exhibited by Morisot in 1880,
Summer (figure 55) and *Winter* (colorplate 38), in which
she integrated the figures and backgrounds as if she were
weaving tapestries with threads of paint. The following
year Manet began an ensemble of similarly decorative

82

COLORPLATE 37

In the Garden (Women Gathering Flowers), 1879
Oil on canvas. 61 x 73.5 cm (24 x 29 in.). Nationalmuseum,
Stockholm.

pictures, hoping to show these in the first Salon des
Arts Décoratifs, which his close friend Antonin Proust
(1832–1905) was organizing.[195] Although this project never
reached fruition, at the Salon of 1881 Manet did exhibit a
decorative half-length female figure titled *Spring* and, on
commission from Proust, began a companion piece,
Autumn (figure 56), as part of a Seasons series.[196]

Meanwhile, in *Portrait of Marcel Gobillard* (colorplate
39), Morisot drew quite openly upon Manet's masterful
portrait of his stepson Léon in *The Luncheon in the Studio*,
1868. Depicted in her portrait, painted around 1880, is her
nephew Marcel (1872–1922), wearing the same sort of dark

jacket and holding a straw hat similar to that Manet used
for his picture. Although Marcel's somewhat formal pose
is completely out of keeping with the rest of Morisot's
portraiture, the casual domestic setting and sweeping
brushwork are entirely characteristic of her work, as is the
poetic color sense—here a "symphony" of silver and gold
tones, the grays in the jacket, shadows, and mirror reflection
contrasting with the blond tones in the child's hair, hat,
and lustrous furniture.

Morisot's command of just such silver and gold harmonies is no less remarkable in a peculiar genre subject,
In the Dining Room (colorplate 40), apparently painted at

FIGURE 54

Edouard Manet, *Boating*, 1874
Oil on canvas. 97.2 x 130.2 cm (38¼ x 51¼ in.). The Metropolitan
Museum of Art, New York, Bequest of H. O. Havemeyer.

COLORPLATE 38

Winter, 1879–80
Oil on canvas. 73.5 x 58.4 cm (29 x 23 in.). Dallas Museum of
Art, Gift of the Meadows Foundation Incorporated.

FIGURE 55

Summer [BW 75], c. 1878
Oil on canvas. 76 x 61 cm (29¹⁵⁄₁₆ x 24 in.). Musée Fabre,
Montpellier.

FIGURE 56

Edouard Manet, *Autumn*, 1882
Oil on canvas. 73 x 51 cm (28¾ x 20 in.). Musée des Beaux-Arts,
Nancy.

COLORPLATE 39

Portrait of Marcel Gobillard (Little Boy in Gray), c. 1880
Oil on canvas. 86 x 62 cm (33⅞ x 24⁷⁄₁₆ in.). Private collection,
Geneva, Switzerland.

COLORPLATE 40

In the Dining Room, 1880
Oil on canvas. 92 x 73 cm (36¼ x 28¾ in.). Private collection.

the same time. It is her decision to depict the figure of a maid from behind, in the spirit of Duranty, that seems odd, for it strictly limits the role of expression or gesture. Instead, Morisot's subject is the shimmering play of light in a dining room, transforming a clutter of mundane objects, including tableware, porcelain, bread, a rustic cupboard, and a maid's uniform, into a faceted, jewellike realm of color. It seems that Morisot never exhibited either of these virtuoso tonal paintings, although she had ample opportunity to do so.

The sixth Impressionist exhibition, held in April 1881, again without Monet, Renoir, and Sisley, and now without Caillebotte as well, lacked the excitement of the early shows.[197] Only Degas, Morisot, Pissarro, and Rouart remained from the original group, and since Degas had devoted most of his energy for the last two years to his extraordinary realist wax sculpture, *The Fourteen-Year-Old Dancer*, Impressionist painting was not extensively represented in this 1881 group show. Morisot and Cassatt were the obvious standard-bearers for the new style as far as most newspaper critics were concerned, and so for the first time in recorded history women artists were singled out as the undisputed leaders of avant-garde painting.[198] Morisot showed eight works, although they were not installed in time for the opening.[199] Most cannot be identified from their titles in the catalogue or from descriptions in the press. Clearly, however, Morisot was even more daring than she had been the year before, when Mantz and Ephrussi applauded the poetic charm inherent in her lack of finish. In 1881 Mantz reported: "Mme Morisot has come—and this is something of a surprise—to exaggerate her manner and to blur the imprecise. She has made no more than beginnings of beginnings: the result is curious, but more and more metaphysical. Evidently a colorist's talents are needed in order to surmise the delicacy in the nothingness."[200] Referring to two pastels, Ephrussi likewise threw up his hands: "One step further and it will be impossible to distinguish or understand anything at all."[201] Evidently referring to one of the same pastels, another critic called a profile of a child (perhaps the work reproduced in figure 57) "cancerous."[202] Judging from the oil that was probably exhibited under the title *Nursing* (colorplate 41), the critics' consternation is understandable. So far as is known, no other artist showed a picture as roughly handled as this at any of the eight Impressionist shows. Without the woman's straw hat with its trailing white ribbons, tossed to the ground at the right, it would be impossible to determine the location of any spatial plane,

FIGURE 57

Baby in Profile [BW 453], 1880
Pastel. 40 x 30 cm (15¾ x 11¹³⁄₁₆ in.). Private collection.

and the only indication of recession into space is an opened green parasol on the ground to the left. Its shape is all but lost in the otherwise chaotic setting, a field of strokes in various shades of green scrawled in every direction. It is difficult to think of a comparably active paint surface by any painter before the advent of Abstract Expressionism in the 1950s.

If we presume that the baby in *Nursing* represents Julie, this remarkable painting must have been executed in 1879, initiating an ongoing series of pictures of the little girl. Whereas Morisot's decision to paint her child was a solution to the problems facing any working mother, Cassatt, who was not a mother, was no less passionately interested in the same theme. She showed her first pictures of babies at the sixth Impressionist exhibition, perhaps in part from awareness of her colleague's work. Although Cassatt's somewhat more finished works were by and large received with greater enthusiasm than Morisot's, critics noted that both artists' oils were characterized by pale colors of the sort found mainly in pastels and frescoes.[203] In his review of the 1881 show, the novelist Joris-Karl

COLORPLATE 41

Nursing, 1879
Oil on canvas. 50 x 61 cm (19¾ x 24 in.). Private collection,
Washington, D.C.

FIGURE 58

Photograph of Eugène Manet, Berthe Morisot, and Julie Manet, c. 1882. Private collection.

Huysmans (1848–1907) confessed that despite a strong prejudice against sentimental pictures of children by women painters, he had to make an exception for Cassatt.[204] But Huysmans neglected to mention Morisot's works on the same theme.

His review does, however, point out that several of the exhibitors had framed their works on paper under glass, and that Pissarro had painted his frames in a variety of tones to complement the dominant colors in his works. Other critics mentioned the introduction of white frames, and one specified that the works of both Morisot and Cassatt were "strangely framed."[205] Although the rationale for such experimentation still has not been explained, it is worth mentioning that for this year's exhibition the walls were hung with "parti-colored calicoes"; this deviation from standard red walls may have discouraged some artists from using conventional gold frames.[206]

FIGURE 59

The Port of Nice [BW 112], 1881–82
Oil on canvas. 53 x 43 cm (20⅞ x 16¹⁵⁄₁₆ in.). Private collection.

FIGURE 60

The Port of Nice [BW 113], 1881–82
Oil on canvas. 41 x 55 cm (16⅛ x 21⅝ in.). Private collection.

COLORPLATE 42

The Beach at Nice, 1881–82
Watercolor on paper. 42 x 55 cm (16½ x 21⅝ in.)
Nationalmuseum, Stockholm

In the summer of 1881 for the first time Morisot and her family rented a country house at 4, rue de la Princesse, in Bougival, a picturesque spot on the Seine not far from Versailles, where Edouard Manet, his health failing, was spending his vacation.[207] Enlisting their maid Pasie, Julie, and even Eugène to model, Morisot started a series of domestic garden pictures. She and Eugène had given up their apartment in Paris after purchasing property on the rue de Villejust in Passy; they had contracted to build a large house there, apparently with the intention of renting the upper floors for a steady source of income. Construction was underway by the end of 1881.[208]

By then the Manets had gone south for what Morisot called "an experiment" in Nice, staying at the Hotel Richemont.[209] This "experiment" may have had to do with her series of pictures of boats in the port at Nice (figures 59 and 60), for Morisot made only one figure painting, *The Beach at Nice* (BW 116), on this trip, done while she

watched Julie at play on the overcast beach and studied the distant view of the waterfront buildings and bridges. She evidently plotted the general composition for this painting in a delicate watercolor (colorplate 42). Leaving most of her sheet uncolored, Morisot indicated background details with squiggles and pinpoints of thinned pigment; in the foreground she represented Julie, her nurse, and the violet shadow they cast to fill the large void in her idiosyncratic composition. It is not known how long Morisot and her family stayed in Nice; nor is it known whether they returned to Paris or Bougival before they set out for Italy around February 1882. In any event, the Italian trip was cut short when Julie came down with bronchitis in Florence.[210]

Leaving Morisot and Julie in Nice, Eugène, who now had a civil-service post, hurried back to Paris and oversaw the arrangements for his wife's participation in the seventh Impressionist show, held in March 1882.[211] This year

FIGURE 61

Young Woman in a Conservatory [BW 110], 1881
Oil on canvas. 80 x 100 cm (31¾ x 39½ in.). Private collection.

FIGURE 62

Eugène Manet and His Daughter at Bougival [BW 103], 1881
Oil on canvas. 73 x 92 cm (28¾ x 36¼ in.). Private collection.

Caillebotte, Pissarro, and Paul Gauguin (1848–1903) made a concerted effort to bring the members of the original Impressionist group back together again for a more exciting show. To this end they excluded the lackluster artists Degas had recruited to replace them in the last two exhibitions. Thanks to the help of Durand-Ruel, who agreed to lend new works by Monet and Renoir—neither of whom could be troubled with such negotiations—these efforts succeeded, except that Degas now refused to take part and Cassatt followed his lead.[212]

As for Morisot, Eugène's last-minute efforts to submit works on her behalf were somewhat ineffective. Before he reached Paris, the other artists had already begun to hang the show, taking almost all the available wall space. He immediately went to Bougival, where Morisot's pictures were stored, and with the help of a locksmith retrieved several suitable examples; but most of them needed frames —Eugène had decided on white ones—and it took several days to make them.[213] Fortunately he was able to borrow a relatively large figure painting of a woman named Marie (figure 61) from the dealer Alphonse Portier (d. 1902), a colleague of Durand-Ruel.[214] Portier's was the only picture by Morisot included in the exhibition during the first days, when most newspaper critics came to prepare their reviews.

Meanwhile, Eugène wrote to Morisot about the other works he had selected: "I took the finished Nice canvases —[along with] Julie with Pasie in the Robin garden [BW

124], Julie with her barrel (a small canvas)[BW 107], me and Julie playing with her houses (unstretched canvas) [figure 62]. I particularly like Pasie sewing on a bench [colorplate 43]."[215] These paintings of Julie and Pasie were all presumably painted the previous summer in Bougival. Eugène's letter also mentioned pastels that he had found but gave no details about them.

Morisot replied that she preferred not to show the picture of Pasie sewing, since it needed more work. In its place, she suggested that Eugène take the small picture of Julie and Pasie that "Manet had admired" (probably *The Balcony*, the picture of Julie and Pasie in the Robin garden, mentioned above). She added: "I don't want to have too many; five or six are enough."[216] Aware, as Morisot herself was not, that the other artists were showing far more (Caillebotte and Renoir each had seventeen works, Sisley had twenty-two, Monet thirty-five, and Pissarro thirty-four), Eugène urged her in vain to paint a few new things and ship them to Paris immediately.[217] But time ran out.

Given the confusion, the exhibition catalogue, which lists only nine works by Morisot, including three pastels, is at best an approximate guide.[218] In any event, Morisot's works, which were in place about a week after the opening, hardly impressed the few journalists with later press deadlines. "The *Port of Nice* is something incomprehensible and senseless, and it is certainly what led one exasper-

COLORPLATE 43

Pasie Sewing in the Garden at Bougival, 1881
Oil on canvas. 81 x 100 cm (31⅞ x 39⅜ in.). Musée des
Beaux-Arts, Pau.

ated gentleman to write in anger and rage on the stairway: 'I protest.'"[219] Durand-Ruel, however, was apparently quite impressed with Morisot's paintings in the exhibition, since he purchased the one of Julie with her "barrel" (undoubtedly a pull toy) from Portier in April (BW 107) and took two other paintings by Morisot on consignment (BW 105 and figure 61), possibly to send them to London for an exhibition at a commercial gallery there in July.[220] Their new house still not completed by the time Morisot and Julie returned to Paris in late March, the family quickly set off for Bougival again.[221] Manet, now gravely ill, summered nearby at Rueil.[222]

Dating the group of closely related pictures that Morisot painted at Bougival during the summers of 1881 through 1884 is especially difficult. The apparent age of Julie, who was nearly three years old the first summer and nearly six by the last, would seem to be the best guide, but it has serious limitations. For example, in the picture of Julie watching Pasie sew that Manet liked (BW 124), Julie looks much younger than she does in the painting of Eugène and his daughter playing with miniature houses (figure 62), yet both were done in 1881 and discussed as possible entries in the March 1882 Impressionist show.

Questions of dating aside, however, it is clear that without relinquishing her free brushwork, Morisot had already begun by 1881 to formulate the more sophisticated approach to theme and color that would characterize all her Bougival pictures. The painting of Eugène seated in the garden with Julie's toy village on his lap, watching her fascination with the miniature trees and houses, exemplifies this group. Looking remains the presiding theme, and Julie's intense absorption reflects Morisot's own absorption as a painter, observing the trees and houses in the distant background setting. Morisot's Bougival pictures are typically meditations on contrasting modes of awareness, recalling her pictures of the early 1870s, and in this masterpiece, Eugène's mood contrasts sharply with that of Julie. He appears deeply pensive and unconcerned with the play of color and shape that preoccupies his daughter.

Whereas Morisot's treatment of color in the 1870s was predominantly descriptive or decorative, these Bougival pictures are characterized both by the calculated interplay of opposing complementary tones that resonate and thus heighten the illusion of space and by the contrasting interplay of closely related tones with just the opposite effect. For *Tea* (colorplate 44) Morisot posed a carrot-topped girl at a little bamboo-motif table next to their garden fence. The related tones of the girl's hair, the orange fur of the cat cuddling against her, and the yellow furniture all inter-

FIGURE 63

The Fable [BW 138], 1883
Oil on canvas. 65 x 81 cm (25 9/16 x 31 7/8 in.). Private collection.

act with the complementary blue tones in her dress and the fence, through the interstices of which bright red flowers punctuate the complementary green landscape.

The Fable (figure 63), to use Mallarmé's title for Morisot's double portrait of Pasie and Julie conversing in the garden, is no less complex. Pasie sits slouched and distracted on a shaded garden bench, her blue uniform juxtaposed with the yellow workbasket alongside her. As in the picture of Julie playing with toy houses, the adult here seems immune to the enthusiasm of the child seated before her, even though Julie's excited mood is evoked by a strong raking light that ripples across her pink dress and obliterates details in the foreground.

The most ambitious and moving picture in this group, however, is *The Garden* (colorplate 45), the largest work Morisot had ever painted. As she had for *Interior* (see figure 28), painted a decade earlier, Morisot posed a fashionably dressed model on a chair as if for a formal portrait, although the informal garden background here—with an abandoned rake and a child wandering off—is at odds with the demands of conventional portraiture. The sitter's dark-blue dress seems to cast a shadow in this light-flooded setting, while her inanimate expression only adds to the atmosphere of melancholy, a mood that is comparable to the air of distraction of the modern women in Tissot's psychologically melodramatic genre scenes or to the states of mind of the so-called Sphinxes portrayed in Stevens's

COLORPLATE 44

Tea, 1882
Oil on canvas. 57.5 x 71.5 cm (22⅝ x 28⅛ in.). Madelon
Foundation, Vaduz.

genre pictures. The unedited appearance of the setting in Morisot's painting and the seeming spontaneity of the brushwork notwithstanding, the artist calculated every nuance. In terms of color, she sought stringent, slightly discordant juxtapositions of nearly identical tones: the blue fan against the blue dress, the green leaves against the green trellis and fence, the straw hat with its highlighted brim darkening the pale blond face.

The Garden may have been one of three paintings by Morisot included in an Impressionist group exhibition organized by Durand-Ruel that opened in London on April 21, 1883.[223] The day before, Manet's left leg had been amputated in a last desperate effort to save his life. His death on April 30 crushed Morisot, who realized, as she wrote to Edma, that her "entire past of youth and work [was] suddenly ending."[224] Proust, Zola, Burty, Stevens, Duret, and Monet served as pallbearers for the funeral on May 3,[225] and they all helped throughout the remainder of the year with arrangements for a memorial exhibition, which opened the following January. With Mallarmé acting as a catalyst, Monet and Morisot now developed an especially close friendship, trading letters and visits. Shortly after the

COLORPLATE 46

Eugène Manet and His Daughter in the Garden, 1883
Oil on canvas. 60 x 73 cm (23⅝ x 28¾ in.). Private collection.

COLORPLATE 45

The Garden, 1882 or 1883
Oil on canvas. 99.1 x 127 cm (39 x 50 in.). The Sara Lee
Corporation.

funeral, Eugène's mother moved into the rue de Villejust
house, which was finally ready for occupancy in early 1883.

That summer in Bougival Morisot continued her garden series; in *Eugène Manet and His Daughter in the Garden*
(colorplate 46), she posed Eugène and Julie by a small
circular pond. Her back turned, Julie watches a red toy
boat, the single complementary accent in this densely
shaded setting. The light-splattered leaves and grass, rendered with dabs of green, yellow, and white arranged
roughly in a circle, form a sort of frame for the figures.
This painting and a luminous, loosely rendered water-

COLORPLATE 47

Julie with Her Toy Boat (Child at Play), c. 1883
Watercolor on paper. 23 x 16 cm (9 1/16 x 6 5/16 in.). Private collection.

COLORPLATE 48

In the Garden at Maurecourt, c. 1883
Oil on canvas. 54 x 65 cm (21¼ x 25⅜ in.). The Toledo
Museum of Art; Gift of Edward Drummond Libbey.

color, *Julie with Her Toy Boat* (colorplate 47), are somewhat nostalgic, if understood in relationship to Morisot's
lifelong predilection for painting real boats, whether at
Lorient, Cherbourg, the Isle of Wight, or Nice. Unfortunately, Morisot's work was interrupted in July when Julie
came down with the whooping cough.[226]

Since the painting of Eugène and Julie at the pond is
remarkably close in style to *In the Garden at Maurecourt*
(colorplate 48), a picture of Edma and a child seated on
the grass in the garden of her father-in-law's country home,
just outside Paris, both could possibly have been painted
this same summer. The figures are surrounded by a flurry

of green brushstrokes, and the red accent of the toy boat in the Bougival double portrait has its counterpart in the red trim of Edma's wide-brimmed hat in the Maurecourt picture. The tiny background details in the latter, including two chairs and a straw basket, are remarkable examples of the accuracy of Morisot's fluid brushwork, while her scumbled rendition of the figures in the foreground describes only the most general characteristics of shape and texture.

In August 1883 Eugène's mother suffered a stroke, which left her paralyzed.[227] When Morisot could return to her painting, she began a group of luminous, utterly simple little landscapes. Working from a boat to depict *The Quay at Bougival* (colorplate 49), she chose to devote the bottom half of her composition to a cavity of space inflected only by the moody play of light and shadow across the water. With the exception of a half dozen accents of color for little green trees and tiny straw hats worn by strollers pausing to gaze at the same lapping river scene, Morisot limited herself to white and pale shades of violet and rose.

Around this time, as the neighborhood farmers harvested, Morisot painted *The Haystack* (colorplate 50) as if it were a monument standing in an empty field, muted with lavender shadows. The conventional composition in a watercolor of the same subject by Eugène Manet (figure 64), painted while Morisot worked on her oil, suggests that by contrast her approach to landscape painting stressed utter simplicity. Without the few lilliputian figures at work off in the distance and a curtain of low trees at the horizon, this picture would be a totally abstract texture of feathered brushwork, recording the pale presence of light and space, a picture as boldly modern as the small oil studies that the young Georges Seurat (1859–1891) began to paint around this same time. Of course, for those familiar with Impressionist art, Morisot's little haystack painting calls Monet to mind most of all. Perhaps by coincidence, he painted his first haystack compositions, with his own unique style of brushwork, the following year at Giverny, where he had settled his family just prior to Manet's death.[228]

During 1883 Monet had devoted himself to painting a series of decorative still-life panels commissioned for the doors of Durand-Ruel's dining room. Putting this project aside, Monet set off for the Mediterranean coast around Christmas and decided to undertake an important group of new landscapes there. When he returned to Paris temporarily in early January 1884 for the opening of the Manet memorial exhibition, Monet promised Morisot a landscape of Bordighera as a decoration for the living room of her house on the rue de Villejust.[229]

Morisot had decided to make this high-ceilinged Empire-style room a combination museum, studio, and salon, displaying her family's extraordinary collection of Manet's pictures around the walls and storing her own painting materials behind a screen.[230] Monet wrote Morisot periodically to assure her that he had not forgotten his promise, but he needed well over a year to deliver his present, *Villas at Bordighera* (figure 65), a profuse garden landscape with rose- and blue-tinted southern villas and mountaintops visible in the distance beyond a foreground of exotic plants, a picture close in spirit to the little Nice landscape by Morisot in the 1882 Impressionist exhibition.[231]

The striking resemblance between Monet's *Villas at Bordighera* and a large summer-garden landscape of Bougival by Morisot (figure 66), which her cataloguers also date 1884, raises a question as to whether she saw Monet's work in progress or the variants of it that he sold to Durand-Ruel in June. Alternatively, Morisot's painting, which perhaps dates from an earlier summer at Bougival, may have inspired Monet, just as Morisot's 1884 painting of Julie and her nurse in a boat on the lake in the Bois de Boulogne (figure 67) apparently inspired Monet's 1887 paintings of his stepdaughters gliding in a boat on the Epte River (figure 68). Whatever the case, in November 1884, when Eugène took a trip to the Mediterranean coast with his brother Gustave and searched for "the villa of our dreams" in the vicinity of Nice, the dream undoubtedly resembled the scene depicted in Monet's present to them.[232] Sadly, Morisot and her husband could not find the means to fulfill this dream for several more years.

Judging from the size of Julie, who was nearly six in the summer of 1884, *On the Veranda* (colorplate 51), a painting that Morisot chose to exhibit on three separate occasions in later years,[233] was produced during her last Bougival vacation. In many respects it is a reprise of the large painting of Marie on the same veranda that was exhibited with the Impressionists in 1882 (figure 61). Julie sits at the same bamboo-motif table that Morisot used for her earlier work, and the same glass pitcher with spiral fluting catches ridges of white light in both pictures. But rather than facing forward for her portrait as Marie had,

COLORPLATE 49

The Quay at Bougival, 1883
Oil on canvas. 55.5 x 46 cm (21⅞ x 18⅛ in.). Nasjonalgalleriet, Oslo.

100

FIGURE 64

Eugène Manet, *Haymaking*, 1883
Watercolor. 21.6 x 27.9 cm (8½ x 11 in.). Private collection.

FIGURE 65

Claude Monet, *Villas at Bordighera*, 1884
Oil on canvas. 115 x 130 cm (45¼ x 51³⁄₁₆ in.). Private collection.

FIGURE 67

On the Lake, Bois de Boulogne [BW 146], 1884
Oil on canvas. 60 x 73 cm (23⅝ x 28¾ in.). Private collection.

FIGURE 68

Claude Monet, *Two Women in a Boat*, 1887
Oil on canvas. 145.5 x 133.5 cm (57¼ x 52⁹⁄₁₆ in.). The National
Museum of Western Art, Tokyo, Matsukata Collection.

FIGURE 66

Garden at Bougival [BW 148], 1884
Oil on canvas. 72 x 92 cm (28⅝ x 36⅜ in.). Private collection.

COLORPLATE 50

The Haystack, 1883
Oil on canvas. 55.3 x 45.7 cm (21¾ x 18 in.). Private collection,
New York.

COLORPLATE 51

On the Veranda, 1884
Oil on canvas. 81 x 100 cm (31⅞ x 39⅜ in.). Collection of
John C. Whitehead.

Julie turns away to examine the petals of a large white flower. Her orange hair glows white along its profile as light streams through the porch windows, beyond which the gables and roofs of neighboring cottages emerge from treetops rendered with strokes of delicately blended greens, blues, and yellows. Divided like a Piet Mondrian by the window framing and the rectangular tabletop, *On the Veranda* is among Morisot's most calculated compositions.

In *Julie with a Doll* (colorplate 52), painted at nearly the same time, a related concern for abstract geometrical structure is evident, even if the excited, scumbled brushwork in this frontal portrait makes it seem unfinished in

comparison with *On the Veranda*. Grasping a doll that resembles her, Julie sits back in a small armchair, her skirt hiked up in the process, recalling Cassatt's saucy *Little Girl in a Blue Armchair* (figure 69), which was rejected by the jury for the International Exhibition of 1878. Although the close similarity underlines the ongoing exchange between these women modernists, the way the light sweeps through the room in Morisot's picture, obliterating details, makes it far bolder in style than Cassatt's picture and more in keeping with the sketchy quality of Morisot's pastels. The flourishes of white and blue chalks in *Little Girl with Her Doll* (colorplate 53), an especially beautiful pastel

COLORPLATE 52

Julie with a Doll, 1884
Oil on canvas. 82 x 100 cm (32⁵⁄₁₆ x 39³⁄₈ in.). Private collection.

portrait of Julie, gives a good idea of how Morisot has transposed the stylistic charactistics of one medium to another. Morisot herself never exhibited the oil version of *Julie with a Doll,* perhaps because she realized the highly controversial nature of such transpositions. Indeed, her family and colleagues excluded this ultramodern painting from the comprehensive memorial exhibition of her works in 1896.

In the autumn of 1884 Morisot used Julie as a model for a series of pictures set on the lake in the Bois de Boulogne. One of these, *By the Lake* (colorplate 54), again a repetition in subject of an earlier work, one exhibited

with the Impressionists in 1880 (see colorplate 36), shows Julie in a boat, attracting the attention of swans and a duck. The way her fawn hat and coat complement the slapping blue water is characteristic of Morisot's decorative sense of color. But Morisot's foremost subject here is the lake's calm surface extending to the far bank, accented by miniature figures, a fluid field of brushstrokes modulated from blue to green. During the next several years, Morisot returned to this same motif of the lake's rippled surface again and again, in pastels and watercolors as well as in oils.

The winter brought more grief. Eugène's brother Gustave died in December, and in early January 1885, his

FIGURE 69

Mary Cassatt, *Little Girl in a Blue Armchair*, 1878
Oil on canvas. 89 x 130 cm (35 x 51 in.). National Gallery of Art,
Washington, D.C., Collection of Mr. and Mrs. Paul Mellon,
1983.1.18.

mother died as well.[234] It was perhaps then that Morisot began a group of highly unusual self-portraits in oil and pastel, none of them brought to conventional resolution. Yet the haunting pastel that records Morisot's haggard, if wide-eyed, features with succinct honesty is utterly finished in its own terse and somber terms (colorplate 55). It is clear from this pastel and from paintings such as *Julie with a Doll* (colorplate 52) that for Morisot it had become essential to stop work as soon as the image began to take shape, without adding any extraneous details. Part of the appeal of the "incomplete" oil self-portrait with Julie (colorplate 56) is likewise the fragile, emergent quality of the forms. Like all her fragmentary or unfinished pictures, this at once crude and sensitive image also reveals Morisot's fundamental studio methods, how she began her works with rough tentative outlines drawn with a thin brush and white highlights that map out the edges of volumes. Left in a raw state, these images are glimpses behind the scenes into the artist's most private creative meditations, comparable to the sculptural fragments that Auguste Rodin (1840–1917) began to exhibit in the 1880s, leaving the casting seams visible to allude to the process of image making. It is important to remember that the unprimed canvas background for this painting would originally have been cotton white, for its subsequent discoloration has exaggerated the unfinished appearance (see William Scott's essay, p. 196).

Portions of the insightful critique by Paul Bourget (1852–1935) of the Goncourt brothers (Edmond [1822–1896]

and Jules [1830–1870]) and their influence on the modern novel fascinated Morisot when it appeared in 1885, and she copied out several passages that refer specifically to the fragmentary nature of all visual experience.[235] According to Bourget, the Goncourts and their followers, including Zola, describe far more details than any person might actually notice. Morisot's own increasing inclination to dispense with all but the most salient details in her pictures should be understood then, at least in part, as an attempt, in the spirit of Bourget, to represent the psychology of visual experience, including its limitations.

It was around 1885 that Morisot began to sketch in small notebooks and to record favorite passages from her reading or the observations made by close friends, including Degas, Mallarmé, and Renoir, when they came to her weekly dinners. The quick sketches in these notebooks are symptomatic of an important change in Morisot's art, since before 1885 she had apparently seldom developed her ideas for pictures in preliminary drawings, for such a method detracted from the Impressionist quest for total spontaneity. For example, there is a luminous pastel study (colorplate 57) for *The Garden Chair* (colorplate 58), a painting of two little girls playing in the garden of the rue de Villejust house. The pastel includes all the elements of the final oil version: the oversized wicker chair, the curving path, the fence, and the children. But in the oil the components are rearranged: the empty chair is turned sideways, and one of the children is brought forward to lean on the fence. Apparently Morisot made the pastel on the spot without editing and subsequently analyzed this impression as a starting point for the oil version. If so, the spontaneous Impressionist brushwork in the oil should now be understood as a strictly stylistic choice, not as an expedient for working as quickly as possible to catch real life on the fly.

Nearly a dozen drawings, watercolors (including a fan [colorplate 59]), and pastels can be understood as studies for or variants of *The Goose* (figure 70), a vertical-format decorative painting that may have been too large for Morisot to transport to the Bois de Boulogne in orthodox Impressionist fashion. The painting, with its emphasis on silhouette and simple horizontal zones of color in the background, has the character of many nineteenth-century Japanese woodblock prints. Perhaps Morisot's immediate source of inspiration, however, considering Mallarmé's enthusiasm for English children's books, was the work of Randolph Caldecott (1846–1886), whose stylized illustrations Gauguin described in 1886 as "the very spirit of

COLORPLATE 53

Little Girl with Her Doll (Julie Manet), 1884
Pastel on paper. 60 x 46 cm (23½ x 18⅛ in.). Private collection.

FIGURE 70

The Goose [BW 179], 1885
Oil on canvas. 165 x 87 cm (64¹⁵⁄₁₆ x 34¼ in.). Private collection.

FIGURE 71

Page with "Dame," "Canard," etc. [BW 694], 1883
Watercolor. 20 x 33 cm (7⅞ x 13 in.). Private collection.

drawing."[236] Morisot herself had begun to make an elementary reading primer for Julie around 1883, using miniature watercolor copies of her own paintings as illustrations for words such as *dame* ("woman") and *canard* ("duck") (figure 71).

Except for *The Goose*, however, Morisot, like Renoir, never adopted the decorative stylizations of Japanese art that obsessed so many colleagues, including Monet. Morisot did, nevertheless, appreciate the finesse with which Japanese artists eliminated inessential details. Referring to her late brother-in-law's watercolors, she explained in a notebook around 1885 that "only Manet and the Japanese can indicate a mouth, eyes, a nose, with a single stroke of the brush so accurate that the rest of the face models itself."[237] She ought to have included herself, for in exhibition watercolors, such as *Woman Seated in the Bois de Boulogne* (colorplate 60), she transcribed the light-struck profile of her redheaded model with only a half dozen minuscule marks and a distant carriage with three or four miniature flourishes of blue.

Morisot had hoped to spend a month working in Venice, but changed her plans when an epidemic of cholera was reported there.[238] Instead, in August she visited her sister Yves at Vieux Moulin, to the north of Paris. While there she painted *Forest of Compiègne* (colorplate 61), rendering the densely shaded forest interior with helter-skelter strokes of every color to describe the kaleidoscopic trails of disoriented space scattered deep among the myriad trees, these revealed by broken lines of white indicating the light filtering through the canopy of leaves. With this remarkable painting in mind, it is possible to understand how disappointed Morisot was with the forest landscapes by the seventeenth-century Dutch masters Meindert Hobbema and Jacob van Ruysdael, which she saw in the museums of Holland and Belgium after she and her family left Vieux Moulin.[239]

COLORPLATE 54

By the Lake, 1884
Oil on canvas. 65 x 54 cm (25⅟₁₆ x 21¼ in.). Private collection.

COLORPLATE 55

Self-Portrait, c. 1885
Pastel on paper. 47.5 x 37.5 cm (18¾ x 14¾ in.). The Art
Institute of Chicago, Helen Regenstein Collection.

COLORPLATE 56

Self-Portrait with Julie, 1885
Oil on canvas. 72 x 91 cm (28⅜ x 35¹³⁄₁₆ in.). Private collection.

COLORPLATE 57

The Garden Chair, 1885
Pastel on paper. 40 x 50 cm (15¾ x 19¹¹⁄₁₆ in.). Private collection.

It was the work by Peter Paul Rubens that she saw on this trip that she most deeply admired, particularly his graceful, airborne, supernatural figures and his incomparable children. In Morisot's opinion, only the eighteenth-century French and English masters approached Rubens's sweeping genius, most of all François Boucher, whose vast decorative painting *Venus at Vulcan's Forge*, 1757 (figure 72), in the Louvre was very much on her mind.[240]

By late 1885 Morisot may already have decided to make a large copy of the same portion of this mythological painting by Boucher that had once intrigued Fantin-Latour.[241] Variously dated 1884 or 1886,[242] Morisot's exquisite copy (colorplate 62) after Boucher's chalky fantasy reveals a great

deal about how her own goals as an artist had developed beyond the descriptive concerns of Impressionism toward more decorative issues.

Her large copy was far more than an idle diversion, and Morisot must have gone back to the Louvre repeatedly to finish it. Fully aware that copies after the old masters are generally considered to be mere student exercises, Morisot, as she reached her mid-forties and was recognized as a leading member of the avant-garde, then hung her finished rendition of a fragment of Boucher's painting in the place of honor over the mantelpiece mirror in her living room.[243] The strikingly modern appearance of Morisot's loosely brushed canvas in tones of blue, white,

COLORPLATE 58

The Garden Chair, 1885
Oil on canvas. 61.3 x 75.6 cm (24⅛ x 29¾ in.). Audrey Jones
Beck.

Fan Decorated with Geese, c. 1884
Watercolor on paper. 47 cm (18½ in.) [diam.]. Mrs. Robert
Cummings.

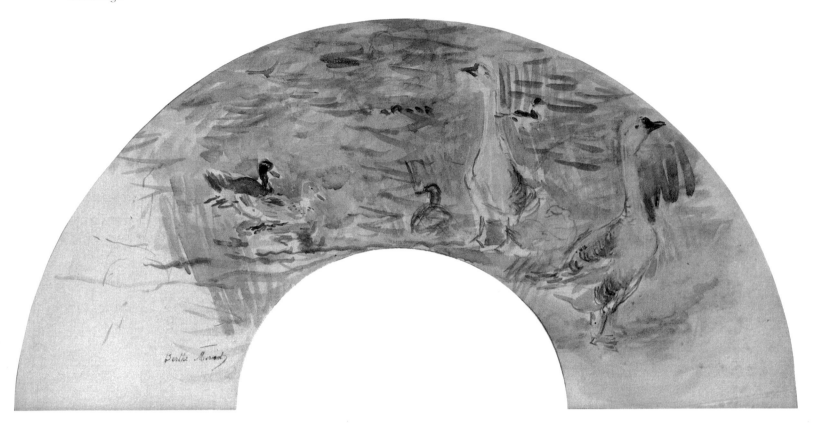

and gold suggests that it may have inspired Monet, who had already presented Morisot with a decorative landscape for this same living-room setting. Seemingly without precedent, his *Nymphéas* murals (e.g., figure 80), begun more than a decade later, were executed with equal flourish in nearly the same ethereal spirit as this copy by Morisot after Boucher. Moreover, since this room was her studio when she was not entertaining guests, the copy must have served as a touchstone for the soft, opulent color harmonies and the rhythmic arabesques that characterize so many of her works from the late 1880s and 1890s.

To the dismay of Durand-Ruel and other early supporters of his art, Renoir shared Morisot's passionate regard for the Rococo masters whom the Goncourts had championed so eloquently. Although he never fully abandoned his Impressionist style, around 1885 Renoir began to concentrate on decorative figure paintings in the art-for-art's-sake tradition. When Morisot visited Renoir's studio

on January 11, 1886, he showed her some large preparatory drawings for his painting *The Bathers,* which he would exhibit the following year.[244] Rendered in red and white chalks like the drawings of Watteau, Boucher, and Fragonard, the figures in Renoir's drawings (figure 73) are posed in the attitudes of the nymphs represented on François Girardon's decorative relief (figure 74) for one of the pools at Versailles dating from the late seventeenth century. Morisot evidently went to Versailles to study this same relief, judging from the quick pencil studies in one of her notebooks (figure 75). Contrary to Impressionist dogma, she began to make red chalk, or sanguine, drawings herself as preparatory studies for an increasing number of her own figure paintings. Describing her visit to Renoir's studio in her notebook, Morisot imagined how an exhibition of these preparatory drawings would surprise the public, for whom Impressionist art was entirely a matter of spontaneity.[245]

COLORPLATE 60

Woman Seated in the Bois de Boulogne, 1885
Watercolor on paper. 19 x 20.8 cm (7½ x 8³⁄₁₆ in.). The
Metropolitan Museum of Art, New York; Harris Brisbane
Dick Fund, 1948.

FIGURE 72

Francois Boucher, *Venus at Vulcan's Forge*, 1757
Oil on canvas. 320 x 320 cm (126 x 126 in.). Musée du Louvre,
Paris.

In the last months of 1885, plans for a new Impressionist exhibition were already under discussion, as Morisot explained in a letter to Edma:

I am working with some prospect of having an exhibition this year: everything I have done for a long time seems to me so horribly bad that I should like to have new, and above all better, things to show to the public. This project is very much up in the air, Degas's perversity makes it almost impossible of realization; there are clashes of vanity in this little group that make any understanding difficult. It seems to me that I am about the only one without any pettiness of character; this makes up for my inferiority as a painter.[246]

Preferring to present their new works at the elegantly decorated gallery of Durand-Ruel's chief rival, Georges Petit (d. 1920), Renoir and Monet refused to participate in this eighth and final Impressionist group exhibition.[247] But as financial backers of this show, Morisot and her husband took an active role in selecting the young artists to replace Monet and Renoir, including Gauguin's friend Emile Schuffenecker (1851–1934) and Pissarro's young associates Georges Seurat and Paul Signac (1863–1935), whose works were based on a scientific system for the applica-

tion of color in little dots.[248] While these debates about the Paris Impressionist show continued, Durand-Ruel organized an exhibition of works by all the disputants—Morisot, Monet, Renoir, and even Seurat—that opened in New York on April 10, 1886. This large, highly successful exhibition designed to introduce Impressionism to the American art market had eight paintings by Morisot, most of them done in the early 1880s at Bougival or Nice.[249]

Despite Morisot's misgivings about her recent works, she had eleven paintings, as well as a group of watercolors, drawings, and decorated fans ready for the Paris group show when it opened on May 15. The critics inevitably stressed her obsession with white-on-white harmonies and her idiosyncratic sketchlike style. Jean Ajalbert (1863–1947), a critic-cum-poet, who published what he called "impressionist verses" in 1886, discussed the nature of this style as if he were discussing Mallarmé's poems: "If I can express myself in such a way, [Morisot's] clear turn of phrase is unencumbered by epithets, weighty adverbs: everything is subject and verb; she has a sort of telegraphic style with glowing vocables; her thought comes across in two words."[250] These remarks are close in spirit to a passage copied out in one of Morisot's notebooks: "I believe that when we think very fast we pass over the verbs and emphasize adjectives. In my opinion that's the way people with cold dispositions think. Myself, I see things."[251]

Among the works she included in this final Impressionist group show were several pictures of a seventeen-year-old model named Isabelle Lambert.[252] One of these, *The Bath* (colorplate 63), may have been a last-minute addition, judging from its number in the catalogue, 94 *bis*. Reminiscent of Morisot's earlier dressing-room pictures, it depicts a behind-the-scenes moment in a woman's life similar to the moments Degas sought to capture with a series of shocking nudes presented in this same exhibition. With her arms raised to fasten her hair, Morisot's figure seems to regard herself; and although the painting contains no specific indication of a mirror, the luminous silvery rose and lavender overtones in the background give her image the quality of a reflection. Indeed, the implied analogy in *The Bath* between the figure's self-scrutiny and the painter's close observation of the model is extended by the hairbrush resting on the woman's lap, since this can be understood as a counterpart to the brush with which the image has been shaped and highlighted by the painter.

Puvis most admired a second painting of Isabelle Lambert in a white chemise for its subtle pose and color tonalities.[253] Like *The Bath*, this second picture, called

COLORPLATE 61

Forest of Compiègne, 1885
Oil on canvas. 54.2 x 64.8 cm (21⅜ x 25½ in.). The Art Institute
of Chicago, Bequest of Estelle McCormick.

COLORPLATE 62

Detail from Boucher's "Venus at Vulcan's Forge," 1884/1886
Oil on canvas. 114 x 138 cm (44⅞ x 54⅜ in.). Private collection,
Paris.

FIGURE 73

Pierre-Auguste Renoir, *Two Nude Women, Study for "The Large Bathers,"* c. 1884
Red chalk on yellowed paper. 125 x 140 cm (49 3/8 x 55 1/8 in.).
Courtesy of the Harvard University Art Museums (Fogg Art Museum, Bequest of Maurice Wertheim, Class of 1906).

FIGURE 75

Two Pages from a Sketchbook (Carnet Vert [a]), 1885–86
Private collection.

FIGURE 74

François Girardon, *Nymphs Bathing,* 1668–70
Iron bas-relief. Fountain of Diana, Allée des Marmousets, Versailles.

Getting Out of Bed (colorplate 64), was conceived first of all as a harmony in white and flesh tones in the spirit of Boucher. Pausing to slide her foot into a slipper before leaving the bed, the figure appears to be still only half conscious of the shimmering play of light and shadow on the rumpled sheets. The rippling whites in *Getting Out of Bed*, taken together with the bordering zones of saturated blues and reds for the walls and carpet, seem to have the nationalistic overtones of the French flag, the *tricolore*. Indeed, this ostensibly modest modern-life genre subject can be understood in terms of the history painting of Boucher and Fragonard, given the Louis XVI bed Morisot chose for a prop.

The striking detail of the opened bottom drawer of the dresser at the far right of this boudoir picture exemplifies a new emphasis upon spatial complexity in several

Getting Out of Bed, 1886
Oil on canvas. 65 x 54 cm (25⅝ x 21¼ in.). Collection Durand-
Ruel, Paris.

COLORPLATE 63

The Bath (Girl Arranging Her Hair), 1885–86
Oil on canvas. 91.1 x 72.3 cm (35⅞ x 28⁷⁄₁₆ in.). Sterling and
Francine Clark Art Institute, Williamstown, Massachusetts.

Gorey, 1886
Watercolor on paper. 17 x 24 cm (6¹¹⁄₁₆ x 9⁷⁄₁₆ in.). Private
collection.

of Morisot's works. This new emphasis is most apparent
in a painting called *The Little Servant* (colorplate 65) in
the 1886 exhibition catalogue and that is a reprise of *In
the Dining Room* of 1880 (see colorplate 40). Pausing from
chores as a little dog at her feet begs for attention, the
servant stands gestureless in the rue de Villejust dining
room, observed from the other side of an open doorway
indicated by a long dark strip along the right edge of the
composition. This sweeping movement from one space
into another is extended by the view out the dining-room
window across the garden to a neighboring house. The

The Little Servant (In the Dining Room), 1885–86
Oil on canvas. 61.3 x 50 cm (24⅛ x 19¾ in.). National Gallery of
Art, Washington, D.C., Chester Dale Collection, 1963.

blurred appearance of this little landscape observed through
the glass pane is matched by the blur of the dishes visible
behind the glass doors of a cupboard at the far left of this
ambitious painting. The cupboard's lower wooden doors
are opened as if Morisot wanted to paint the ambient
light refracted from every possible angle and thus to trans-
mute a simple genre scene into an antic play of paint.

In June of 1886 Morisot took a family vacation on the
Channel Island of Jersey, evidently hoping to make paintings of the port of Gorey and coastal landscapes. She
filled a notebook with pencil sketches and painted remarkable landscapes in watercolor, some—for example, *Gorey*
(colorplate 66)—as summary in execution as the luminous
pictures that Henri Matisse (1869–1954), André Derain

FIGURE 76

Interior at Jersey [BW 197], 1886
Oil on canvas. 50 x 60 cm (19¹¹⁄₁₆ x 23⅝ in.). Musée d'Ixelles, Belgium. Collection F. Toussaint.

(1880–1954), and the other so-called Fauves painted on the Mediterranean coast some fifteen years later.[254] But Morisot was unable to make headway with her oil paintings, and she confided in a letter to her niece that the motifs on Jersey would be more suitable for Monet than for herself. Although she complained about Monet's tendency to paint too many variations of a single motif, she realized that her friend "had exhausted the subject matter of simple landscape and no one feels brave enough to attempt what he has thoroughly covered."[255]

Of course Morisot had worked in a similar vein for years, repeating the basic elements of her figure compositions in variations, and her reservations about Monet's serial methods notwithstanding, she continued to work in this way. Her most important Channel Island picture, *Interior at Jersey* (figure 76), the composition·of which she plotted in a preliminary pastel (colorplate 67), is fundamentally a variation on the interior scenes that had preoccupied her since the early 1880s: a round tabletop still life in the foreground juxtaposed with a rectangular background landscape view visible out the window. Pentimenti visible near the middle of the pastel study indicate that Morisot at first wished to portray Julie seated next to her father by the table. She then covered over this initial image with one of Julie standing, her back turned, and looking at the harbor view. For the subsequent oil version, Morisot decided to omit the figure of Eugène and to pose Julie at the window with a blond doll, as if to suggest a parity between her own painter's observations of a model and the child's play. What most distinguishes the oil version of *Interior at Jersey*, so named when exhibited by Morisot on two separate occasions the following year, is the calculated interplay of whites: Julie's dress, a sheet draped over a screen, the breakfast table with a white tablecloth and white dishes waiting to be cleared away.

But if Morisot continued to produce compositional variations, she nevertheless sought greater variety in her work around 1886–87 by exploring new mediums: sculpture and drypoint. The very lack of color in these modes of expression apparently challenged her widely acknowledged virtuosity as a colorist. Referring to the straightforward sculpture of Julie's head (figure 77), which Monet encouraged her to exhibit in May 1887, Morisot confided in her notebook: "I am a slave to this idea: white plaster."[256]

In February 1887 Morisot showed five paintings in Brussels at an invitational exhibition of avant-garde trends organized by an artists' group called Les Vingt;[257] Pissarro and Seurat were among the other foreign exhibitors. Following the lead of Monet and Renoir, who had shown works at the lavish International Exhibition staged by

FIGURE 77

Portrait of Julie Manet, 1886
Plaster. Height 26.7 cm (10½ in.). Private collection.

COLORPLATE 67

Interior at Jersey, 1886
Pastel on paper. 46 x 60 cm (18⅛ x 23⅝ in.). Private collection.

Georges Petit in 1886, Morisot agreed to participate in the 1887 edition of this commercial showcase, along with Whistler, Rodin, Pissarro, and Monet, who showed the rugged landscapes that he had just brought back from Belle Isle. Renoir was represented by his large *Bathers*. More hardheaded about his business than Durand-Ruel, Petit received works from participants to offset his overhead expenses,[258] and he refused to allow artists to use white frames.[259] Yet, although Morisot acceded to Petit's demands, he was apparently unable to sell any of the seven works by her in the International, among them the sculpture of Julie, *On the Veranda* (colorplate 51), *Interior at Jersey* (figure 76), and a portrait in whites of her niece Paule Gobillard (BW 210).

Although the single pastel presented on this occasion has not yet been identified, it may well have been one of the half-draped nudes that Morisot undertook in response to her study of Boucher and her admiration for Renoir's new works. Petit's negative attitude to white frames notwithstanding, one would have been well suited to the pale silvery tonalities of *Young Woman in White* (colorplate 68), a signed bust-length "portrait" of Isabelle Lambert wearing only a white sheet. Morisot's treatment of Isabelle's foreshortened arm, supporting her head, suggests a sculptor's sensitivity to volume as much as the chalky whites evoke plaster. Of course, the very fact that Morisot had begun to work from nude models, as Degas, Puvis, Renoir, and Rodin did, is indicative of a change in her

COLORPLATE 68

Young Woman in White, 1886
Pastel on paper. 41.5 x 53 cm (16⅜ x 20⅞ in.). Collection of
John C. Whitehead.

premises. In addition to Isabelle, Carmen Gaudin posed nude for Morisot around 1887 (BW 761 and 762). Although closely related works by Morisot in oil (BW 207), pastel (colorplate 69), charcoal (colorplate 70), watercolor (BW 762), and pencil record Carmen in a seated pose, drying her back with a towel in the same attitude as Rodin's plaster *Zoubaloff Bather* (figure 78), Morisot's images of this particular model are most intriguing when considered in relation to works by Henri de Toulouse-Lautrec (1864–1901). According to Lautrec's biographers, he discovered Carmen and persuaded her to model for him in 1885, but, unlike Morisot, he never painted her in the nude.[260]

Morisot's new interest in the nude as a subject coincides with her new interest in preparatory drawings. When she arranged to have Renoir make a portrait of Julie in the spring or early summer of 1887 (see figure 106), she could witness his progress from one stage of realization to the next. Indeed, she acquired all five preliminary drawings and tracings that Renoir made for the final portrait in oils, and her own drypoint (figure 79) after Renoir's painting is rendered in a crisp linear style that marks a turning point in her work.[261]

During the summer of 1887, Morisot and her family visited Mallarmé at his country house on the Seine near

COLORPLATE 69

Young Woman Drying Herself, 1886–87
Pastel on paper. 42 x 41 cm (16⁹⁄₁₆ x 16⅛ in.). Courtesy of
Galerie Hopkins and Thomas, Paris.

Valvins, before touring the Loire Valley in late August, when she executed *View of Tours* (colorplate 71). Like Renoir, of course, Mallarmé was a regular at the weekly rue de Villejust soirées, and by the end of the year the poet had persuaded these painter friends, as well as Degas, Monet, and the sporting artist John Lewis-Brown (1829–1890), to make illustrations for a limited-edition anthology of some of his poems to be called "Le Tiroir de laque."

Although the project was never realized, Morisot made a serious effort to illustrate Mallarmé's "The White Water Lily," a prose poem about a quiet riverside reverie. It was evidently thanks to her collaborator on this project, Lewis-Brown, who was familiar with the possibilities of color lithography, that Morisot began to do three-pencil drawings with pale red, yellow, and blue pencils as trials for the Mallarmé project.[262] Although she eventually made just one color lithograph, Morisot continued to make colored-pencil drawings for the rest of her life, fashioning images so fragile in appearance that the lines seem about to evaporate or disperse. An especially beautiful example is the *Portrait of Paule Gobillard* (colorplate 72); the sitter wears a straw hat indicated by just a dozen delicate yellow lines and the pale yellow shadows it casts on her cheeks and throat. To suggest the greens in the landscape setting here, Morisot hatched blue lines with yellow ones, thus achieving a trembling optical mixture in the spirit of Seurat.

Unfortunately, her three-pencil drawing for "The White Water Lily" is lost. It has always been presumed that it would have been similar to the two sketches of the lake in the Bois de Boulogne that Morisot executed as drypoints, perhaps with the technical guidance of Cassatt, but nei-

FIGURE 78

Auguste Rodin, *Zoubaloff Bather,* 1888
Tinted plaster. Musée Rodin, Paris.

FIGURE 79

Julie Manet with a Cat, c. 1887
Drypoint. 14.5 x 11.3 cm (5¹¹⁄₁₆ x 4⁷⁄₁₆ in.). National Gallery of Art, Washington, D.C., Rosenwald Collection, 1953.

Nude from the Back, 1886–87
Charcoal on paper. 57 x 43 cm (22⁷⁄₁₆ x 16⁷⁄₈ in.). Private
collection, Paris.

COLORPLATE 71

View of Tours, 1887
Pastel on paper. 30 x 47 cm (11¾ x 18½ in.). Private collection,
Paris.

ther of the drypoints actually includes a water lily.[263] Since
this aquatic flower would, of course, become Monet's preferred subject immediately after Morisot's death, Mallarmé's
report that Monet was charmed by Morisot's lost drawing
is especially noteworthy.[264] In color and touch, Morisot's
pastels and watercolors of white swans gliding on a lake's
surface (colorplate 73) and her views of the lake observed
beyond trees on its bank (colorplate 74) anticipate Monet's
last paintings so closely that this lost drawing may somehow
have been a missing link between Mallarmé, Morisot, and
the famous *Nymphéas* (figure 80).

From Antibes, where he had gone in January 1888 to
undertake a second series of Mediterranean landscapes,
Monet wrote to Morisot, Renoir, and other colleagues,

encouraging them to participate in another International
Exhibition at Petit's.[265] Although Morisot was agreeable to
his idea, she had been unable to work much because of
poor health.[266] By May she had but three paintings, a pastel (colorplate 71), and a watercolor ready to present pub-
licly—not at Petit's, whose demands led to a falling out
with Monet, but at Durand-Ruel's, where, as Renoir
pointed out, "the only expense will be that of sending
one's pictures."[267]

A watercolor listed in the catalogue as *Bather* is probably the nude in a lakeside setting (BW 762) for which
Carmen Gaudin posed.[268] Lautrec apparently saw this exhibition, to judge from *Woman with Red Hair Seated in
the Garden of M. Forest* (figure 81) and other pictures of
Carmen that he painted in the following months.[269] Furthermore, the freely painted wicker chairs in these paint-

COLORPLATE 72

Portrait of Paule Gobillard, c. 1887
Colored pencil on paper. 27.9 x 22.9 cm (11 x 9 in.) [sight]. The
Reader's Digest Association, Inc.

COLORPLATE 73

Swans, c. 1887
Watercolor on paper. 19 x 26 cm (7½ x 10¼ in.). Private
collection.

COLORPLATE 74

The Lake, Bois de Boulogne, c. 1887
Watercolor on paper. 29.5 x 22.2 cm (11⅝ x 8¾ in.). The
National Museum of Women in the Arts, Washington, D.C.,
The Holladay Collection.

COLORPLATE 75

Little Girl Reading, 1888
Oil on canvas. 74.3 x 92.7 cm (29¼ x 36½ in.). Museum of Fine
Arts, St. Petersburg, Florida. Gift of Friends of Art in memory
of Margaret Acheson Stuart.

COLORPLATE 75A

Little Girl Reading [detail]

FIGURE 80

Claude Monet, *Clear Morning with Willows*, 1921–22
Oil on canvas. 200 x 425 cm (78¾ x 172½ in.). Musée d'Orsay,
Paris.

ings and the contrast between Carmen's red hair and the lush green fronds in the background suggest that such details in Morisot's *Little Girl Reading* (colorplate 75) in the same show greatly impressed him. Whistler, also among the exhibitors on this occasion, was likewise impressed with Morisot's works, or so he told Mallarmé.[270]

The redheaded model for *Little Girl Reading*, a repetition of *On the Veranda* (see colorplate 51), was Jeanne Bonnet, who must have appealed to Morisot because of her striking resemblance to Julie.[271] Jeanne sits reading a book next to a window overlooking the rue de Villejust garden, her face dappled with sunlight. Although the theme is simple, Morisot carefully integrated every detail of *Little Girl Reading*: the soft colors are all matched complementaries (blues and yellows, greens and reds) for heightened vibrancy, and every object included in the setting has the same latticelike texture (wicker chair, palms, trellises) to filter and atomize the play of light. The most remarkable detail of all, and perhaps to be understood as symbolizing Morisot's fundamental concern with the integration of figure and setting, is the windowpane at the far right, through which a corner of the garden is visible; yet superimposed upon it is the faint reflection of the model's back. Although Morisot used a stand-in for Julie in *Little Girl Reading*, her daughter's own features were nevertheless on view in this same exhibition at Durand-Ruel's, since Morisot lent Renoir's recent portrait of Julie (see figure 106).

Thanks to the efforts of the young dealer Theo van Gogh (1854–1891, Vincent's brother), Monet, who chose not to participate in the Durand-Ruel exhibition, was able to show ten of his new Mediterranean landscapes in June at the Boussod and Valadon gallery. Morisot wrote Monet

that the new work "dazzled" her,[272] but she never managed to visit him that summer in Giverny, where he was working on several figure paintings as a surprise for her.[273]

As for her own paintings, the integration of figure and setting remained her foremost concern, exemplified in a watercolor of riders in *Path in the Bois de Boulogne* (colorplate 76). Adding long vertical washes to indicate a screen of trees in the immediate foreground, Morisot nearly masked her primary subject in the picture, and the densely textured result is among the most abstract that she or any Impressionist ever realized.

By November 1888, Morisot was in the South of France, enjoying the same sort of scenery that Monet had portrayed.[274] Fulfilling their longstanding dream, Morisot and her family rented a spacious villa with a garden at Cimiez, just outside of Nice, for the winter. "I was very happy to see this setting again," Morisot wrote to Edma, "since I am not interested in new places."[275] She urged Puvis, Monet, and Mallarmé to visit them, and Renoir

FIGURE 81

Henri de Toulouse-Lautrec, *Woman with Red Hair
Seated in the Garden of M. Forest*, 1889
Oil on canvas. 64.8 x 53 cm (25½ x 20⅞ in.). Private collection,
U.S.A.

COLORPLATE 76

Path in the Bois de Boulogne, c. 1888
Watercolor on paper. 24 x 20 cm (19⁷⁄₁₆ x 7⁷⁄₈ in.). Private
collection, Courtesy of Galerie Hopkins and Thomas, Paris.

COLORPLATE 77

Nice, View from Cimiez, 1888–89
Watercolor on paper. 21 x 29 cm (8¼ x 11⅜ in.). Private
collection.

promised to make the long trip on his tricycle, but never did.[276] She recorded the luxuriant garden and the panoramic view from the villa with remarkable economy in watercolors (colorplate 77) and pencil drawings (colorplate 78). But what her friends missed when they failed to visit is perhaps most splendidly evoked by a drawing done with orange, yellow, blue, and green pencils and showing Julie's pet parakeet in its cage set on the sill of a window opened to the Mediterranean view (colorplate 79).

When Puvis had received a commission in February 1888 from the museum in Rouen for decorative murals (figure 82), he found inspiration in the celebrated *Primavera* by the fifteenth-century painter Sandro Botticelli. The orange trees in the garden at Nice reminded Morisot of the same masterpiece, which she had seen in Florence eight

years earlier.[277] A pastel study (figure 83) of a woman reaching up to pick fruits embodies her memories of Botticelli's decoration, and there developed from it a full-scale painting. Perhaps these pictures together constitute an early phase in the development of Morisot's *Cherry Tree* (see figure 89 and colorplate 89), the important decorative project that she would begin in earnest in 1891. The heavily laden branch in the upper-right corner of *Under the Orange Tree* (colorplate 80), an Arcadian portrait of Julie, is no less Botticelliesque. Seated in the blue-green shade of

COLORPLATE 78

Villa Ratti, 1888–89
Pencil on paper. 29 x 23 cm (11⅜ x 9⅟₁₆ in.). Private collection.

Pierre Puvis de Chavannes, *Inter Artes et Naturam*, 1890
Oil on canvas. 40.3 x 113.7 cm (15 ⅞ x 44 ¾ in.).
The Metropolitan Museum of Art, New York,
Gift of Mrs. Harry Payne Bingham.

Pierre-Auguste Renoir, *Alexander Thurneyssen as a Shepherd*, 1911
Oil on canvas. 75.3 x 92.7 cm (29 ⅝ x 36½ in.). Museum of Art,
Rhode Island School of Design, Providence, Museum Works of
Art Reserve.

Picking Oranges [BW 542], 1889
Pastel. 61 x 46 cm (24 x 18⅛ in.). Collection du Musée d'Art et
d'Histoire de Provence, Grasse.

this overladen little tree with her parakeet, Julie wears a broad-brimmed straw hat that gives her a slightly Japanese appearance. Although the free brushwork suggests that Morisot executed the picture outdoors, she in fact studied Julie's pose in a preliminary pastel (BW 549). Renoir greatly admired *Under the Orange Tree*, the memory of which may have inspired his fanciful portrait of the son of a German collector painted in 1911 (figure 84). He also admired *The Mandolin* (colorplate 81), a simple portrait of Julie in white playing a musical instrument the color of her own golden hair.[278] Although the treatment of the white dress, rippled with blue shadows, is a tour de force of drawing in oils, the monochromatic background, an exquisite blend of blues and greens, must have appealed most to Renoir. A feathered texture of vertical strokes

COLORPLATE 79

Parakeet at a Window, 1889
Colored pencil on paper. 19 x 21 cm (7½ x 8¼ in.). Courtesy of
Galerie Hopkins and Thomas, Paris.

COLORPLATE 80

Under the Orange Tree, 1889
Oil on canvas. 54 x 65 cm (21¼ x 25⁹⁄₁₆ in.). Private collection,
Courtesy of Galerie Hopkins and Thomas, Paris.

COLORPLATE 81

The Mandolin, 1889
Oil on canvas. 55 x 57 cm (21⅝ x 22½ in.). Private collection.

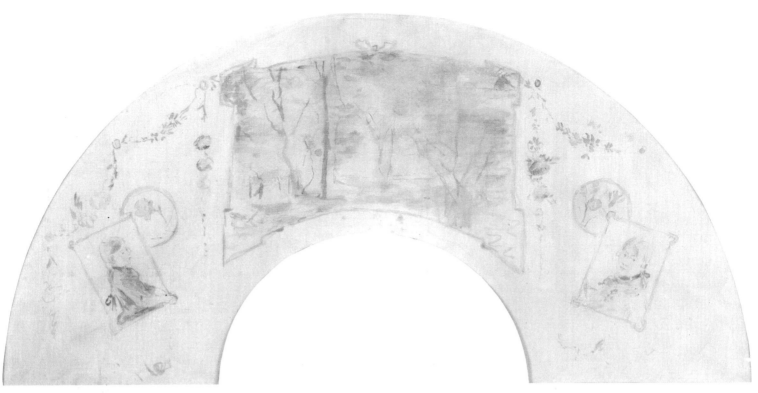

COLORPLATE 82

Fan Decorated with Vignettes, 1887
Watercolor on silk. 50 cm (19⅝ in.) [diam.]. Private collection.

more evocative of watered silk than of any shaded landscape setting, this decorative background initiated a series of similar, often more refined abstract backgrounds for dozens of subsequent works by both Renoir and Morisot herself.

Characteristically, Morisot complained that her work in Nice was going badly.[279] Perhaps she was referring to her inability to bring a new project to resolution. During her stay she kept a notebook in which she drafted several similar lists of some dozen subjects, as if she were considering publishing a book; and indeed Mallarmé, Lewis-Brown, and Cassatt had all encouraged her to make prints. What seemed to be the title page had Julie's portrait in a medallion surrounded by oranges and flowers, and subsequent pages of this unrealized book consisted of landscape panoramas, gardens, and the port.[280] A silk fan painted in watercolor (colorplate 82) seems to suggest the intended decorative layout, with garland motifs and tiny portraits of Julie as well as Morisot herself.[281]

Back in Paris in May 1889, Morisot enjoyed the World's Fair, which boasted such exotica as the Javanese dancers who would help to lure Gauguin to the South Seas. A special survey of the century of French art since the 1789 Revolution included a room of Manet's masterpieces, among them the *Olympia*. Monet, upon seeing it again at the World's Fair, decided to organize a fund-raising campaign to buy it as a gift for the Louvre, a time-consuming and frustrating effort given the government's lack of enthusiasm for this bequest, which was not presented at the Louvre until 1907.[282]

Most of the relatively few works that Morisot undertook in 1889 depict boating in the Bois de Boulogne. In one of these (colorplate 83), a trio of geese on the bank seems to stare bemused as Julie rows off in the distance. Morisot's whimsical paintings of boating on the lake in the park apparently inspired other artists to make similar pictures. For example, Cassatt's *Summertime*, painted around 1894 (figure 85), shows a woman and a child in a boat feeding ducks, and *On the Lake, Central Park* (figure 86) by William Merritt Chase (1849–1916) is also a reverie in the manner of Morisot. Chase, who often came to Paris in the early 1880s, had bought Morisot's *Woman at Her Toilette* (see colorplate 35) for his own collection.

Presumably Morisot's limited output at this time was the result of Eugène's failing health. He was well enough in late February 1890 to arrange a special soirée for Mallarmé to read his lecture on the fantastical novelist and poet Villiers de l'Isle-Adam (1838–1889); but in April the family left Paris for Mézy, a village in the valley of the Seine northwest of Paris.[283]

FIGURE 85

Mary Cassatt, *Summertime*, 1894
Oil on canvas. 73.4 x 100 cm (28⅞ x 39⅜ in.). The Armand
Hammer Collection.

FIGURE 86

William Merritt Chase, *On the Lake, Central Park*, c. 1894
Oil on canvas. 35.5 x 40.6 cm (14 x 16 in.). The Alexander
Gallery, New York.

Disregarding her own expressed opinion that Monet had exhausted the possibilities of landscape painting, Morisot began to portray the sweeping view from the garden. Using a pale palette limited to yellows, blues, and greens, as if she were working with colored pencils, she painted *View from the Terrace at Mézy* (colorplate 84), recording a tapestry of budding and flowering trees and the rolling hills extending to the horizon. Mary Cassatt, who rented a house in the nearby village of Septeuil, urged Morisot to make a trip back to Paris to see the important exhibition of Japanese art on view that spring at the Ecole des Beaux-Arts.[284] Although Cassatt's work was profoundly affected by the color prints they saw together, Morisot's response to Japanese art is less obvious. Nevertheless it was probably not long after seeing this exhibition that she traded two of her own paintings to the dealer Tadamasa Hayashi (1853–1906) for some Japanese prints for her own collection.[285] Moreover, by the end of the following summer Morisot would again consider making suites of illustrations, perhaps inspired by the portfolios that Japanese printmakers often produced.[286]

Morisot began to reflect upon her career. She felt that she and her husband were growing old somewhat prematurely, and she was nostalgic for her own youth as she watched her daughter and nieces learn to draw, paint, and play music. Referring to the autobiographies of the painter Marie Bashkirtseff (1860–1884) and the novelist Pauline Algae (1808–1891) in one of her Mézy notebooks, Morisot concluded: "The truth is that our value lies in feeling, in intention, in our vision that is subtler than that of men, and we can accomplish a great deal provided that affectation, pedantry, and sentimentalism do not spoil everything."[287]

Using local children of Mézy as models and a barn for a studio, Morisot painted the sort of bucolic figure pieces that had absorbed her in Nice. The most surprising project, a large work of a Mézy child as the infant Saint John the Baptist, failed to develop to Morisot's satisfaction, and she destroyed it, although studies survive (BW 252 and 558). Julie, however, who celebrated her First Communion in September 1890, was Morisot's preferred model. In a letter to Edma, Morisot explained that in her will she had specified her wish that Mallarmé become Julie's guardian. The same letter gives an account of an important printmaking project in progress: "My attempts at color prints are disappointing and that was all that interested me. I worked all summer with a view to publishing a series of drawings of Julie. Worst of all I am approaching the end of my life, and yet I am still a mere beginner."[288] Like the previous summer's portfolio project in Nice, the Julie portfolio was never to be realized. A single trial proof of a color lithograph showing Julie playing a flute (figure 87) perhaps gives an idea of what she had planned. Presumably some of Morisot's three-pencil drawings of Julie can also be associated with this same project.

COLORPLATE 84

View from the Terrace at Mézy, 1890
Oil on canvas. 53 x 65 cm (20⅞ x 25⁹⁄₁₆ in.). Private collection,
Washington, D.C.

COLORPLATE 83

View of the Bois de Boulogne, 1889
Oil on canvas. 65.4 x 54.6 cm (25¾ x 21½ in.). National Gallery
of Art, Washington, D.C., Ailsa Mellon Bruce Collection, 1970.

FIGURE 87

Julie Playing the Flute, c. 1890
Lithograph. 21.6 x 27.9 cm (8½ x 11 in.). Private collection.

Although because of poor health Morisot declined an invitation to send works to Brussels for the early 1891 exhibition of Les Vingt,[289] her works were featured in an exhibition at Durand-Ruel's gallery in April.[290] In a notebook she expressed her dismay that Julie's portrait looked harsh installed in a hallway rather than in one of the large rooms.[291] Durand-Ruel had for this occasion commissioned Mallarmé's colleague Théodor de Wyzewa (1862–1917) to write a catalogue essay, and he produced the longest appreciation of Morisot's art yet published. This essay appeared in the March 28, 1891 issue of the gallery's periodical, *L'Art dans les deux mondes.* For the most part a general discussion of the feminine character of Morisot's style, Wyzewa's article pointed out that her influence on contemporary artists exceeded that of her better-known male colleagues, including Renoir and Monet. Furthermore, his article is illustrated with engravings after "a recent series of three-pencil drawings" of Julie and Alice Gamby, Tiburce's stepdaughter, which Wyzewa called "impressions." Although he was the only critic ever to suggest that Morisot's works in colored pencils should be considered Impressionist drawings—and indeed they are the ultimate examples of this genre—Wyzewa failed to specify whether such drawings were included in the exhibition or whether they were related to Morisot's projected portfolio of images of Julie.[292] The drawing of Julie and Alice seated on an Empire sofa attests to Morisot's renewed interest in the early-nineteenth-century furniture that her father had treasured. Of course, as props these pieces of furniture add an historical dimension to her modern-life genre paintings.[293]

Morisot evidently never fulfilled the commission to illustrate Mallarmé's "White Water Lily," at least not to her own satisfaction, and when Mallarmé's anthology, now entitled *Pages,* appeared in 1891, it had only one illustration, by Renoir. Morisot brought a copy to read at Mézy, to which she returned for the summer of 1891. Her masterful drawings and pastels of the sun-swept gardens (colorplates 85 and 86), rendered in three or four colors, are highly decorative, with the play of light and shadow orchestrated as sweeping arabesques integrating near and far. None of these excels *Pears* (colorplate 87), a close-up view of slender branches with broad blue leaves and ripe yellow pears that seem to swing like pealing bells silhouetted against the vibrant yellow fields and azure skies of Mézy, here poetically transformed into a sort of El Dorado.

The especially decorative character of Morisot's work this summer is most pronounced in a group of oil paintings that may have been conceived as an ensemble for a specific room. She and Eugène had decided by early July to buy a seventeenth-century château at nearby Juziers, as Morisot explained in a letter to Mallarmé: "We are carried away by the desire to be in a beautiful setting before we die."[294] Although the negotiations for the purchase of the château at Mesnil, as the property is called, continued into October,[295] her summer's work may have been motivated by the anticipation of redecorating a new home.

By early summer she had begun a suite of colored-pencil and charcoal drawings, as well as transfer tracings like those Renoir used, for *The Little Flute Players* (colorplate 88), a horizontal, overdoor-format double portrait of Julie and her cousin Jeanne Gobillard, seated under apple trees.[296] In both a preliminary oil and in this final painting, the muted, somewhat indistinct background is rendered in feathery strokes that evoke rather than describe the garden setting. This suggests that both versions were done in her studio rather than outdoors in typical Impressionist fashion. Renoir, who had been a guest at Mézy the previous summer, returned briefly in August 1891 from Paris, where he too had decided to paint outdoor pictures in the studio. Since Renoir began to use similiarly general background settings for a series of

COLORPLATE 85

Path in the Garden at Mézy, 1891
Pastel on paper. 60.1 x 45.1 cm (23⅝ x 17¾ in.). Private collection.

COLORPLATE 86

Sunflowers, c. 1891
Colored pencil on paper. 27.3 x 19.1 cm (10¾ x 7½ in.). Mr. and
Mrs. Richard A. Hess.

COLORPLATE 87

Pears, 1891
Pastel on paper. 42 x 48 cm (16½ x 18⅞ in.). Private collection,
Courtesy of Galerie Hopkins and Thomas, Paris.

COLORPLATE 88

The Little Flute Players (Julie Manet and Jeanne Gobillard), 1891
Oil on canvas. 56 x 87 cm (22 x 34¼ in.). Josefowitz Collection.

standard-format pictures of two young girls reading (figure 88), picking flowers, or playing the piano, it seems likely that these colleagues shared ideas about the subject matter of decorative art and the need to integrate figure and background as fully as possible. Shortly after his visit to Mézy, on August 17 Renoir wrote Morisot that he would be buying the dresses for his models, presumably so that he could begin these decorative paintings.[297]

In the same letter he urged her to finish her "painting with the cherry trees," referring to the largest of her new decorative works, for which Julie posed standing on a ladder while Jeanne held a basket to collect the fruit. The fulfillment of an idea that Morisot had formulated in Nice in 1888, to make a decorative picture in the spirit of Botticelli's *Primavera, The Cherry Tree* (colorplate 89) was developed from the largest group of preliminary studies Morisot had ever made for any of her paintings. One of the very earliest in the sequence would appear to be a

pastel on heavy pink paper (colorplate 90) of a ladder set between two flowering trees, but with no figures. Rendered like her colored-pencil drawings with short hatchings in alternating tones of blue, olive, yellow, and pink, this luminous study for the background trembles with suffused light like the laboriously dotted paintings that Seurat and Signac had developed during the last few years.

Morisot experimented with the full composition —including the figures, their white dresses splattered with shadows—in a colored-pencil drawing and two watercolors (BW 791 and 792). She constantly modified Julie's position on the ladder and the disposition of her raised arms, which at first hid her face. A pastel study of Julie's figure by itself, the face still hidden (BW 572), apparently belongs to this early phase of the painting's development, as does a vibrant pastel study of the figure of Jeanne, her head hidden by her wide-brimmed straw hat and her intense strawberry-blond hair tumbling down her back (BW 571).

152

COLORPLATE 89

The Cherry Tree, 1891–92
Oil on canvas. 136 x 89 cm
(53⁹⁄₁₆ x 35¹⁄₁₆ in.). Private collection.

FIGURE 88

Pierre-Auguste Renoir, *Reading*, 1890
Oil on canvas. 54 x 66 cm (21¼ x 26 in.). Musée d'Orsay,
Paris.

The fact that the figures in these pastels are on the same
scale as those in the final oil versions of *The Cherry Tree*
suggests that Morisot had already started to block out her
idea on a large canvas.

Even so, a smaller oil version (BW 274), in which Julie's
arms are slightly lower, revealing the upper part of her
face, indicates that Morisot continued to modify and refine
details after completing the full-figure studies in pastel.
Morisot's numerous red-chalk drawings and tracings for
this project (colorplates 91 and 92), which stress the graceful contours of the figures, are no less revealing about her
working methods. Apparently tracing the contours from
such chalk drawings onto her canvas, Morisot was in effect adapting a technique that fresco painters had used for
centuries.

It is necessary to digress and continue the discussion
of the complex evolution of *The Cherry Tree* before returning to the other important decorative projects done in
Mézy in 1891. No more capable of satisfying herself than
were Manet and Degas, both of them notorious for their
constant revisions, Morisot evidently became dissatisfied
with her large oil version of the subject and decided to
make a second full-scale version after she returned to Paris
in the fall (colorplate 89).[298] Since Morisot omitted both

FIGURE 89

The Cherry Tree [BW 275], 1891
Oil on canvas. 135.9 x 88.9 cm (53½ x 35 in.). Private collection.

versions from the retrospective of her works that opened
in May 1892, it seems that she still considered them unfinished, continuing to refine them throughout the next year.

Later in 1892, for example, she returned to the first
large oil and changed the figure on the ladder, replacing
Julie, who was ill, with a professional model named Jeanne
Fourmanoir, who also posed for Renoir.[299] Modifying the
gesture of the upraised arms again, Morisot fully revealed
Jeanne's face for this ultimate modification of *The Cherry
Tree* (figure 89).

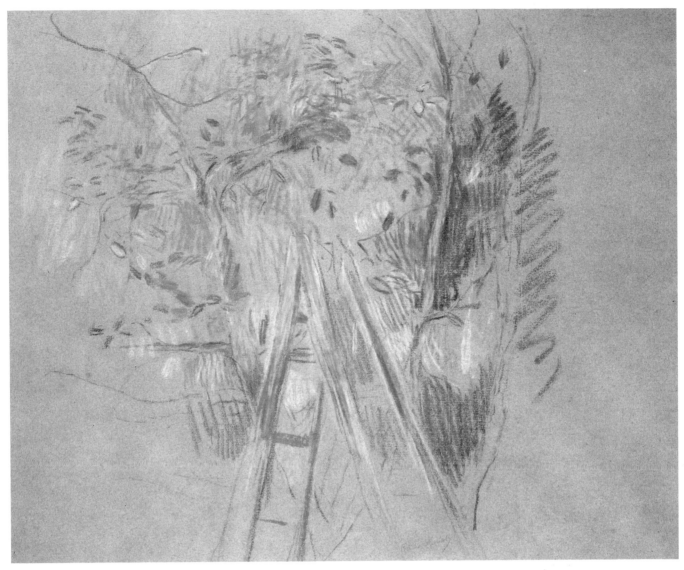

COLORPLATE 90

Study for "The Cherry Tree," 1891
Pastel on paper. 45.7 x 48.9 cm (18 x 19¼ in.). The Reader's
Digest Association, Inc.

Despite the delays owing to Morisot's perfectionist re-visions, her project apparently became familiar to col-leagues, who were so impressed that they developed decorative works on the same theme. The young artist Maurice Denis (1870–1943), commissioned by Henry Lerolle (1848–1929), the painter-collector who owned works by Renoir and Degas, to create a decoration for his ceil-ing, executed a large stylized canvas of women on ladders picking fruit (figure 90). And Mary Cassatt, commissioned by June 1892 to create a vast mural for the tympanum of

the Women's Building at the 1894 World's Columbian Ex-hibition in Chicago, also selected women picking fruit as her central motif.[300]

In the summer of 1891 at Mézy, in addition to *The Cherry Tree* and *The Little Flute Players*, Morisot began two other decorative compositions, *The Reclining Shepherd-ess* and *The Haymaker*, the first of a peasant girl lying in the grass and the second of the same girl raking hay (colorplate 93). Gabrielle Dufour, who had posed the pre-vious summer, again served as the model.[301] Using prelim-

COLORPLATE 92

Young Woman Gathering Cherries, 1891
Red chalk on paper. 55.8 x 43.1 cm (22 x 17 in.). Collection of
John C. Whitehead.

COLORPLATE 91

Girl Picking Cherries, 1891
Red chalk on paper. 74.3 x 50.8 cm (29¼ x 20 in.). From the
Collection of Mr. and Mrs. Paul Mellon, Upperville, Virginia.

Maurice Denis, *Women on a Ladder in the Leaves,* 1892
Oil on canvas. 235 x 172 cm (92½ x 67¾ in.). Musée Départemental
du Prieuré, Saint-Germain-en-Laye, France.

inary drawings and tracings in red chalk, just as she had in
developing *The Cherry Tree,* Morisot executed three versions of *The Reclining Shepherdess,* each on a different scale
and each with a slightly different background. In the smallest and largest versions (BW 279 and figure 91), the figure
is fully clothed and accompanied by a goat; in the third
version, which has the same dimensions as *The Little Flute
Players* and should probably be considered its pendant,
the model posed as a nude bather resting on the bank of a
stream (BW 282). It is unclear which of these three versions Morisot selected for her 1892 exhibition.[302]

Although Morisot continued working on *The Cherry
Tree* after she returned to Paris in the fall of 1891, she also
began several new easel paintings with Julie and family
friends as models. *Young Girl Writing,* 1891 (colorplate 94),
a portrait of Julie seated at a table, is haunted by moody
green and violet shadows. Oblivious to the view through

the window in the background, Julie sits at the edge of
her chair, her head propped on her hand. More than any
other painting by Morisot, this one seems to register the
mental suffering that pervaded the household in the winter of 1891–92, as the health of the fifty-nine-year-old
Eugène Manet grew progressively worse and his family
anticipated the outcome.[303] He died on April 13, 1892.

With him died their shared dream to live in the château at Mesnil. Morisot rented it out and stayed in Paris
during the summer of 1892. Although Morisot retained
control of the house on the rue de Villejust, she was evidently too depressed to remain there, and by the end of
the year she took a smaller apartment not far away on the
rue Weber for herself and Julie.[304] She turned down another invitation to exhibit with Les Vingt in Brussels at
the beginning of 1892, but since Eugène had urged her to
stage a large individual exhibition at the Boussod and
Valadon gallery, Morisot did so, barely a month after his
death.[305]

The most complete exhibition of Morisot's works organized in her lifetime, it comprised forty oils, along with
pastels, drawings, and watercolors, including works borrowed from collectors and dealers, all installed in two adjacent rooms. Monet's journalist friend Gustave Geffroy
(1855–1926) wrote a poetic preface for the catalogue,
applauding Morisot's ability to render the most delicate
oscillations of light and describing her art as a "delightful
hallucination, a vaguely fantastic truth." For once even
Morisot was pleased: "All in all," she wrote her friend
Louise Riesener, "I shall tell you frankly that the whole
seemed to me less bad than I had expected, and that I did
not dislike even the very old pieces. Let us hope that twenty
years from now the new ones will have the same effect on
me."[306] Several works sold, including *On the Veranda*
(colorplate 51), which was acquired by the composer Ernest Chausson (1855–1899).

Morisot's work changed dramatically thereafter. Working again with the beautiful model Jeanne Fourmanoir,
Morisot painted a group of sexually charged images: Jeanne
asleep, her long hair caressing her naked body (figure 92);
Jeanne holding a wide-eyed cat (BW 312); Jeanne, like a
modern Leda, in a boat confronting a swan (BW 308). All
were painted directly, without preliminary drawings, and

COLORPLATE 93

Study for "The Haymaker," 1891
Pencil on paper. 29 x 21.2 cm (11⅜ x 8⅜ in.). M. and Mme
Bernard Foray-Roux.

FIGURE 91

Shepherdess [BW 280], 1891
Oil on canvas. 64 x 116 cm (24⅜ x 45⅝ in.). Private collection.

FIGURE 93

Lucie Léon at the Piano [BW 317], 1892
Oil on canvas. 65 x 80 cm (25⅝ x 31½ in.). Private collection.

all were observed from close up. Indeed, in the painting of Jeanne seated in the bow of a rowboat, Morisot evidently worked from the stern.

In September Morisot, with her tenants' permission, briefly visited the château at Mesnil, where she made a variety of landscape and figure studies.[307] For the most ambitious of these works, *Girls at a Window* (colorplate 95), two local redheaded children named Bodeau posed with their pet cats on the sill of an open window overlooking the garden.

FIGURE 92

Young Girl Sleeping [BW 313], 1892
Oil on canvas. 38 x 46 cm (14¹⁵⁄₁₆ x 18⅛ in.). Private collection.

Traveling with Julie later in the year, Morisot stopped at the museum in Tours, where she made a faithful copy of two embracing water nymphs in the corner of another of Boucher's mythologies, *Apollo Revealing His Divinity to the Shepherdess Issé* (see figures 111 and 112).[308] The dominant blue-green tonalities in the landscape background may have reminded Morisot of the saturated blues in her own *Lucie Léon at the Piano* (figure 93), or alternatively, Boucher's sense of color may have influenced Morisot's portrait. Morisot developed this picture with careful preliminary studies, the way she had worked at Mézy in 1891, but relatively few of her late paintings progressed in this fashion. She sent the finished painting and a portrait of Louise Riesener (BW 222) to the annual group exhibition of the Association pour l'Art in Antwerp in May 1893. That same spring one of her early port scenes of Fécamp was included in an exhibition organized by the progressive New English Art Club in London.[309] However, the death of her sister Yves in early June overshadowed her professional aspirations that year, just as Eugène's death had the year before.

Morisot's prolonged grief left her art relatively unaffected, which seems to call into question the notion ex-

COLORPLATE 94

Young Girl Writing, 1891
Oil on canvas. 57.7 x 46 cm (22¹¹⁄₁₆ x 18⅛ in.). Private collection, New York.

Young Girl Reclining, 1893
Oil on canvas. 65 x 81 cm (25⅝ x 31⅞ in.). Private collection,
New York.

COLORPLATE 95

Girls at a Window, 1892
Oil on canvas. 65 x 49 cm (25⁹⁄₁₆ x 19¼ in.). Courtesy of Galerie
Hopkins and Thomas, Paris.

pressed by the poet Paul Valéry (1871–1945) that her art
was her life.[310] Indeed, although Morisot's art often portrayed her immediate surroundings, family members, and
friends, it was often a form of escape, and the goal of her
ostensibly mundane pictorial ideas was to record the experience of reverie that transcends routine appearances.

In the summer of 1893 Morisot hired one of Renoir's
models to portray such reverie more explicitly than ever
before. Posed in a white dress that registers every colored

nuance of the ambient light, the model reclines on an
Empire chaise longue decorated with a swan's-neck motif.
Resting her head on her right hand, she looks off at nothing in particular, perhaps dreaming of a different time or
place—such as the lake in the Bois de Boulogne with its
gliding swans. Only one of the three versions of this image
actually contained a specific setting (figure 94). A small
pastel (BW 592) observed from close up, including only
the model's reclined head resting on her hand, is perhaps
a preliminary study for the oil version with an interior
background, yet the pastel may be Morisot's ultimate re-

FIGURE 94

Young Woman Reclining [BW 339], 1893
Oil on canvas. 55 x 73 cm (21⅝ x 28¾ in.). Private collection.

FIGURE 95

Photograph of Julie Manet with her greyhound, Laërtes, c. 1893.
Private collection.

finement of this captivating image. The largest version, *Young Girl Reclining* (colorplate 96), which includes only slight fragments of the setting—merely the swan's neck carved on the back of the chaise longue and some white curtains with a faint floral motif—is perhaps the most successful of all in evoking the semiawareness of a daydream.

Morisot's *Girl with a Greyhound* (colorplate 97), her "unfinished" portrait of Julie with Laërtes, the greyhound that Mallarmé had just given to her (figure 95), is no less telling with regard to the artist's preoccupation with setting. Here Morisot merely suggests the room's furniture and a framed Japanese print on the wall with a few thin outlines and general areas of scumbled pale colors. A few strokes of white along the right edge barely indicate a curtain pulled open, allowing daylight to rake across the space and obliterate irrelevant details. Without the figure of Julie in her dark dress, the illusion of space would evaporate. The very fragility of the setting, however, seems to characterize Julie's mood, as she absentmindedly strokes the throat of her new pet. As always, Morisot's lack of finish is to be understood as a refinement.

At the end of the summer, Morisot, Julie, and Laërtes set off to visit Mallarmé at his country house in Valvins. Thanks to the diary that Julie began to keep as they ar-

rived there, the final two years of Morisot's career are better recorded by far than any earlier phase. Almost immediately Julie and her mother stationed themselves side by side at their hotel window to make paintings of Mallarmé's sailboat on the Seine (colorplate 98 and figure 96).[311] Mother and daughter now often worked together this way, just as Morisot and Eugène Manet had done since their courtship. Morisot made a present of her "portrait" of the boat to its owner. Painted in the style of her Impressionist landscapes of the 1870s, with a variety of short strokes that both draw and color the most essential forms without regard for details, *Mallarmé's Sailboat* is the visual counterpart to the exquisite quatrains with which Mallarmé addressed his letters to friends.

Back in Paris, Morisot devoted herself almost entirely to portraits of Julie. *Julie Daydreaming* (colorplate 99), perhaps Morisot's simplest, most concentrated, lyrical, and modern painting, anticipates the decoratively stylized pictures that Pablo Picasso (1881–1973) and Matisse created a decade later; she eliminated setting per se, although the saturated green background, in the spirit of such so-called primitive masters as Hans Holbein, in itself sets a cool, fresh, sylvan mood. Julie's blank, masklike expression is formed by a few elegant arcs for the eyes, nose, and lips, and her body is a carefully orchestrated sequence of sup-

COLORPLATE 97

Girl with a Greyhound (Julie Manet), 1893
Oil on canvas. 73 x 80 cm (28¾ x 31½ in.). Musée Marmottan, Paris.

ple arabesques—the tumbling tendrils of her hair, fingers, shoulders, lap, and hips all curve as gracefully as the neck of a swan. These sensual outlines are animated by the arcing strokes of white that highlight her chalky flesh and her dress. The exquisite balance between Julie's emerging sexuality and her lack of self-awareness creates a mood of mystery and reverie that none of Morisot's colleagues ever surpassed.

Slightly later Morisot began a group of portraits of Julie playing her violin in their rue Weber apartment. In these pictures the setting dominates rather than the figure, whose performance is evoked by the rhythms and color harmonies of Morisot's own sweeping brushwork. For *Julie Playing the Violin* (colorplate 100), the most complex version of this theme, Morisot worked from an adjacent room and incorporated the frame of the doorway

FIGURE 96

Julie Manet, *Mallarmé's Sailboat,* 1893
Oil on panel. 35 x 28.5 cm (13¾ x 11½ in.). Private collection.

between them as part of her composition. Looking beyond Julie, she recorded two portraits hanging on the far wall —Manet's portrait of herself and Degas's portrait of Eugène (see figure 39). These, of course, are emblems of Julie's parents, but they can also be understood as emblems of Morisot's own artistic past.

Between sittings for such portraits, Morisot and her daughter traveled to visit friends: Mallarmé again at Valvins, Monet at Giverny, Sisley at Moret.[312] During these trips, mother and child worked together making water-color landscapes. Early in March 1894 they set off for Brussels to see the museums and a large group exhibition of modern art organized under the auspices of the Libre Esthétique by Octave Maus (1856–1919), who had earlier assembled such exhibitions for Les Vingt. Morisot showed four works on this occasion, in the same room with two works by Renoir.[313] However, a new generation of painters, such as Denis, Redon, and Gauguin, were now the center of debate.

Not that the Impressionist revolution was already a dead issue; it was quite the contrary, as Renoir discovered in his role as executor of the estate of Caillebotte, who died on February 21, 1894, leaving his vast collection of Impressionist paintings to the Luxembourg Museum on condition that they be put on display rather than hidden

in a storage basement. In early March no one could have foreseen that it would take more than a year before the museum would finally agree to accept the paintings in Caillebotte's bequest—and then only thirty-eight of the sixty-six offered—and nearly three years before the museum placed them on exhibition. Since Caillebotte had never acquired one of Morisot's works, Mallarmé was immediately concerned that her key role in the movement might be overlooked; to ensure that Morisot's contribution would not go unrecognized, he used his influence to persuade the Ministry of Fine Arts to buy her *Young Woman in a Ball Gown* (see figure 45) from the sale of Duret's paintings on March 19, 1894.[314]

Morisot and her daughter were at this auction, determined to bid on two portraits of Morisot by Manet. Bids for *Repose* (see figure 23), which had been exhibited at the Salon of 1873, went far beyond their means. But with the help of Durand-Ruel, they were able to acquire a haunting image of Morisot in black silhouetted against a curtain aglow with filtered light.[315] This would become one of Julie's most precious souvenirs of her mother, along with a double portrait by Renoir for which they posed a few weeks after the Duret sale (figure 97).[316] Although a little etching by Renoir of Morisot's head in profile (figure 98) just as it appears in this painting was not published until 1924, he may possibly have executed it to use as a frontispiece for the 1896 memorial exhibition catalogue.

During the early summer of 1894 Morisot painted what amounts to her most ambitious late work in terms of scale, a portrait of Jeanne Pontillon (colorplate 101) destined to hang in the white living room of the apartment that Edma had recently taken in the rue de Villejust building. Evidently developed from a small watercolor (BW 799) in the spirit of Morisot's earliest portraits of her sisters in this medium (see colorplate 17), the large oil shows her niece seated on the Empire chaise longue. Placed somewhat whimsically in front of the mantelpiece in Morisot's rue Weber apartment where presumably it would never have been positioned in daily life, the chaise longue here evokes memories of the sitter's grandparents to whom it had belonged, while a framed photograph of Morisot with Eugène Manet and Julie visible on the wall preserves the memory of a more recent phase of the family's history. This impressive portrait is far more than an exercise in nostalgia for the past, however, for set against the pale apricot wall and the somber upholstery of the chaise longue, Jeanne's orange dress is altogether up-to-date. Moreover, the full hydrangea blossoms on the nearby man-

COLORPLATE 98

Mallarmé's Sailboat, 1893
Oil on canvas. 28.4 x 34.9 cm (11³⁄₁₆ x 13¾ in.). Mr. and Mrs.
Palmer Stearns.

COLORPLATE 99

Julie Daydreaming, 1894
Oil on canvas. 70 x 60 cm (27½ x 23⅝ in.). Private collection.

COLORPLATE 100

Julie Playing the Violin, 1894
Oil on canvas. 65 x 54 cm (25⅝ x 20¼ in.). Mr. Hermann Mayer.

telpiece characterize her as a voluptuous young modern woman.

Intrigued by a travel poster on display at the Gare Saint-Lazare that same summer, Morisot rented a house at Portrieux on the Channel coast and took Julie and her nieces, Paule and Jeanne, for a holiday. They saw the sights and painted together before returning to Paris via Brittany in late September.[317]

Morisot now finished her double portrait *The Children of Gabriel Thomas* (colorplate 102); Thomas, her first cousin, had been one of her earliest patrons.[318] Although she managed to get the children to keep still, Laërtes could evidently not be restrained from joining them, and in the final portrait the dog seems to look at them, baffled by their stiff formality. Morisot also developed a series of watercolors and paintings of models at rest or dressing one another, decorative harmonies in pale pinks, greens, and blues. Behind-the-scenes meditations on female vanity, this group of pictures would turn out to be Morisot's final statement as an artist. In *The Coiffure* (colorplate 103), the brunette model is seated and the blond one is standing behind her to arrange her hair, a motif that had preoccupied Renoir and Degas for the last few years. On the wall behind the models is one of Morisot's own earlier pictures, *The Black Bodice* (see colorplate 30). This image of a model dressed in the fashion of a different generation adds a nostalgic perspective to this late genre scene, suggesting that once the model's hair is arranged she will be ready to pose for the painter as others had before her, and suggesting as well that Morisot's paintings continued to be about the dialogue between art and life. Just such a dialogue is evident in her late watercolors (e.g., colorplate 104), which show models in the rue Weber apartment. Domestic details, such as the paintings on the walls or the family's parakeet cage, can be understood as reminders of Morisot's long-standing predilection to merge her daily private life with her studio life. Much more tightly defined

FIGURE 97

Pierre-Auguste Renoir, *Berthe Morisot and Her Daughter, Julie Manet,* 1894
Oil on canvas. 81.3 x 65.4 cm (32 x 25¾ in.). Private collection.

FIGURE 98

Pierre-Auguste Renoir, *Berthe Morisot,* c. 1896
Etching. 11.5 x 9.2 cm (4½ x 3⅝ in.).

COLORPLATE 101

Portrait of Jeanne Pontillon, 1894
Oil on canvas. 116 x 81 cm (45⅝ x 31⅞ in.). Private collection,
Switzerland.

COLORPLATE 102

The Children of Gabriel Thomas, 1894
Oil on canvas. 100 x 80 cm (39³⁄₁₆ x 31½ in.). Musée d'Orsay,
Paris.

COLORPLATE 103

The Coiffure, 1894
Oil on canvas. 55 x 46 cm (21⅝ x 18⅛ in.). Museo Nacional de
Bellas Artes, Buenos Aires.

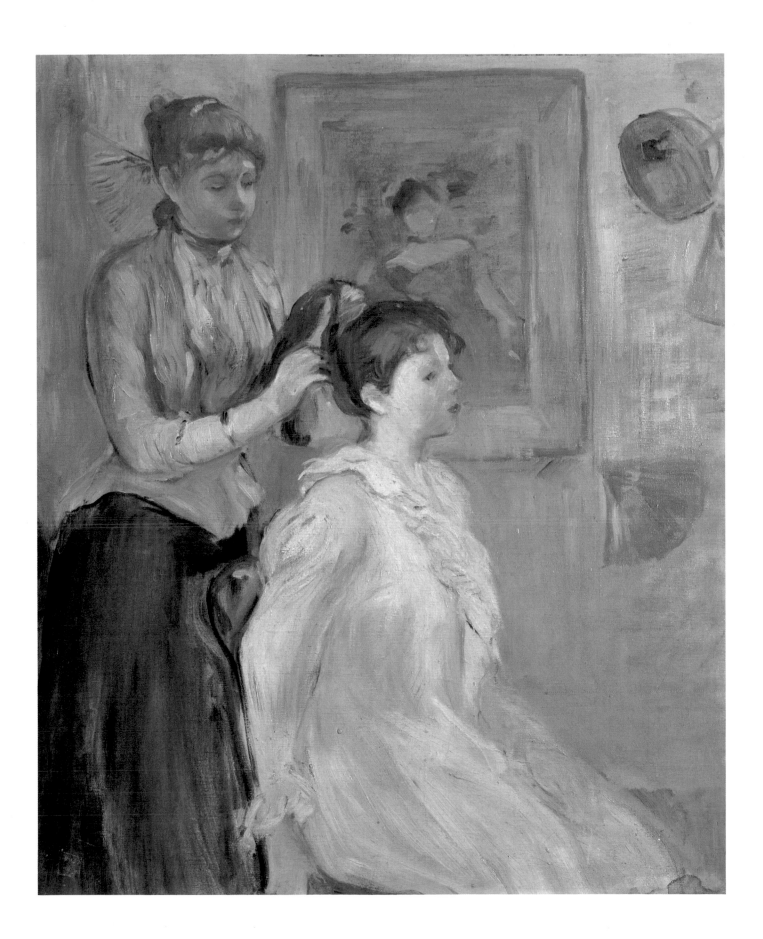

Seated Model, 1894
Watercolor and pencil on paper. 23.1 x 16.8 cm (19⅛ x 6⅝ in.).
Philadelphia Museum of Art: The Louis E. Stern Collection.

than the figures in Morisot's antic Impressionist watercolors of the 1870s and 1880s, these late images of models seem to be recollections of her first mature works in the spirit of Manet done twenty-five years earlier.

In February 1895 Morisot fell ill with pulmonary congestion; she died on March 2 at the age of fifty-four. The death certificate described her as "without any profession."[319] Mallarmé sent wires to her closest friends notifying them of her death. Renoir, who was in Aix working with Cézanne when he received the message, immediately put down his brushes and rushed to the train station. "I had a feeling of being all alone in a desert," he remembered later.[320] Pissarro, who attended the funeral, wrote to his son Lucien in London: "You can hardly conceive how surprised we all were and how moved, too, by the disappearance of this distinguished woman, who had such a splendid feminine talent and who brought honor to our impressionist group, which is vanishing—like all things."[321]

On March 6 Morisot was buried in the Manet family tomb in Passy, joining her husband, Eugène, and her closest professional colleague, Edouard. Understandably, Julie omitted any description of the funeral or burial from her diary.

*J*ulie Manet moved back to the rue de Villejust house that her parents had built, and she lived there with her cousins Paule and Jeanne Gobillard. Friends referred to them as "the little Manets." Only three years later, her guardian Mallarmé died. Degas, who not without regret had never married, played matchmaker to bring Julie together with Ernest Rouart, one of the sons of Henri Rouart, his wealthy schoolmate who had exhibited with the Impressionists from the start and formed an unsurpassed collection of nineteenth-century French art.[322] Degas's efforts led to a double wedding: Jeanne Gobillard married the poet Paul Valéry at the same ceremony, and both couples took up residence with Paule in the rue de Villejust (now rue Paul Valéry).

Notes

Key to sources cited in abbreviated form:

ARCHIVES

DRB Brouillard (Daily Ledger), Durand-Ruel Archives, Paris.

DRC Correspondence, Durand-Ruel Archives, Paris.

DRD Livres des Dépôts (Deposit Books), Durand-Ruel Archives, Paris.

DRS Livres du Stock (Stock Books), Durand-Ruel Archives, Paris.

Carnet beige Morisot, Berthe. *Carnet beige*. c. 1885–88. Private collection. Berthe Morisot's notebook, identified by the color of the cover.

Carnet noir Morisot, Berthe. *Carnet noir*. 1890–? Private collection. Berthe Morisot's notebook, identified by the color of the cover.

Carnet vert (a) Morisot, Berthe. *Carnet vert (a)*. 1885–86. Private collection. Berthe Morisot's notebook, identified by the color of the cover.

Carnet vert (b) Morisot, Berthe. *Carnet vert (b)*. 1888–89. Private collection. Berthe Morisot's notebook, identified by the color of the cover.

PUBLICATIONS

Angoulvent Angoulvent, Monique. *Berthe Morisot*. Paris, 1933.

Bataille-Wildenstein/BW Bataille, Marie-Louise, and Georges Wildenstein. *Berthe Morisot: Catalogue des peintures, pastels, et aquarelles*. Paris, 1961. BW denotes catalogue numbers.

Blanche Blanche, Jacques-Emile. "Les Dames de la grande-rue, Berthe Morisot," in *Les Ecrits nouveaux*. Paris, 1920.

Fourreau Fourreau, Armand. *Berthe Morisot*. Paris, 1925.

Journal Manet, Julie. *Journal (1893–1899)*. Paris, 1979.

Louis Rouart Rouart, Louis. "Berthe Morisot (Mme Eugène Manet)," *Art et décoration* (May 1908), 168–76.

Mallarmé Mallarmé, Stéphane. "Preface," in *Berthe Morisot (Mme Eugène Manet): 1841–1895*, exh. cat., Durand-Ruel. Paris, 1896. First edition and second revised edition.

Manet *Manet, 1832–1883*, exh. cat., Metropolitan Museum of Art. New York, 1983.

Monneret Monneret, Sophie. *L'Impressionnisme et son époque*, 4 vols. Paris, 1978.

New Painting *The New Painting: Impressionism 1874–1886*, exh. cat., Fine Arts Museums of San Francisco and National Gallery of Art. Washington, D.C. Geneva, 1986.

Rewald, 1973 Rewald, John. *The History of Impressionism*, 4th rev. ed. New York, 1973.

Rouart, 1950 Rouart, Denis, ed. *Correspondance de Berthe Morisot*. Paris, 1950.

Rouart, 1957 Rouart, Denis, ed. *The Correspondence of Berthe Morisot*. Translated by Betty W. Hubbard. New York, 1957. A second, small-format edition with identical pagination was published in London in 1959 by Lund Humphries.

Rouart, 1986 Rouart, Denis, ed. *The Correspondence of Berthe Morisot*. Translated by Betty W. Hubbard. Introduction and notes by Kathleen Adler and Tamar Garb. London, 1986.

Rouart-Wildenstein/RW Rouart, Denis, and Daniel Wildenstein. *Edouard Manet: Catalogue raisonné*, 2 vols. Lausanne and Paris, 1975. RW denotes catalogue numbers.

Valéry Valéry, Paul. "Tante Berthe," in *Berthe Morisot*, exh. cat., Musée de l'Orangerie. Paris, 1941.

Wildenstein Wildenstein, Daniel. *Claude Monet: Biographie et catalogue raisonné*, 4 vols. Lausanne and Paris, 1974–85.

1 *Carnet noir*, in Angoulvent, 96–97.

2 *Journal*, 77. As a rental fee for the use of the gallery, Paul Durand-Ruel received *Tea*, 1882 (colorplate 44), from Julie Manet; DRB (vol. June 1893–97, no. 3683, 25 March 1896).

3 *Journal*, 79.

4 *Journal*, 80–93.

5 Bataille-Wildenstein, 5.

6 Birth certificate in "Pièces justificatives et bibliographie," Angoulvent, after p. 152.

7 Marie Elisabeth Yves Morisot, born 4 October 1838 (Actes de mariage, V4E 1948, registration no. 354, Yves Morisot, Archives de la Ville de Paris), died c. 8 June 1893 (*Journal*, 166); Marie Edma Caroline Morisot, born 13 December 1839 (Actes de mariage, V4E 1966, registration no. 83, Edma Morisot, Archives de la Ville de Paris), died 1921 (letter dated 17 May 1974 from Denis Rouart to unknown correspondent, Doc-

umentation du Département des Peintures, Musée d'Orsay, Paris). Information about Tiburce is scant and confused: according to Fourreau, 9 n. 1, he was four years younger than Berthe, placing his birth date in 1845; according to Bataille-Wildenstein, 13, he was born in 1848; the date of his death, although after 1925 (Fourreau, 9), is unknown.

8 The move to Passy was in 1852, according to Fourreau, 8, and in 1851, according to Rouart, 1950, 8; 1957, 13; 1986, 18.

9 *See* David H. Pinkney, *Napoleon III and the Rebuilding of Paris* (Princeton, 1958).

10 Claude Roger-Marx, "Berthe Morisot: Les Femmes peintres et l'impressionnisme," *Gazette des beaux-arts*, ser. 3, 38 (December 1907), 491. M. Morisot's death certificate (Actes de décès, V4E 4662, registration no. 79, Tiburce Morisot, Archives de la Ville de Paris) identifies his parents as Tiburce Pierre Morisot and Claudine Elisabeth Duch[esne] of Paris, similar to Bataille-Wildenstein, 13 (Edme Tiburce Morisot). Curiously, however, according to Fourreau, 7, n. 1, M. Morisot's father

was an architect named Joséphin, probably Joseph-Madeleine-Rose Morisot, 1767–1821 (see Michaud, Biographie universelle, rev. ed., 29:337).

11 Fourreau, 9.

12 Thieme-Becker, s.v. "Chocarne, Jeoffroy Alphonse"; Fourreau, 10.

13 For a general discussion of art education for women in France, see Charlotte Yeldham, Women Artists in Nineteenth-Century France and England (New York and London, 1984), 1:40–62; see also Linda Nochlin, "Women Artists after the French Revolution," Women Artists 1550–1950, exh. cat., Los Angeles County Museum of Art (New York, 1976), 45–67; Jacques Lethève, Daily Life of French Artists in the Nineteenth Century, trans. Hilary E. Paddon (New York, 1972), 26; Germaine Greer, The Obstacle Race: The Fortunes of Women Painters and Their Work (New York, 1979); and Tamar Garb, Women Impressionists (New York, 1986), 6–8.

14 Fourreau, 11–14; Henry Dérieux, "Joseph Guichard, peintre lyonnais (1806–1880)," Gazette des beaux-arts, ser. 5, 5 (March 1922), 181–94; and Thieme-Becker, s.v. "Guichard, Joseph."

15 Jean Gigoux, Causeries sur les artistes de mon temps (Paris, 1885), 57; and Robert Ricatte, ed., Edmond et Jules du Goncourt, Journal: Mémoires de la vie littéraire (Monaco, 1956), 1:213.

16 Fourreau, 11–12.

17 Fourreau, 14; Theodore Reff, "Copyists in the Louvre, 1850–1870," Art Bulletin 46 (December 1964), 556; and Paul Duro, "The 'Demoiselles à copier' in the Second Empire," Woman's Art Journal 7 (Spring/Summer 1986), 1–7.

18 Cartes des permissions, 1858, no. 176, and 1865, no. 177, Archives du Louvre, Paris; in Reff (see n. 17 above), 556. This record only extends to 1865; the rest allegedly was destroyed. According to Reff, Morisot copied Peter Paul Rubens's Debarkation of Marie de' Medici at Marseilles (BW 15) in 1865. According to Bataille-Wildenstein, 14, she copied works by Titian at this time.

19 Fourreau, 15. The two copies are BW 2 and 3.

20 Fourreau, 14.

21 Elizabeth Pennell, The Life of James McNeill Whistler, 5th ed. (Philadelphia, 1911), 53; A. Tabarant, Manet et ses oeuvres (Paris, 1947), 30.

22 LouiRouart, 173. For Lecoq, see Judith Wechsler, "An Aperitif to Manet's Déjeuner sur l'herbe," Gazette des beaux-arts, ser. 6, 91 (January 1978), 32–34.

23 Louis Rouart, 174; or Guichard took them to Corot, who took them to Oudinot; Fourreau, 16–17.

24 Quoted in Charles F. Stuckey, "Monet's Art and the Act of Vision," in John Rewald and Frances Weitzenhoffer, eds., Aspects of Monet (New York, 1984), 110.

25 Fourreau, 18.

26 Jules Claretie, "Millet et Corot," L'Art et les artistes contemporains (Paris, 1876), 393.

27 Louis Rouart, 174; Fourreau, 18. Only one copy after Corot by Morisot, BW 4, survives. Contrary to most accounts, Alfred Robaut claims that this copy was painted after 1873; L'Oeuvre de Corot (Paris, 1905), 2:164, no. 457. According to Fourreau, 19, Julie Manet acquired BW 4 from Mme Pissarro; according to Rouart (1950, 14; 1957, 18; 1986, 23), Pissarro saved it from destruction without giving a date for the episode.

28 Fourreau, 18–20; Rouart, 1950, 10; 1957, 14; 1986, 19. There is disagreement on that date; Roger-Marx (see n. 10 above), 492, places the

date of their work with Corot at Ville d'Avray in 1862, with Guichard's departure for Lyons.

29 Fourreau, 21–22; Rouart, 1950, 10–11; 1957, 15; 1986, 20. The latter, however, quotes a passage from a reminiscence by Tiburce Morisot that calls the date into question. He describes a visit to the Daubignys' house with Daumier, Oudinot, and the landscape painter Antoine Guillemet, where they saw a "fresco" by Daumier. The painting in question (probably Don Quixote and the Dead Mule [Louvre, R.F. 1965–67]) is usually dated 1867–68, but an earlier date of 1864 has also been proposed; Daumier's canvas may have been undertaken in tandem with Daubigny's own series of decorative panels painted in 1864 (Etienne Moreau-Nélaton, Daubigny raconté par lui-même [Paris, 1925], 85–89).

30 Rewald, 1973, 102.

31 Morisot kept Corot's title, Souvenir, in mind for many years: she later claimed not to have known precisely what he meant until her second visit to Nice in 1888–89, when the landscape moved her to write Edma: "It is extraordinary how much of Corot there is in the olive trees and the backgrounds. Now I can understand the title he loves—Souvenir of Italy" (Rouart, 1950, 144; 1957, 146; 1986, 164). Although BW 6 has been identified as Morisot's other entry in the Salon of 1864, entitled Vieux Chemin à Auvers (Old Road to Auvers), it does not seem to depict a road.

32 Angoulvent, 18–19.

33 Fourreau, 25–26; cited in excerpt in Rouart, 1950, 12; 1957, 16–17; 1986, 21–22. One of the 1864 paintings described in Millet's letter may be BW 1, usually dated 1859, which is remarkably close to a painting by Corot; see Robaut (see n. 27 above), no. 404. For Millet, see Stanislas Lami, Dictionnaire des sculpteurs de l'école française au dix-neuvième siècle (1919; reprint, Nendeln, 1970), 3:451–59.

34 Charles Clément, "Exposition de 1965: 8ᵉ article," Journal des débats (25 June 1965), n.p.

35 Wildenstein, 1:421, letter 11.

36 Evidently the expense of the studio prevented the family from taking a trip to Italy; see Rouart, 1950, 15; 1957, 20; 1986, 25.

37 Fourreau, 22.

38 See n. 17 above. See also Geneviève Viallefond, Le Peintre Léon Riesener 1808–1878 (Paris, 1955).

39 Viallefond (see n. 38 above), 29.

40 See Henriette Bessis, "Delacroix et la duchesse Colonna, L'Oeil 14 (March 1967), 29; O. d'Alcantara, Marcello: Adèle d'Affry, Duchesse Castiglione-Colonna 1836–1879 (Geneva, 1961); and Henriette Bessis, Marcello sculpteur (Fribourg, 1980). Regarding Morisot's close but little-known friendship with the Duchess Colonna, see Rouart, 1950, 99, 101; 1957, 101, 103; 1986, 115, 117. According to Morisot, the only true friendship a woman could have was with another woman, and none in her life equaled that with the Duchess Colonna (Carnet noir).

41 Angoulvent, 16.

42 Rouart, 1950, 12; 1957, 16; 1986, 21. The medallion is reproduced in Monneret, 2:87.

43 Angoulvent, 14. The piano was an upright, probably a Pleyel like those Rossini owned; it may be the one depicted in several works by Morisot (BW 229–31, 316–17, 336, 376–77, and 532).

44 Gonzague Privat, Place aux jeunes! Causeries critiques sur le Salon de 1865 (Paris, 1865), 146–47; paraphrased and quoted in part, without reference to source, in Angoulvent, 19–20.

45 Charles F. Stuckey, "What's Wrong with This Picture?" *Art in America* 69 (September 1981), 96–98.

46 Angoulvent, 32; Rouart, 1950, 28; 1957, 32; 1986, 37.

47 Rouart, 1950, 14; 1957, 19; 1986, 24.

48 Robaut (*see* n. 27 above), nos. 1333, 1334, and 1337, among others.

49 Paul Mantz, "Salon de 1865: IV," *Gazette des beaux-arts* 19 (1 July 1865), 30.

50 *Manet*, no. 64.

51 *Fourreau*, 14–15, claims that the Morisot sisters noticed Manet copying Venetian paintings at the Louvre in 1860.

52 Angoulvent, 21.

53 Yet Fourreau, 19, proposes that this painting may be a copy after Corot. But all related works by Corot postdate Morisot's picture except one, Robaut (*see* n. 27 above) no. 815, dated approximately 1855–65; considering Morisot's commitment to originality, this too may postdate *Thatched Cottage in Normandy* (colorplate 2).

54 Rouart, 1950, 15; 1957, 20; 1986, 25; Bataille-Wildenstein, 14–15.

55 Charles Sterling and Margaretta M. Salinger, *French Paintings: A Catalogue of the Collection of The Metropolitan Museum of Art*, vol. 3, *XIX–XX Centuries* (New York, 1967), 164. The picture is now in private hands.

56 *See* Patricia Mainardi, "Edouard Manet's View of the Universal Exposition of 1867," *Arts Magazine* 54, no. 5 (January 1980), 108–15; and Theodore Reff, *Manet and Modern Paris*, exh. cat., National Gallery of Art (Washington, D.C., 1982), no. 2. According to Blanche, 19, Morisot watched Manet working on his view of the World's Fair.

57 Rouart, 1950, 16–17; 1957, 21; 1986, 26.

58 Rouart, 1950, 17–18; 1957, 22; 1986, 27.

59 Actes de mariage, Yves Gobillard (*see* n. 7 above). In the civil marriage certificate, Théodore Gobillard is described as a "receveur des finances particulier," and in the religious marriage certificate (Registre des actes de mariage, Paroisse de l'Annonciation de Passy, Archevêché, 1335, no. 111), as a "receveur particulier des finances."

60 Rouart, 1950, 13; 1957, 18; 1986, 23. According to Pinkney (*see* n. 9 above), 174, Ferry's arguments were fairly commonncy.

61 First published as articles in *Le Temps* (Paris, 20, 24, and 31 December 1867; 10 January, 17 March, 11 April, and 5 and 11 May 1868), then as a brochure (1868).

62 Rouart, 1950, 22; 1957, 26; 1986, 31.

63 Actes de mariage, Edma Pontillon (*see* n. 7 above); Etienne Moreau-Nélaton, *Manet raconté par lui-même* (Paris, 1926), 1:14 n. 2.

64 Rouart, 1950, 17; 1957, 22; 1986, 27.

65 Rouart, 1950, 16; 1957, 21; 1986, 26.

66 Angoulvent, 25–26; Rouart, 1950, 21–22; 1957, 26; 1986, 30–31.

67 Moreau-Nélaton (*see* n. 63 above), 103.

68 Peter Mitchell, *Alfred Emile Léopold Stevens, 1823–1906*, exh. cat., John Mitchell and Son (London, 1973), 17, pl. 6.

69 Rouart, 1950, 25; 1957, 29; 1986, 34.

70 Rouart, 1950, 25; 1957, 29; 1986, 34. For Manet's portrait, *see Manet*, no. 97, where it is misdated.

71 Blanche, 19–20.

72 Rouart, 1950, 24; 1957, 28; 1986, 33; Louise d'Argencourt, Marie-Christine Boucher, Douglas Druick, and Jacques Foucart, *Puvis de Chavannes*, exh. cat., National Gallery of Canada (Ottawa, 1977), 95–98, nos. 74–76.

73 Actes de mariage, Edma Pontillon (*see* n. 7 above).

74 Rouart, 1950, 26, 30; 1957, 30, 34; 1986, 35, 39. *See* Puvis (*see* n. 72 above), nos. 74–76, for the critical reviews.

75 Letter dated 1 May 1869; Moreau-Nélaton (*see* n. 63 above), 108; Rouart, 1950, 27; 1957, 31; 1986, 36 (erroneously dated 2 May).

76 Rouart, 1950, 28; 1957, 32; 1986, 37 (translation slightly corrected). Letter dated 5 May 1869 from Berthe to Edma.

77 Rouart, 1950, 29; 1957, 33; 1986, 38.

78 The canvas with peonies was found on the same stretcher as *Laundresses Hanging Out the Wash* (colorplate 25; BW 45) when it was undergoing treatment for conservation in 1980.

79 Rouart, 1950, 31; 1957, 35–36; 1986, 40–41.

80 Rouart, 1950, 31–32, 39; 1957, 35–36, 43; 1986, 40–41, 51.

81 Rouart, 1950, 33, 35; 1957, 36, 39; 1986, 43, 45.

82 Rouart, 1950, 32–34; 1957, 36–38; 1986, 41–44.

83 Rouart, 1950, 35; 1957, 40; 1986, 46.

84 Rouart, 1950, 34–35; 1957, 37–40; 1986, 44–46. For a psychoanalytic reading of this painting, *see* Matthew Rohn, "Berthe Morisot's *Two Sisters on a Couch*," *Berkshire Review* (Fall 1986), 80–90.

85 Stuckey (*see* n. 45 above), 100–101.

86 *Degas*, exh. cat., Musée de l'Orangerie (Paris, 1937), cat. 185; P. A. Lemoisne, *Degas et son oeuvre 2* (Paris, 1946–49), no. 173; Marc Gerstein, "Degas's Fans," *Art Bulletin* 64 (March 1982), 106 (*see also* n. 281 below).

87 Rouart, 1950, 38–39; 1957, 43; 1986, 51.

88 Rouart, 1950, 37; 1957, 41; 1986, 48.

89 Rouart, 1950, 38; 1957, 42; 1986, 49 (translation slightly corrected).

90 Rouart, 1950, 39; 1957, 44; 1986, 52.

91 Marcel Crouzet, *Un Méconnu du réalisme: Duranty (1833–1880)* (Paris, 1964), 290–94. Crouzet also identifies Morisot as the inspiration for Duranty's Lucie Hambert in his story "L'Atelier," but the arguments are not convincing.

92 Rouart, 1950, 40; 1957, 44; 1986, 52.

93 *Manet*, no. 122; Charles F. Stuckey, "Manet Revised: Whodunit?" *Art in America* 71 (November 1983), 167. According to Moreau-Nélaton (*see* n. 63 above), 114, 140, Manet painted *In the Garden* under Morisot's influence. For the list of paintings that Manet sent to Duret, *see* Tabarant (*see* n. 21 above), 182–83.

94 Bernice Davidson, "'Le Repos': A Portrait of Berthe Morisot by Manet," *Rhode Island School of Design Bulletin* 46 (December 1959), 7; *Manet*, no. 121.

95 Théodore Duret, "Salon de 1870," in *Critique d'avant-garde* (Paris, 1885), 19–20.

96 Rouart, 1950, 46–47; 1957, 50–51; 1986, 58–60.

97 Rouart, 1950, 41–42; 1957, 45–46; 1986, 53–54.

98 Rouart, 1950, 45–46; 1957, 49–50; 1986, 57–58.

99 A. Tabarant, ed., *Une Correspondance inédite d'Edouard Manet: Les Lettres du siège de Paris (1870–1871)* (Paris, 1935).

100 Rouart, 1950, 45; 1957, 49; 1986, 57.

101 Rouart, 1950, 49–56; 1957, 54–61; 1986, 62–71. Valéry, 6, claims that M. Morisot's father had once been secretary general to Thiers, who was also a personal friend of the Morisot family, appearing as a

witness at both Yves's and Edma's weddings (Actes de mariage, Yves Gobillard and Edma Pontillon; *see* n. 7 above).

102 Fourreau, 33–34.

103 Rouart, 1950, 52; 1957, 57; 1986, 66.

104 Just when Morisot began to make watercolors is an unresolved issue. According to Fourreau, 34, her first were done at Versailles in 1870–71, when she copied a fan by Degas (which he had given her), presumably BW 19; according to Angoulvent, 36, Morisot began to paint them earlier but identifies none dating before 1870–71. In Bataille-Wildenstein, six watercolors date from the 1860s: BW 609–14, beginning allegedly in 1864. Since Edma apparently had never painted in watercolor at the time, Morisot's efforts may postdate their training and work together (Rouart, 1950, 67; 1957, 71; 1986, 82).

105 Rouart, 1950, 53; 1957, 58; 1986, 67.

106 Rouart, 1950, 56; 1957, 60–61; 1986, 70–71.

107 Rouart, 1950, 61–64; 1957, 65–69; 1986, 75–80. The reason for her parents' apparent hostility to Puvis is unknown, but Puvis and Morisot disregarded it, seeing each other secretly (Rouart, 1950, 62–64; 1957, 66–69; 1986, 76–80; and letter dated 16 August 1871 from Puvis to Morisot, private collection). The true nature of the relationship is still little understood, but they remained warm friends and colleagues for the rest of her life.

108 Rouart, 1950, 68; 1957, 72; 1986, 83.

109 Rouart, 1950, 67; 1957, 71; 1986, 82.

110 Rouart, 1950, 67; 1957, 71; 1986, 82. Paule Gobillard was born 3 December 1867 (*Journal*, 74).

111 The models are variously identified as Valentine and Marguerite Carré (BW 23) or Yves, Edma, and Paule (Reff [*see* n. 56 above], no.3).

112 *Manet*, no. 133.

113 Later Morisot and her child, Julie, would describe what they saw on walks in chromatic terms: "[Julie] sees rose in the light and violet in the shadows" (*Carnet beige*); with evident pleasure Morisot would record Julie's bedazzlement at natural phenomena such as the first snowfall in the Bois (*Carnet vert* [a]).

114 *Journal*, 81.

115 Letter dated 28 April 1872 from Puvis de Chavannes to Morisot, private collection.

116 Edma Pontillon had come to Paris to await the birth of her second daughter, Blanche, born 23 December 1871 (Actes de naissance, V4E 4644, registration no. 717, Blanche Pontillon, Archives de la Ville de Paris).

117 Fourreau, 31, described a related small pastel, now apparently lost, which he dated 1867.

118 For Morisot's use of Millet's studio, *see* Angoulvent, 38. For Manet, *see* Rouart, 1950, 67; 1957, 71; 1986, 82.

119 Tabarant (*see* n. 99 above), 33.

120 RW 228 is usually considered a mourning portrait of Morisot, following the death of her father in January 1874; but she apparently always wore black or white (Blanche, 17), and the painting hardly suggests sadness even if Manet wished to record his friend's grief or if she consented to let him try. None of the nine paintings for which Morisot posed is listed in Manet's 1872 studio inventory. He sold or gave away only two of them, RW 179 (figure 32, upon which he based both an etching and two lithographs) and RW 181 (figure 30), which is possibly the *Woman with a Fan* sold to Duret in 1873 for 600 francs and

acquired by de Bellio before 1884. All the others were listed in the inventory of Manet's estate in 1883.

121 DRS, vol. 1868–73, nos. 2045–47.

122 DRS, vol. 1868–73, nos. 20490–91.

123 Rouart, 1950, 70–73; 1957, 74–77; 1986, 85–89.

124 DRB, vol. 1873–76, no. 20819, 21 March 1873; sold to Durand-Ruel on 28 April 1873 for 500 francs, given inventory no. 2934, and sold that very day to Hoschedé. For a recent discussion of the history of Hoschedé's collection, which omits this information on his earliest purchases of Impressionist paintings, *see* Hélène Adhémar, "Ernest Hoschedé," in Rewald and Weitzenhoffer (*see* n. 24 above), 54–71. For a comparison of Morisot's prices with those of her contemporaries, *see* Paul Tucker, "The First Impressionist Exhibition in Context," in *New Painting*, 106, 116 n. 76.

125 *Vente au bénéfice des Alsaciens-Lorrains émigrés en Algérie . . . offerts par les artistes*, 18–19 April 1873, cat. 106, *La Jetée*, 22 x 48 cm, bought for 300 francs; DRB, vol. 1873–76, no. 3159, 3 July 1873. It is unknown why the date of purchase is several months later than that of the auction.

126 Angoulvent, 44, identifies this pastel as Morisot's entry in the 1873 Salon. The model is too old to be Edma's daughter Blanche.

127 Rewald, 1973, 302–4.

128 Charles S. Moffett, "Introduction," in *New Painting*, 17.

129 DRB, vol. 1873–76, no. 20861, 24 May 1873; *Seventh Exhibition of the Society of French Artists*, 168 New Bond Street, London, c. July 1873, cat. 62. Although this double portrait eventually belonged to the Pontillon family, it was originally intended for the art market. At the 1874 Impressionist exhibition its price was 800 francs (unpublished prices annotated by the artists themselves in Philippe Burty's copy of the catalogue; *see* Claude Roger-Marx, "En marge de la première exposition du groupe dit impressionniste," *Cent ans d'impressionnisme*, exh. cat., Durand-Ruel (Paris, 1974), n.p. Morisot quoted the same price in 1873 to Durand-Ruel for the picture to be exhibited in London, but he doubled it to 1,500 francs.

130 "Société anonyme coopérative d'artistes-peintres, sculpteurs, etc., à Paris," *Chronique des arts et de la curiosité* (17 January 1874), 19; cited in Hélène Adhémar, "Introduction," *L'Exposition de 1874 chez Nadar (retrospective documentaire)*, in Anne Dayez et al., *Centenaire de l'impressionnisme*, exh. cat., Grand Palais (Paris, 1974), 223.

131 This document is in a private collection. Degas also invited Edma to consider exhibiting with them if she was still painting.

132 Rouart, 1950, 76; 1957, 80; 1986, 92.

133 This unpublished letter is in a private collection.

134 Rouart, 1950, 76; 1957, 80; 1986, 92. Guichard's reference to himself as a physician may allude to his having served during the Commune in the medical and ambulance corps; Ricatte (*see* n. 15 above), 9:210, 239, 241.

135 For facsimiles of the catalogues for the eight Paris Impressionist exhibitions, *see New Painting*. We have in several instances proposed alternate identifications for the works Morisot showed.

136 Giuseppe de Nittis, "Corrispondenze: Londra," *Il Giornale artistico* (1 July 1874), 26: "As to the portrait by Mlle Morisot, it is a colored pastel of a bust of a pale woman dressed in black with crossed arms."

137 Philippe Burty, "Exposition de la Société anonyme des artistes," *La République française* (25 April 1874); Jules Castagnary, "Exposition du boulevard des Capucines: Les impressionnistes," *Le Siècle* (29 April 1874), 3.

138 Jean Prouvaire, "L'Exposition du boulevard des Capucines," *Le Rappel* (20 April 1874), 3. In *New Painting*, 134, following information supplied in Oskar Reutersvärd, *Impressionisterna inför publik och kritik* (Stockholm, 1952), 261, it is claimed that "Jean Prouvaire" is a pseudonym for Pierre Toloza, but Roger-Marx (*see* n. 10 above), 496, claims that it is a pseudonym for Catulle Mendès (1841–1909). However, in the *Catalogue général des imprimés* of the Bibliothèque Nationale, Paris, it is claimed that both Prouvaire and Toloza are pseudonyms of the Languedoc Parnassian poet Auguste Fourès (1848–1890). Infrared reflectography indicates that originally Morisot painted the figure in *Reading* with wide eyes glancing to the right; *see* William A. Real, "Exploring New Applications for Infrared Reflectography," *The Bulletin of the Cleveland Museum of Art* 72, no. 8 (December 1985), 410.

139 Louis Leroy, "L'Exposition des impressionnistes," *Le Charivari* (25 April 1874).

140 DRB, vol. 1873–76, no. 3051, 25 June 1873. Lucien Boursier was her paternal cousin. A witness cited in M. Morisot's death certificate of 24 January 1874, he is described as a nephew, thirty-one years of age, an inspector general of the gas company, living on rue de la Tour, Paris. Only one work by Morisot can be documented as part of Stevens's collection: BW 35 can be seen on the upper tier of the wall at left in *Salon of the Painter*, 1880 (William A. Coles, *Alfred Stevens*, exh. cat., Ann Arbor, University of Michigan Museum of Art; Baltimore, Walters Art Gallery; Montreal, Musée des Beaux-Arts [1977–78], cat. 32), a painting of his studio on rue de Martyrs. *See also Journal*, 82–83.

141 Blanche, 21.

142 Rouart, 1950, 76–77; 1957, 81; 1986, 93. *See also Journal*, 81. The tradition that they became formally engaged during this holiday is open to question, given his insecurity about other suitors and about her apparent disinterest in him, expressed in letters written by Eugène immediately after this trip (Rouart, 1950, 77–79; 1957, 81–83; 1986, 93–95).

143 Rouart-Wildenstein, 1:9, n. 4, describes Eugène as a "rédacteur de ministère," but which ministry he was associated with is unknown. Eugène's 347-page novel *Victimes!* (Clamecy: A. Staub) is about (and dedicated to) those persecuted or exiled on the occasion of Louis-Napoleon's coup d'état on 2 December 1851, which led to the inauguration of the Second Empire (1852–70). For the marriage certificate, *see* Angoulvent, after p. 152.

144 Lemoisne (*see* n. 86 above), no. 339.

145 Letter dated 16 November 1885 from Stéphane Mallarmé to Paul Verlaine, in Henri Mondor and Lloyd James Austin, eds., *Stéphane Mallarmé: Correspondance* (Paris, 1965), 2:303, letter 438.

146 This sitter was the wife of Nicolas-Gustave Hubbard (1828–1888), an economist and secretary general of the quaestorship of the Chamber of Deputies (G. Vapereau, *Dictionnaire universel des contemporains*, 1893, s.v. "Hubbard, Gustave-Adolphe"); she died around March 1894 (*Journal*, 27). Their son was Gustave-Adolphe Hubbard, a distinguished extreme leftist who served both national governmental chambers (Vapereau). Morisot turned the affairs of Eugène's estate over to him in 1892, when he was deputy from Seine-et-Oise; his daughter Gaby (perhaps Gabrielle) was a friend of Julie (*Journal*, 28).

147 Jean Renoir, *Renoir: My Father*, trans. Randolph and Dorothy Weaver (Boston and Toronto, 1962), 158. René Gimpel, *Journal d'un collectionneur-marchand de tableaux* (Paris, 1963), 28.

148 "Mémoires de Paul Durand-Ruel," in Lionello Venturi, *Les Archives de l'impressionnisme* (Paris, 1939), 2:201. For the auction, *see* also Angoulvent, 50–52; Reutersvärd (*see* n. 138 above), 39–40; Merete Bodelsen, "Early Impressionist Sales 1874–94 in the Light of Some Unpublished 'procès-verbaux,'" *Burlington Magazine* 110, no. 783 (June 1968), 333–36; and Rewald, 1973, 353–54.

149 Quoted in Rewald, 1973, 351.

150 For the price and buyer, *see* Bodelsen (*see* n. 148 above), 335. The dimensions of BW 61 (figure 41), 54 x 45 cm, correspond to those listed for *Intérieur* in the 1875 *procès-verbaux*, 56 x 47 cm; moreover, BW 61 was later put up for auction by Hoschedé on 14 April 1876 under the title *La Coquette*. For Hoschedé's participation in this sale, *see* Adhémar, in Rewald and Weitzenhoffer (*see* n. 24 above), 61. Apparently bought in at the 1876 sale, BW 61 was subsequently sold at the Hôtel Drouot auction of 18 February 1878, cat. 57, again as *La Coquette*.

151 Bodelsen (*see* n. 148 above), 335, cat. 21, *Chalet au bord de la mer*, 51 x 61 cm. Bataille-Wildenstein's claim that *Villa at the Seaside*, BW 38, belonged to Hoschedé seems to be erroneous. Degas acquired BW 38 at some unknown date before the Morisot memorial exhibition of 1896.

152 Gabriel Thomas, who owned at least eleven works by Morisot at one time or another, was a collector of avant-garde art throughout his life, and his patronage deserves to be studied in detail. According to an unpublished family legend, Thomas, who was head of the consortium financing the construction of the Eiffel Tower, had to sell part of his collection, perhaps including four important paintings by Morisot (BW 14 [colorplate 20], 158, 181 [colorplate 58], and 219 [colorplate 75]), around 1888 when he lost money in a bank failure. However, no record of Thomas's alleged transactions has been found in any auction catalogue or dealer's archives. This information was supplied by Dr. Paul Denis, Paris, in a letter to the author of 15 September 1986. Later, around 1894, Thomas tried to acquire one of the large versions of *The Cherry Tree*, but Morisot was unwilling to sell and promised to make another decorative painting specifically for him; *see Journal*, 84.

153 Rouart, 1950, 81–90; 1957, 84–94; 1896, 97–107. Mme Morisot's unpublished letters (27 May [1875], 7 and 12 June [1875], 20 July [1875], and 26 and 28 August [1875] private collection) indicate that one of the possible positions in the Middle East may have been with an international organization, for it had French and English committees that were responsible for selecting the job candidates. Mme Morisot hoped that the couple would settle in Paris, but they still considered living abroad as late as January 1876, when the Duchess Colonna wrote Berthe from Florence: "Your letter . . . awakened some old pains . . . you give the impression of being always on the way to some other path on the globe where I won't be able to see you. . . . For the moment you enhance Paris with your fascinating grace and I believe you will stay, since it's your true environment. The rest of the world is merely provincial, I assure you" (letter dated 19 January 1876 from the Duchess Colonna to Berthe Morisot, private collection).

154 Rouart 1950, 90; 1957, 93–94; 1986, 106–7. Mme Morisot refers to "your dealer" without naming him. There seems to be no reference to these paintings in any of the Durand-Ruel gallery ledgers for 1875. The following year, however, Durand-Ruel showed a painting by Morisot entitled *Cornfield*, probably BW 46, in *French and Other Foreign Painters*, Durand-Ruel-Deschamps, 168 New Bond Street, London, April 1876, cat. 146. See Kate Flint, ed., *Impressionists in England: The Critical Reception* (London, Boston, Melbourne, and Henley, 1984), 360.

155 For discussions of the impact on modern painting of the project to irrigate market gardens in the area of Gennevilliers and Argenteuil

with sewage water from Paris, *see* Paul Tucker, *Monet at Argenteuil* (New Haven and London, 1982), 149–53; and particularly T. J. Clark, *The Painting of Modern Life* (New York, 1985), 161–63.

156 Rouart, 1950, 85; 1957, 89; 1986, 101. It is possible that they either went to the Normandy coast first or to England instead, as a possible visit to Sainte-Adresse is discussed by Mme Morisot in late May (letter dated 27 May 1875 from Mme Morisot to Berthe Morisot, private collection).

157 Rouart, 1950, 87; 1957, 91; 1986, 104.

158 Rouart, 1950, 86–87; 1957, 90–91; 1986, 102–4. Among the paintings made at the window were BW 50–54 (figure 42, colorplates 26 and 27); apparently BW 49, 56, 431, 432, 630 (colorplate 28), and 632 were painted in a boat.

159 Rouart, 1950, 89; 1957, 93; 1986, 106.

160 Rouart, 1950, 92; 1957, 96; 1986, 109.

161 Rouart, 1950, 93, 97; 1957, 97, 99; 1986, 110, 113. Mme Morisot's death certificate, however, identifies her residence in 1876 as 2, rue Jean Bologne, several blocks away from rue Guichard (Actes de décès, V4E 4675, registration no. 1042, Marie Cornélie Thomas Morisot, Archives de la Seine).

162 DRB, vol. 1873–76, no. 22320, 23 January 1877. This same transaction is also recorded in DRS, vol. 1877 (where the painting is entitled *Seated Woman in White*, which Durand-Ruel purchased from M. Jacque, c/o Munroe and Co.). The London exhibition (Durand-Ruel-Deschamps, 168 New Bond Street, April 1876) included BW 46 and perhaps BW 54 (colorplate 27), listed as *The Harbor*.

163 Albert Wolff, "Le Calendrier parisien," *Le Figaro* (3 April 1876); quoted in Rewald, 1973, 368–69.

164 Rouart, 1950, 94; 1957, 98; 1986, 111.

165 Emile Porcheron, "Promenades d'un flâneur: Les Impressionnistes," *Le Soleil* (4 April 1876), 3.

166 Louis Enault, "Mouvement artistique: L'Exposition des Intransigeants dans la galerie de Durand-Ruel," *Le Constitutionnel* (10 April 1876).

167 Paul Mantz, "Le Salon de 1863: III," *Gazette des beaux-arts*, 15 (1 July 1863), 38.

168 Arthur Baignères, "Exposition de peinture par un groupe d'artistes," *L'Echo universel* (13 April 1876).

169 The paintings by Morisot from the Isle of Wight were BW 51, 53, and 56 and probably 50 and 52 or 54. The figure paintings with the same model were BW 59, 60, 61, and 73. Armand Silvestre refers to BW 59 as a portrait of "Mlle M." ("Exposition de la rue le Peletier," *L'Opinion nationale* [2 April 1876], 3).

170 Hoschedé, although not identified as a lender in the catalogue, did lend several works by Monet to the 1876 exhibition. Some of Hoschedé's pictures, including BW 61 (figure 41), were removed from the exhibition prematurely to be sold at auction on 14 April 1876. *See* Adhémar, in Rewald and Weitzenhoffer (*see* n. 24 above), 61, 68, n. 17.

171 Alex[andre] Pothey, "Chronique," *La Presse* (31 March 1876); Silvestre (*see* n. 169 above).

172 Degas, of course, borrowed this portrait from Morisot and her husband (Rouart, 1950, 93–94; 1957, 97; 1986, 110). Desboutins's drypoints were simply titled *Portraits and Studies* or *Portraits* (cats. 68–71). His portrait of Morisot (figure 46), taken from life about this time, was certainly exhibited later in his individual show at Durand-Ruel, July–August 1889, as cat. 12.

173 Stéphane Mallarmé, "The Impressionists and Edouard Manet," trans. George T. Robinson, *The Art Monthly Review and Photographic Portfolio* (London), 1, no. 9 (30 September 1876), 117–22. Reprinted with commentary and bibliography in *New Painting*, 27–35. For a discussion of the critical reaction to women painters in the nineteenth century and an analysis of the "feminine" nature of their work, *see* Kathleen Adler and Tamar Garb, "Introduction," in Rouart, 1986, 1–11.

174 This unpublished letter, private collection, mentioned but not quoted in Monneret, 2:90, is the earliest documented communication between them.

175 Morisot's mother died 15 December 1876 (Actes de décès, *see* n. 161 above). Rouart (1950, 97; 1957, 99; 1986, 113) dates her death to October of that year.

176 Rouart, 1950, 98; 1957, 100; 1986, 114.

177 Charles-Albert d'Arnoux [Bertall, pseud.], "Exposition des impressionnistes," *Paris-Journal* (9 April 1877), 7; Roger Ballu, "L'Exposition des peintres impressionnistes," *La Chronique des arts et de la curiosité* (14 April 1877), 147, 434.

178 Théodore Duret, *Les Peintres impressionnistes* (Paris, 1878), 29–30.

179 François Daulte, *Auguste Renoir: Catalogue raisonné de l'œuvre peint*, vol. 1, *Figures, 1860–1890* (Lausanne, 1971), no. 94; RW 160.

180 See d'Arnoux (*see* n. 177 above).

181 The address was 9, avenue Eylau (Rouart, 1950, 98; 1957, 100; 1986, 114).

182 See Adhémar, in Rewald and Weitzenhoffer (*see* n. 24 above), 62–63. For Chocquet, *see* John Rewald, "Chocquet and Cézanne," *Gazette des beaux-arts*, ser. 6, 74 (July–August 1969), 33–96; reprinted in Irene Gordon and Frances Weitzenhoffer, eds., *John Rewald: Studies in Impressionism* (New York, 1985), 121–87.

183 *See* Bodelsen (*see* n. 148 above), 340. Bataille-Wildenstein suggests that Cassatt owned BW 63, but that picture, in which the figure is standing, was never owned by Hoschedé. Both Morisot dressing-room pictures in his collection, *Interior* (BW 61; figure 41) and *Woman at Her Toilette* (BW 73; figure 44), show seated figures (*see* n. 150 above for BW 61 and n. 162 above for BW 73). Although BW 72 might seem to be a possible candidate for the picture that passed from Hoschedé's collection to Cassatt's, BW 73 is more likely, since it was exhibited in 1876 at the second Impressionist show, to which Hoschedé was a lender (*see* n. 170 above); BW 61 and 73 moreover correspond to details in reviews by Philippe Burty, "The Exhibition of the 'Intransigeants,'" *The Academy* (London, 15 April 1876), and by Emile Porcheron (*see* n. 165 above).

184 Ronald Pickvance, "Contemporary Popularity and Posthumous Neglect," in *New Painting*, 244–49. The fans that Morisot apparently intended to show cannot be identified.

185 Actes de naissance, V4E 4682, registration no. 872, Eugénie Julie Manet, Archives de la Seine. Eugène was then forty-four and Morisot thirty-seven.

186 Rouart, 1950, 100; 1957, 102; 1986, 116.

187 Nancy Mowll Mathews, *Cassatt and Her Circle: Selected Letters* (New York, 1984), 149.

188 Charles S. Moffett, "Disarray and Disappointment," in *New Painting*, 293–309; Henry Havard, "L'Exposition des artistes indépendants," *Le Siècle* (2 April 1880), 2; Jules Claretie, "M. de Nittis et les impressionnistes," *Le Temps* (6 April 1880), 3.

189 Odilon Redon, *A soi-même: Journal (1867–1915)* (Paris, 1922), 154–55.

190 Paul Mantz, "Exposition des oeuvres des artistes indépendants," *Le Temps* (14 April 1880).

191 Charles Ephrussi, "Exposition des artistes indépendants," *Gazette des beaux-arts*, ser. 2, 21 (1 May 1880), 487.

192 Mallarmé, 9, was the first to mention her relationship to Fragonard; he may have been speaking figuratively, thus confusing later writers, as in Blanche, 19; Angoulvent, 72, where Morisot is called a cousin of Fragonard on her father's side; and Bataille-Wildenstein, 13, which refers to a portrait of Morisot's paternal grandmother by Fragonard's son. Mary Cassatt refutes the claim in a letter to the Philadelphia painter Carroll Tyson, dated 9 July [postmarked 1905] (Archives of American Art, Philadelphia Museum of Art): "She was not at all a grandaughter [*sic*] of Fragonard though, nor any relation to him. I assisted at the birth of that legend [but] when I spoke of it to her sister, the latter assured me she had never heard it mentioned, the only connection was that the two families were originally from the town of Grasse. It was Mallarmé who first mentioned the story to me."

193 Edmond Duranty's text is published, with commentary, in *New Painting*, 37–49 (English translation) and 477–84 (original French).

194 Rouart, 1950, 100; 1957, 102; 1986, 116.

195 Léon Leenhoff, register of works by Manet, 1883, Bibliothèque Nationale, Paris, Estampes Yb³4649 Rés. nos. 11, 12.

196 *Manet*, no. 215.

197 Fronia E. Wissman, "Realists among the Impressionists," in *New Painting*, 337–52. All details about this exhibition cited here derive from this source.

198 Elie de Mont, "L'Exposition du boulevard des Capucines," *La Civilisation* (21 April 1881); Auguste Dalligny, "Sixième Exposition," *Le Journal des arts* (8 April 1881).

199 Henry Havard, "L'Exposition des artistes indépendants," *Le Siècle* (3 April 1881), 2.

200 Paul Mantz, "Exposition des oeuvres des artistes indépendants," *Le Temps* (23 April 1881).

201 C[harles] E[phrussi], "Exposition des peintres indépendants," *La Chronique des arts et de la curiosité* (23 April 1881), 134.

202 Henry Trianon, "Sixième Exposition de peinture par un groupe d'artistes," *Le Constitutionnel* (24 April 1881), 2.

203 Havard (*see* n. 199 above).

204 J.-K. Huysmans, "L'Exposition des indépendants en 1881," *L'Art moderne* (Paris, 1883), 232.

205 Jules Claretie, *La Vie à Paris: 1881* (Paris, 1881), 150: Havard (*see* n. 199 above). There is a painting in a white frame in the background of BW 264.

206 Anonymous, *Artiste* (1 May 1881), in Flint (*see* n. 154 above), 41–43.

207 Angoulvent, 60; Tabarant (*see* n. 21 above), 415.

208 Rouart, 1950, 101; 1957, 103; 1986, 117.

209 Rouart, 1950, 101; 1957, 103; 1986, 117. A letter from Morisot to an unknown dealer dated 10 December 1881 is return-addressed Hotel Richemont, av. Delphine, in Nice; f. 419 NAF 24839, Marcel Guérin collection, Département des Manuscrits, Bibliothèque Nationale, Paris.

210 Angoulvent, 62.

211 Rouart, 1950, 103; 1957, 105; 1986, 118–19.

212 For a general discussion of this exhibition, *see* Joel Isaacson, "The Painters Called Impressionists," in *New Painting*, 373–93.

213 Rouart, 1950, 103–5; 1957, 105–7; 1986, 119–21. However, although Eugène borrowed a white frame for BW 116 and ordered similar ones for the other works, including BW 110 (figure 61), he later reported that except for BW 124, in a white frame with gold decorations, all of Morisot's works in the exhibition ultimately had gray frames decorated with gold.

214 Rouart, 1950, 104; 1957, 106; 1986, 120. The painting of Marie on the porch is possibly BW 110 (figure 61).

215 Slightly varied translation. Rouart, 1950, 103; 1957, 105; 1986, 119. BW 124 is traditionally identified as a view from Eugène's own balconied bedroom at Bougival (*Journal*, 82), but the hilly topography does not conform to any other scenes of the garden. Dr. Albert Robin (b. 1847), a friend of Mallarmé who lived in the same building in which Edouard Manet had his studio from 1872 to 1878, also had a summer home in Bougival, where BW 124 and also 149 were painted. The barrel (tonneau) could be the cask-shaped push toy in BW 107.

216 Rouart 1950, 105; 1957, 107; 1986, 121.

217 Rouart 1950, 105; 1957, 107; 1986, 121.

218 Rouart 1950, 107; 1957, 109; 1986, 123.

219 Paul de Charry, "Beaux-Arts," *Le Pays* (10 March 1882), 6.

220 DRB, vol. 1881–84, no. 2271, 4 April 1882, *Enfant dans un jardin* (BW 107); no. 3579, 20 April 1882, *Femme étendant du linge* (BW 105); and no. 3585, 25 April 1882, *Femme dans un jardin* (BW 110; figure 61). This last was sent to Durand-Ruel's associate in London, Marriott, on 12 June 1882. No catalogue for this exhibition in London has been found, but Flint (*see* n. 154 above), 44–55, reprints several reviews.

221 In Paris they rented a furnished apartment at 3, rue Mont-Thabor during March and April (Angoulvent, 65; Rouart, 1950, 113; 1957, 115; 1986, 130). By 3 May, however, they were at the house at 4, rue de la Princesse in Bougival (DRC, letter dated 3 May 1882 from Morisot to Durand-Ruel).

222 Tabarant (*see* n. 21 above), 450. A relatively large unfinished oil sketch by Manet showing Julie with a watering can in a garden documents how he tried to paint together with Morisot, whose finished picture of Julie (BW 120) was observed from only a few feet to the left of where her brother-in-law was at work.

223 "Paintings, Drawings, and Pastels by Members of 'La Société des impressionistes,'" Dowdeswell and Dowdeswell's, 133 New Bond Street, London. The opening date, not published in the catalogue, is suggested by a letter from Pissarro to his son Lucien, dated 22 April 1883, which claims the show opened the day before; in Janine Bailly-Herzberg, ed., *Correspondance de Camille Pissarro* (Paris, 1980), 196–97, letter 140. DRB, vol. 1881–84, 12–13 April 1883, lists six paintings sent to London for this exhibition, although the catalogue includes only three of these, all lent by Morisot: no. 14, *Femme dans un jardin* (perhaps BW 142); no. 26, *Femme étendant du linge* (BW 105); and no. 57, *Sur la plage* (perhaps BW 116). Flint (*see* n. 154 above), 55–64, reprints several reviews of this show.

224 Rouart, 1950, 114; 1957, 116; 1986, 131.

225 Tabarant (*see* n. 21 above), 477.

226 Rouart, 1950, 116; 1957, 118; 1986, 133.

227 Rouart, 1950, 116; 1957, 118; 1986, 133.

228 Charles S. Moffett, in "Monet's Haystacks," Rewald and Weitzenhoffer (*see* n. 24 above), 142, points out that Monet had already depicted the motif as a minor element in a landscape from 1865.

229 Rouart, 1950, 121; 1957, 123; 1986, 138. He had still not given it to her by 1885 (Rouart, 1950, 124; 1957, 126; 1986, 141).

230 *See* Mallarmé, 6; Louis Rouart, 169; Blanche, 23; and Rosamond Bernier, "Dans la lumière impressionniste," *L'Oeil* (May 1959), 42.

231 BW 118, a signed painting that was included in the 1896 memorial exhibition (*Journal*, 86), is more likely to be the version exhibited that year, contrary to the proposal in *New Painting*, 395, of the variant, BW 117.

232 Rouart, 1950, 123; 1957, 125; 1986, 140.

233 International Exhibition of Georges Petit, May–June 1887, cat. 99; *Exposition de tableaux, pastels, et dessins par Berthe Morisot* at Boussod & Valadon, 25 May–18 June 1892, cat. 7; and the exhibition at the Libre Esthétique in Brussels, 17 February–15 March 1894, cat. 320.

234 Rouart, 1950, 123; 1957, 125; 1986, 140.

235 *Carnet vert (a)*, from Paul Bourget, "Edmond et Jules de Goncourt," *La Nouvelle Revue* (1 October 1885), 449–81.

236 "Memoirs of Archibald Standish Hartick," in Victor Merlhes, ed., *Correspondance de Paul Gauguin: Documents, témoignages* (Paris, 1984), 440.

237 *Carnet vert (a)*, quoted in Angoulvent, 69–70.

238 Rouart, 1950, 126–27; 1957, 128–29; 1986, 143–44.

239 *Carnet vert (a)*, quoted in Angoulvent, 73–74.

240 *Carnet vert (a)*, quoted and paraphrased in Angoulvent, 73–75.

241 Fantin-Latour's copy is in the Musée Magnin, Dijon, France.

242 BW 143; Angoulvent, cat. 284.

243 *Journal*, 83.

244 *Carnet vert (a)*, in Rouart, 1950, 128; 1957, 130; 1986, 145.

245 *Carnet vert (a)*.

246 Rouart, 1950, 126; 1957, 128; 1986, 143.

247 Martha Ward, "The Rhetoric of Independence and Innovation," in *New Painting*, 425–27.

248 Richard Thomson, *Seurat* (Oxford, 1985), 95–96. Cassatt's father identifies Morisot as one of the principal backers, along with Degas, a certain Lenoir, and Cassatt herself; Mathews (*see* n. 187 above), 197–98.

249 *Works in Oil and Pastel by the Impressionists of Paris*, American Art Galleries; extended for an additional month but moved to the National Academy of Design; Morisot's entries were cat. 139, *In the Garden* (BW 107); cat. 140, *Peasant Hanging Out Linen* (BW 105); cat. 141, *La Toilette*; cat. 142, *Portrait of Mme X* (BW 67); cat. 143, *Port of Nice* (perhaps BW 113; figure 60); cat. 144, *Beach at Nice* (perhaps BW 116); cat. 147, *Marine View* (perhaps BW 42 or 43); and cat. 148, *Young Girl with Umbrella* (BW 104). For details about the exhibition, *see* Lionello Venturi, "Introduction," in Venturi (*see* n. 148 above), 1:77–78 and 2:216–18; Hans Huth, "Impressionism Comes to America," *Gazette des beaux-arts*, ser. 6, 29 (April 1946), 225–26, 237–43; Rewald, 1973, 523–24; and Frances Weitzenhoffer, *The Havemeyers: Impressionism Comes to America* (New York, 1986), 39–42.

250 Jean Ajalbert, "Le Salon des impressionnistes," *La Revue moderne* (20 June 1886), 388.

251 *Carnet beige*.

252 Julie also identifies her as the model for three pictures, including BW 173 (*Journal*, 87–89), and Bataille-Wildenstein identifies her as the model for BW 174, 175, 496, 498, and 504.

253 Letter dated 24 May 1886 from Puvis de Chavannes to Morisot (partially quoted in Rouart, 1950, 128–29; 1957, 131; 1986, 146, erroneously dated 14 May 1886).

254 *Carnet beige*.

255 Letter dated (inscribed) Jersey 1886 from Morisot to Paule Gobillard, private collection.

256 *Carnet beige*, quoted in Angoulvent, 81. On 4 March 1887, Monet asked Rodin to give Morisot advice on casting (Wildenstein, 3:221, letter 774). The head was cast in bronze, probably in an edition of eight, around 1964; Alan DuBois, "Ma Petite Julie," *Pharos* 6 (Summer–Fall 1968), 16. Around 1894 Morisot also executed a bas-relief, the composition of which is a variant of BW 364. Curiously, the first edition of the catalogue for the 1896 Morisot memorial exhibition lists three sculptures: the head, the bas-relief, and a *Mother and Child*. This last probably refers either to a lost work or to the pewter cast of the bas-relief.

257 Annual exhibition of Les Vingt; according to the critical reviews, it ran from 5 February to 5 March 1887. Her entries were cat. 1, *Young Girl on the Grass* (BW 173); cat. 2, *Getting Out of Bed* (BW 191; colorplate 64); cat. 3, *Little Servant* (perhaps BW 194; colorplate 65); cat 4, *The Port of Nice* (BW 113; figure 60); and cat. 5, *Interior at Jersey* (BW 197; figure 76). She refused their invitation to participate in 1886. Letter A.A.C. no. 4743, Fonds Octave Maus, Archives de l'Art Contemporain, Musées Royaux des Beaux-Arts de Belgique: Art Moderne, Brussels; cited in a letter dated 3 September 1986 to Dr. Suzanne Lindsay from Mme Micheline Colin, Chargé de mission, Musées Royaux des Beaux-Arts de Belgique —Art Moderne.

258 Morisot gave him *Getting Out of Bed* (colorplate 64).

259 Undated letter, before 1 May 1887, from Morisot to unnamed woman, probably Mme Hoschedé, private collection.

260 In her *Carnet beige*, Morisot noted Carmen's address, which is unfortunately nearly illegible (109, Bd. B[?]er). Gaudin posed for BW 207, perhaps 264, 518 (colorplate 69), 519, 761, and 762. For Gaudin and Lautrec, *see* Charles F. Stuckey and Naomi Maurer, *Toulouse-Lautrec Paintings*, exh. cat., Art Institute of Chicago (Chicago, 1978), cats. 15, 28, and 39. According to Françoise Gauzi, in *Lautrec et son temps* (Paris, 1954), 129, it was this model's slightly brutal facial features that appealed to Lautrec. In a related spirit, around 1885 Cassatt made a wager with Degas that she could produce a masterpiece (*Girl Arranging Her Hair*, National Gallery of Art, Washington, D.C.) from a model with an ugly face; *see* Achille Segard, *Mary Cassatt* (Paris, 1913), 184–86.

261 Rouart, 1950, 131; 1957, 133; 1986, 148; Barbara E. White, *Renoir: His Life, Art, and Letters* (New York, 1984), 175–76. For Morisot's etching, *see* Janine Bailly-Herzberg, "Les Estampes de Berthe Morisot," *Gazette des beaux-arts*, ser. 6, 93 (May–June 1979), 223, no. 6.

262 The most complete discussion of Morisot's prints and the Mallarmé project is in Bailly-Herzberg (*see* n. 261 above), 215–27. According to Angoulvent, 92–93, Morisot began these colored-pencil drawings after 1890, after she gave a set of these pencils to Julie as a Christmas present. Given Morisot's support of Seurat (*see* n. 248 above), reference should also be made to his colored-pencil drawings; *see* C. M. de Hauke, *Seurat et son oeuvre* (Paris, 1961), nos. 364–69, 370, 380, 383–85.

263 Bailly-Herzberg (*see* n. 261 above), 220–22, nos. 1, 2.

264 Rouart, 1950, 145; 1957, 147; 1986, 165.

265 Wildenstein, 3:222, letter 782.

266 Rouart, 1950, 134; 1957, 136; 1986, 152.

267 Rouart, 1950, 135; 1957, 137; 1986, 153.

268 The group exhibition at Durand-Ruel took place from 25 May to 25 June 1888; Morisot's other entries were cat. 53, *Little Girl Reading* (perhaps BW 219; colorplate 75); cat. 54, *Study of a Child* (perhaps BW 218); cat. 55, *View of Tours* (pastel) (BW 523; colorplate 71); and cat. 56, *Garden* (perhaps BW 201).

269 See M. G. Dortu, *Toulouse-Lautrec et son oeuvre* (New York, 1971), cat. nos. 342, 343.

270 Letter dated 21 May 1888 from Mallarmé to Morisot, in Mondor and Austin, 1969, 3:200, letter 644. *See* n. 145 above.

271 Bonnet may also have posed for BW 218–21 and BW 528–31.

272 Rouart, 1950, 135–36; 1957, 138; 1986, 154.

273 Rouart, 1950, 141; 1957, 143; 1986, 161.

274 Rouart, 1950, 140; 1957, 142; 1986, 160.

275 Rouart, 1950, 140; 1957, 142; 1986, 160.

276 Rouart, 1950, 141–42, 146; 1957, 143–44, 149; 1986, 161–62, 168.

277 Rouart, 1950, 144; 1957, 146; 1986, 164.

278 *Journal*, 87.

279 Rouart, 1950, 146; 1957, 149; 1986, 168.

280 *Carnet vert (b)*; two similar lists of subjects begin with the medallion of Julie, followed by a view of the mountain and chateaux; the port; Célestine with a basket; Villefranche; a child; the port at night; orange trees; the house with aloes; Julie gathering flowers with the olive trees in the background; figures and orange trees; carnival; and the entrance to the church.

281 Marc Gerstein, "Impressionist and Post Impressionist Fans," Ph.D. dissertation, Harvard University (1978), 68, no. 12. He points out that the vignette portrait of Morisot in this fan design is a rendition of BW 166. This is of special interest because although BW 166 might appear "unfinished," Morisot evidently considered it otherwise.

282 Rouart, 1950, 149–51; 1957, 151–53; 1986, 170–72. For Monet's voluminous correspondence related to this campaign, *see* Wildenstein, 3:250–59, letters 1000–1081.

283 Rouart, 1950, 151–52; 1957, 153–54; 1986, 172–73. Angoulvent, 90, refers to the house that they rented at Mézy as "la Maison Blotière," where Morisot worked in the attic studio with floral-pattern wallcovering.

284 Rouart, 1950, 153, 57, 155; 1986, 174.

285 *Journal*, 90.

286 Rouart, 1950, 157; 1957, 159; 1986, 179.

287 Excerpt from an unidentified notebook, in Rouart, 1950, 156; 1957, 158; 1986, 177.

288 Rouart, 1950, 157; 1957, 159; 1986, 179.

289 Document A.A.C. no. 5718, Fonds Octave Maus, in Colin (*see* n. 257 above).

290 Although there was no catalogue, the works included probably correspond to DRB, vol. 1888–91, nos. 7786–90, 7794–96, 20–27 April 1891.

291 *Carnet noir*, in Rouart, 1950, 157–58; 1957, 159–60; 1986, 179–80.

292 Théodor de Wyzewa, "Mme Berthe Morisot," *L'Art dans les deux mondes* 19 (23 March 1891), 223–24.

293 For Morisot's interest in Empire furniture, *see* Rouart, 1950, 159–60; 1957, 162; 1986, 182. Around this time Morisot became increasingly nostalgic, telling Puvis: "I often live in the past; I was seeing Passy again (*Carnet noir*, in Rouart, 1950, 158; 1957, 160; 1986, 180).

294 Rouart, 1950, 160; 1957, 162; 1986, 182.

295 Rouart, 1950, 162; 1957, 165; 1986, 185. The original is dated 12 October.

296 Rouart, 1950, 159; 1957, 161; 1986, 181.

297 Rouart, 1950, 154, 161; 1957, 157, 163; 1986, 176, 183. Renoir's decorative-figure series (Daulte [*see* n. 179 above], 599–602, 604, and 610), heretofore dated 1890, should probably be dated late 1891; the models always wear the same dresses, presumably those mentioned by Renoir in this letter (Rouart, 1950, 161; 1957, 163; 1986, 183). In any case none of these so-called 1890 pictures seems to have been included in Renoir's exhibition at Durand-Ruel in July 1891. The claim that Julie posed for his series during Renoir's visits to Mézy has been disproved (*see* Sterling and Salinger [*see* n. 55 above], 158).

298 *Journal*, 84.

299 For Julie's health, *see* Philippe Huisman, "Julie Manet," *Connaissance des arts* 183 (May 1967), 78. Angoulvent, 101, claims that Zandomeneghi recommended Jeanne Fourmanoir to Morisot as a model.

300 Cassatt's mural is lost, and Puvis's murals for the museum in Rouen may have been her major source of inspiration; *see* Adelyn Breeskin, *Mary Cassatt: A Catalogue Raisonné of the Oils, Pastels, Watercolors, and Drawings* (Washington, D.C., 1970), cat. 213; Nancy Hale, *Mary Cassatt* (Garden City, N.Y., 1975), 159–66; and Mathews (*see* n. 187 above), 229, 232–33, 235–38, 335.

301 Angoulvent, 95, calls her Gabrielle Joye.

302 Angoulvent, 100, n. 4.

303 *Journal*, 85.

304 Rouart, 1950, 169, 172; 1957, 171, 174; 1986, 194, 197. She retained ownership of the house at 40, rue de Villejust but evidently rented all the apartments to tenants until her orphaned nieces moved into the top-floor apartment. They were joined by Julie after her mother's death.

305 Document A.A.C. no. 6291, Fonds Octave Maus, in Colin (*see* n. 257 above). For Eugène's encouragement, *see* Angoulvent, 99.

306 Rouart, 1950, 169; 1957, 171; 1986, 194.

307 Rouart, 1950, 171; 1957, 173; 1986, 196.

308 Rouart, 1950, 172; 1957, 174; 1986, 197. Boucher, *Apollo Revealing His Divinity to the Shepherdess Issé*, Musée des Beaux-Arts, Tours.

309 Flint (*see* n. 154 above), 364.

310 Valéry, 119.

311 *Journal*, 10; and Rouart, 1950, 177; 1957, 179; 1986, 203.

312 *Journal*, 19–23.

313 *Journal*, 28–29. The works Morisot lent were singled out for praise in a review by Paul Gauguin, "Exposition de la libre esthétique," *Essais d'art libre* 5 (April 1894), 31.

314 *See* Théodore Duret, *Histoire des peintres impressionnistes*, rev. ed. (Paris, 1919), 112.

315 *Journal*, 30. Julie claimed the portrait cost 4,500 francs, but according to DRB, vol. 1893–97, no. 2973, the dealer purchased the painting at the sale for 5,100 francs (*see also* Bodelsen [*see* n. 148 above], 344–45) and resold it that very day to Morisot for 5,325 francs, which she paid in installments.

316 Rouart, 1950, 179; 1957, 181; 1986, 205; *see also* White (*see* n. 261 above), 200.

317 Rouart, 1950, 181; 1957, 183; 1986, 207; *Journal*, 31–47.

318 Begun 19 October 1893 (*Journal*, 22) and worked on intermittently until finally signed 28 October 1894 (*Journal*, 49).

319 *Journal*, 52; extracts of the death certificate, in "Pièces justificatives," Angoulvent, after p. 152.

320 Henri Mondor, *La Vie de Mallarmé* (Paris, 1941), 709; Renoir (*see* n. 147 above), 300–301.

321 John Rewald, ed., *Camille Pissarro: Letters to His Son Lucien* (Santa Barbara and Salt Lake City, 1981), 333.

322 *Journal*, "Epilogue," opp. p. 288; Huisman (*see* n. 299 above), 81.

Morisot's Style and Technique

The work of Berthe Morisot is perhaps the least familiar of all the Impressionist artists. It is not well represented in museums, nor is it reproduced widely in art-history books and magazines. Furthermore, accounts of her life tend to be strictly biographical and include little information about her working methods. Yet Morisot was a painter's painter; during her lifetime, her patrons included artists Mary Cassatt (1844–1926), William Merritt Chase (1849–1916), Edgar Degas (1834–1917), Alfred de Knyff (1819–1885), Giuseppe de Nittis (1846–1884), Edouard Manet (1832–1883), Claude Monet (1840–1926), Camille Pissarro (1830–1903), Auguste Renoir (1841–1919), Henri Rouart (1833–1912), and Alfred Stevens (1828–1906). Other patrons were writers Stéphane Mallarmé (1842–1898) and George Moore (1852–1933) and composer Ernest Chausson (1855–1899). That her art was important to some of the greatest artists of her time makes its relative obscurity all the more surprising.

The observations that follow are those of a painter. Based on nearly fifteen years' study of Morisot's work, they are inevitably incomplete and personal but are made from the conviction that without considering her techniques and materials, one can lose sight of what is most fundamental in her art. Some of the practices she followed at the start of her career remained constant throughout her life. The scale of her work, for example, was almost always small. Her palette was rather limited, yet most of her contemporaries considered her a virtuoso colorist. Indeed color was as vital to her work as it was later to that of Henri Matisse (1869–1954) and Pierre Bonnard (1867–1947).

Despite the consistency of her palette and format, however, she loved to experiment, and new techniques significantly changed her working methods as she matured. Around 1880 Morisot and her colleagues Edouard Manet and Eva Gonzalès (1849–1883) began to paint on unprimed canvas; its rough surface considerably affected the pull of her brush, the way heavily textured papers tend to crumble the otherwise smooth application of charcoal or pastel stick. Her brushwork became increasingly looser, to the extent that many viewers complained that her oil paintings resembled rapidly sketched drawings and watercolors. And she increasingly sought to solve color decisions with drawing and drawing decisions with color. From 1885 on, however, she developed most of her oil paintings from carefully prepared preliminary drawings on paper. In a sense, everything about her technique contributes to the impression that she painted without effort; yet her obsession with grace and spontaneity, although remaining her uppermost goal as a stylist, often involved a struggle. Her mother observed, "Whenever she works she has an anxious, unhappy, almost fierce look," adding, "This existence of hers is like the ordeal of a convict in chains."[1] No matter how improvisational her works appeared, there was always an underlying control.

Upon looking at her pictures in the 1880 Impressionist group show, Odilon Redon (1840–1916) observed, "Berthe Morisot retains the marks of an early artistic education which sets her distinctly apart, with Degas."[2] Unquestionably, her most influential teachers were Camille Corot (1796–1875) and Edouard Manet, yet she never received

FIGURE 99

Edouard Manet, *Linen,* 1875
Oil on canvas. 145 x 115 cm (57⅛ x 45¼ in.). The Barnes
Foundation, Merion, Pennsylvania.

FIGURE 100

Edouard Manet, *Young Woman in a Garden,* 1880
Oil on canvas. 151 x 115 cm (59½ x 45¼ in.). Private collection.

conventional art lessons from either man. As a mature
artist she hung paintings by them in her studio out of
veneration for the basic principles that sustained her own
creativity. Jacques-Emile Blanche (1861–1942) reported that
a landscape study by Corot hung in her Paris bedroom-
studio on the rue Guichard.[3] And Morisot's daughter, Julie
Manet (1878–1966), remembered that two large paintings
by Manet, *Linen,* 1875 (figure 99), and *Young Woman in a
Garden,* 1880 (figure 100), hung on the walls of her mother's Paris salon-studio on the rue de Villejust.[4]

Like Manet, whose passion for the old masters is leg-
endary, Morisot was receptive to what the art of the past
could teach her. As a student she copied works by Peter
Paul Rubens and Paolo Veronese, and when she was in her
forties she copied a detail from an eighteenth-century allegorical painting by François Boucher (see colorplate 62),
hanging the copy in her studio next to the paintings by

Manet. Although she never overtly incorporated specific
elements from works by Boucher in her own pictures, the
luminosity and what Morisot called the "restrained
voluptuousness"[5] in his art and that of other Rococo masters pervaded all her late pictures.

No matter how important the example of Corot and
Manet was for Morisot, her work never mimicked theirs.
She was distraught when in the 1860s her paintings were
compared to Corot's, and evidently she destroyed anything
she had made that was thus tainted for her. In her later
years she grew especially self-critical with regard to
Manet's influence, and in 1871 complained about a painting
in progress: "My work is losing all its freshness. Moreover,
as a composition it resembles a Manet. I realize this and
am annoyed."[6]

The qualities Morisot valued most highly in her work
were spontaneity, individuality, and originality. When her

niece Jeanne Pontillon began to keep a diary in 1884, Morisot shared some of her ideas: "To record [one's] thoughts every day is an excellent idea; nothing forms one's style more effectively. And by that I mean not the habit of turning out fine phrases but of putting one's thoughts into words. It even seems to me that we ought to be very lenient, to condone lack of correctness, provided that the feeling is real, and that the ideas are personal."[7]

Morisot reflected on the problems of painting in her own notebook:

It is impossible to say how it is done . . . the words, value, chiaroscuro, half-tones, are just so many scrawls to be imposed on the artists; but real painters understand through the brush . . . is it really necessary to submit to such a vulgarization of art?

And of what use are the rules? None at all. It is only necessary to feel and to see things in a different way and where can that be learned? All painting is in some measure taken from nature, so that copying after Boucher or Holbein is of equal truth. One is as good as the other. The eternal question of drawing and color is futile because color is only an expression of form. You can't train a musician by scientific explanations of sound vibrations, nor the eye of a painter by explaining the relationship between line and tone.[8]

Morisot apparently did not have a set working routine.[9] According to the poet Paul Valéry (1871–1945), when she painted "she would take up the brush, leave it aside, take it up again, in the same way as a thought will come to us, vanish, and return."[10] Her biographer, Armand Fourreau, noted, "In Paris she was accustomed to paint in her drawing-room, laying aside her canvas, brushes, and palette in a cupboard as soon as an unforeseen visitor was announced."[11] Such anecdotes are telling, but to understand more fully Morisot's technique, individual pictures must be examined. An attempt must be made to raise the sort of painter's questions that Morisot apparently posed for herself and to chart the most significant technical changes from one phase of her career to the next.

Harbor Scene, Isle of Wight (colorplate 105 and detail; see also colorplate 27), painted in 1875 when Morisot was thirty-four years old, exemplifies her mature vision and the brushwork that she favored for the rest of her life. Drawing attention to the surface of the canvas, Morisot illuminated with her brushwork the process of painting itself, which on one occasion she compared to being "engaged in a pitched battle."[12] Evidently improvising as she went along, she applied unblended color with rapid strokes, sometimes modulating them by wiping, thinning, and blotting. As if to record the act of painting as well as the scene before her, she left her mistakes and alterations, only partly overpainting unwanted passages or half-wiping or scraping them out with a palette knife. (In leaving pentimenti as symbols of process, she anticipates a major development of twentieth-century art.) Such imprecise, semi-effaced, even crude marks with the brush constituted a visual language to describe motion. In an 1875 letter to her sister Edma Pontillon (1839–1921), she expressed her concern for this point—perhaps with regard to this very painting: "People come and go on the jetty, and it is impossible to catch them. It is the same with boats. There is extraordinary life and movement, but how is one to render it?"[13]

Morisot had adopted this bold brushwork in an attempt to find a new and uniquely personal style after years of working in the mode of Corot and Charles Daubigny (1817–1878). Yet although she sought to make her own style different from theirs, her motivation to do so was the logical outcome of Corot's teaching: "While trying for the conscientious imitation [of nature]," said Corot, "I never for a single instant lose the emotion which first seized me."[14]

Figure painting outdoors in works such as *In the Garden*, 1879 (colorplate 106 and detail), presented Morisot with different challenges. Still, she brought to pictures such as this the same informality she had previously given to the English scene. Indeed, the arrangement of figures in this composition is so clumsy by any standard—even that of Manet—that such notions as pose, gesture, and composition hardly apply. Although ostensibly a document of an episode in real life, observed spontaneously with the strictest candor in the modern-life tradition advocated by Charles Baudelaire (1821–1867), it depicts a brief interlude of such utter insignificance that it is as if Morisot had reversed the priorities of subject matter and paint, making subject matter an excuse for paint, rather than vice versa. What she has captured is apparently of so little concern that all her attention (and, by extension, ours) is on pattern and color. Dominating the subject matter, Morisot's paint is a texture of seemingly random jabs and slashes, what the American painter and critic Fairfield Porter described as "a tactile continuum like petals falling from overblown peonies."[15] The vigorous, diagonal brushstrokes that describe the skirt of the model seated on a chair at left almost dissolve into the foliage. The illusion of space is created primarily by Morisot's use of color, rather than by drawing; and as drawing and color become one, there is sureness and accuracy in her touch, color values, and placement.

COLORPLATE 105

Harbor Scene, Isle of Wight, 1875
Oil on canvas. 38 x 46 cm (14¹³⁄₁₆ x 18¼ in.). Private collection.

COLORPLATE 105A

Harbor Scene, Isle of Wight [detail]

COLORPLATE 106

In the Garden (Women Gathering Flowers), 1879
Oil on canvas. 61 x 73.5 cm (24 x 29 in.). Nationalmuseum,
Stockholm.

COLORPLATE 106A

In the Garden (Women Gathering Flowers) [detail]

COLORPLATE 107

Cows, 1880
Watercolor on paper. 20 x 26 cm (7⅞ x 10¼ in.). Mount
Holyoke College Art Museum, South Hadley, Massachusetts,
Museum Purchase: Gift of Alice Hench Fiske in memory of
Paula Radway Utell and the Warbeke Art Museum Fund, 1985.

Morisot's working methods were fundamentally the same in both oil and watercolor. For example, before painting the watercolor *Cows*, 1880 (colorplate 107), undoubtedly situating herself outdoors, before the motif, she began by making a light pencil sketch, still visible under the translucent washes. Such a technique is hardly unusual. More important, as she worked she disregarded the rectangular shape of the sheet. Leaving the corners unpainted, she developed the picture in an oval format, as she would the oil *Eugène Manet and His Daughter in the Garden,* 1883 (see colorplate 46). Although it is true that many painters who worked outdoors left the outer edges of their paint-

ings bare to facilitate handling, filling in these blank, unpainted areas only in a last stage after transporting the pictures back to the studio, Morisot seldom bothered with this last step, perhaps as a result of her perception that one's field of vision is rounded rather than rectangular and because of her aesthetic disposition toward an unfinished look.

Morisot's presiding ambition was to give her oil paintings the same spontaneous, informal appearance as her watercolors and pastels, in which areas of blank paper are visible between and around the marks of color. The color of the paper becomes an essential factor in the intricate

194

FIGURE 101

Woman Hanging Out the Wash [BW 105], 1881
Oil on canvas. 46 x 67 cm (18⅛ x 26⅜ in.). Ny Carlsberg
Glyptotek, Copenhagen.

FIGURE 103

Eugène Manet and His Daughter at Bougival [BW 103], 1881
Oil on canvas. 73 x 92 cm (28¾ x 36¼ in.). Private collection.

FIGURE 102

At Bougival [BW 122], 1882
Oil on canvas. 58 x 71 cm (22⅞ x 28 in.). National Museum of
Wales, Cardiff.

mechanics of these works. Morisot began to use unprimed canvas in paintings such as *Woman Hanging Out the Wash*, 1881 (figure 101), *At Bougival*, 1882 (figure 102), and *Eugene Manet and His Daughter at Bougival*, 1881 (figure 103).[16] Noted for her virtuoso harmonies in related white, silver, blue, and pink tones, Morisot allowed the areas of bare canvas to play an especially important role. For these first experiments she chose lightweight, finely woven, unprimed linen, slightly off-white, perhaps in the hope of making her oils look even more like works on paper. However, just as many papers discolor with age or exposure to light, so can unprimed canvas darken, and this has happened to some of Morisot's pictures from the 1880s.

Without a knowledge of oil-painting techniques, modern viewers might not understand that there had been a change. Before a fabric such as linen is painted on, it is normally protectively sealed with a glue sizing; otherwise it will eventually become brittle or decay as it reacts to the oil paint. According to conventional painting practice, the sized canvas is usually primed with one or more coats of paint, which assures the artist a smooth surface on which to work. Like most painters, Morisot simply bought canvases prepared with a white ground from an art supplier. It can be assumed that the works she painted on such canvases have remained relatively unchanged in terms of color to the present day.

Two other factors have affected the appearance of Morisot's paintings on unprimed canvas: varnishing and lining. The effects of varnish can be seen in *Eugène Manet and His Daughter at Bougival* and *At Bougival*, in which the unpainted areas, once varnished, today appear brownish orange in color rather than white. It is virtually certain the varnish was not applied by Morisot, however. Artists have often applied varnish to finished oil paintings to protect the surface from dirt. The use of varnish poses a problem, however, for as soon as it is applied, it can give a painting a highly glossy finish. Morisot may have objected to this effect, for as early as 1865 her mother reprimanded her for not varnishing a painting that was exhibited at the Salon: "This is being too careless of the appearance of painting when the aim is to please the untrained eyes susceptible to a first impression."[17] In an attempt to avoid the drawbacks of varnish as a protective shield, some artists began to cover their unvarnished paintings with glass. James Tissot (1836–1902) is known to have done so by the late 1870s, and Georges Seurat (1859–1891) glazed his paintings no later than 1886. For all we know, Morisot, Degas, and other Impressionists did likewise. This would seem especially likely with regard to her paintings on unprimed canvas.

Lining is a measure that is taken when the original canvas has become weakened with age. Put simply, a fresh piece of canvas is attached with a suitable adhesive to the back of the original painting to strengthen it. Unfortunately, if glue or wax is used, it soaks through to the front, causing significant discoloration if the original canvas was unprimed. This effect is most apparent in the *Self-Portrait with Julie*, 1885 (colorplate 108 and detail), a picture on unprimed canvas that has been lined. Morisot left nearly three-quarters of the canvas unpainted, and today it is predominantly brownish orange in color. Since the artist undoubtedly worked originally on a white or off-white surface, it is likely that the tones of the pale blue and white areas behind Morisot's head were very close to those of the unpainted canvas and did not dominate it in the way they do today. Against the white canvas, surely the contrasting areas of this painting would have been the darker strokes accentuating Morisot's face, blouse, and collar, as well as the strokes of ultramarine blue with which she had begun to plan the rest of the composition. The original color relationship of the paint to the canvas perhaps would have resembled that of the watercolor to the white paper in *Portrait of Berthe Morisot and Her Daughter*, 1885 (figure 104), by Morisot's husband, Eugène Manet (1833–1892).

FIGURE 104

Eugène Manet, *Portrait of Berthe Morisot and Her Daughter*, 1885
Watercolor. 19.1 x 27.3 cm (7½ x 10¾ in.) [sight]. Private collection.

Other paintings by Morisot on unprimed canvas, all of them lined, include *By the Lake*, 1884 (see colorplate 54); *The Garden Chair*, 1885 (see colorplate 58); *Forest of Compiègne*, 1885 (see colorplate 61); *The Little Servant*, 1885–86 (see colorplate 65); and *The Cherry Tree*, 1891–92 (see colorplate 89); each has discolored to a degree.[18] An idea of their original appearance can perhaps be gleaned by comparing them with *The Bath*, 1885–86 (see colorplate 63), a painting whose unprimed canvas has discolored only minimally. This picture was lined only in 1980.[19]

Although Morisot's colors remain vital and distinctive, her use of certain oil paints whose colors are "fugitive," that is, whose chemical mixtures are impermanent and therefore change color as they oxidize, has also brought about some variation in her pictures. One such fugitive color is a red called "lac de garance," which Morisot is thought to have used in the early 1880s but which cannot be seen in her paintings today.[20] Such a situation perhaps explains why nineteenth-century descriptions of paintings by Morisot—or by Manet or Renoir for that matter—now seem inaccurate. According to Julie Manet, for example, the color of the model's dress in Morisot's large picture *The Garden*, 1882 or 1883 (see colorplate 45), is violet, whereas today it appears to be blue.[21]

Although a close study of Morisot's palette has shown that she used a variety of colors—lead white, black, chrome yellow, cadmium yellow, yellow ocher, vermillion, cobalt and ultramarine blue, viridian green, and chrome green[22]—the most significant for Morisot was white. Many of her best works can be described as orchestrations of white tones. No other artist, with the possible exception of Paul Cézanne (1839–1906), used the color with such intelligence. It appears in every Morisot painting, whether in a model's dress, a vase on a tabletop, or a swan on the lake in the Bois de Boulogne. Indeed, a painting such as *The Quay at Bougival*, 1883 (colorplate 109 and detail), is *about* the color white. It is applied with splintered, energetic brushstrokes as a pure, unmixed color. Rather than using other colors to record the physical appearance of her subject matter, in effect she has created a color field of white that anticipates its use by the Abstract Expressionist painters Bradley Walker Tomlin, Giorgio Cavallon, and Joan Mitchell.

Morisot uses white in a considerably different way in *The Haystack*, 1883 (colorplate 110 and detail), an example of tonal painting. For this work her palette consisted only of yellow, blue, and green mixed with varying amounts of white to obtain a broad spectrum of tones. It brings the various colors into harmony with one another, integrating figure and ground rather than accentuating disparate shapes or spaces as in *The Quay at Bougival*. This use of white to integrate the entire surface of a painting in a decorative manner is part of the heritage of Rococo painting. Morisot's intense interest in eighteenth-century techniques at this time is symbolized by her copy after Boucher's *Venus at Vulcan's Forge*, 1884/1886 (see colorplate 62). Keenly aware of her obsession with white, she noted in her journal that by comparison, "everything else seems indifferent."[23]

The Haystack is very thinly painted. Morisot's short, choppy brushstrokes dissolve form and at the same time define it. As if to compensate for this effect, she expresses the solidity of her subject in compositional terms by isolating it, surrounding it with open space. She thus draws attention to its sculptural mass, just as she would express the mass of a birdcage (figure 105) or a bowl of flowers in one of her still lifes by placing it in isolation on a tabletop. The loose, unintegrated brushstrokes suggest speed and movement. Although accounts of Morisot's working methods vary, they lead to the conclusion that she painted *The Haystack* in no more than two or three short sessions. Like any Impressionist, Morisot hoped to work quickly but realized that this presents a great challenge, which she had expressed in a letter to her sister Edma in 1871: "I feel quite stupid setting up my easel before something and fancying myself able in an hour's time to reproduce nature."[24] Nearly a decade later Morisot had apparently mastered her craft and had an enviable ability to paint with sureness. By 1882, her husband noted that she could complete two canvases in a week.[25]

However, Morisot herself rarely seemed satisfied with her progress and often complained to her sister of the problems she encountered: "My work is going badly. . . . It is always the same story. I don't know where to start. I made an attempt in a field, but the moment I had set up my easel more than fifty boys and girls were swarming about me, shouting and gesticulating."[26] Morisot also noted that when using her young daughter as a model, "one can advance only very slowly unless one wants to risk ruining everything."[27]

Morisot addressed these and other challenges faced by landscape painters. It was her "principle never to try to rectify a blunder,"[28] and she adhered to this principle throughout her life, rarely reworking an unsatisfactory start. She attempted to recreate in the studio the environment of working outdoors. Thus, her studio–dining room in Bougival, where she painted *On the Veranda*, 1884 (see

FIGURE 105

The Cage [BW 171], 1885
Oil on canvas. 55 x 38 cm (21¾ x 15 in.). The National Museum of Women in the Arts, Washington, D.C., Gift of Wallace and Wilhelmina Holladay.

COLORPLATE 108

Self-Portrait with Julie, 1885
Oil on canvas. 72 x 91 cm (28⅜ x 35¹³⁄₁₆ in.). Private collection.

COLORPLATE 108A

Self-Portrait with Julie [detail]

colorplate 51), was enclosed by a glass wall, admitting light and allowing a view of the verdant garden beyond, and her studio on the rue de Villejust in Paris faced south, so that the light by which she worked was shifting, ever-changing, not like the steady northern light traditionally preferred by artists. Landscape painting may have been particularly on her mind in Bougival, for it was at this time, in 1884, that she acquired several works by Edouard Manet, including two large landscapes with figures, which she hung in her studio (see figures 99 and 100). Claude Monet was then preparing a large landscape for her studio, too (see figure

65). And it was probably in the same studio that she painted *Julie with a Doll,* 1884 (colorplate 111 and detail), a portrait of her daughter in which the paint is applied as if the work had been executed outdoors; that is, Morisot painted from the center of the composition, apparently without having a set goal in mind for how the painting would appear. She improvised, applying strokes of thin paint, searching for the right placement of Julie's feet. By leaving several of these attempts visible, she suggests movement. Her paint application is differentiated, and her preference for blues and greens may have been intensified

COLORPLATE 109

The Quay at Bougival, 1883
Oil on canvas. 55.5 x 46 cm (21⅞ x 18⅛ in.). Nasjonalgalleriet,
Oslo.

COLORPLATE 109A

The Quay at Bougival [detail]

COLORPLATE 110

The Haystack, 1883
Oil on canvas. 55.3 x 45.7 cm (21¾ x 18 in.). Private collection,
New York.

COLORPLATE 110A

The Haystack [detail]

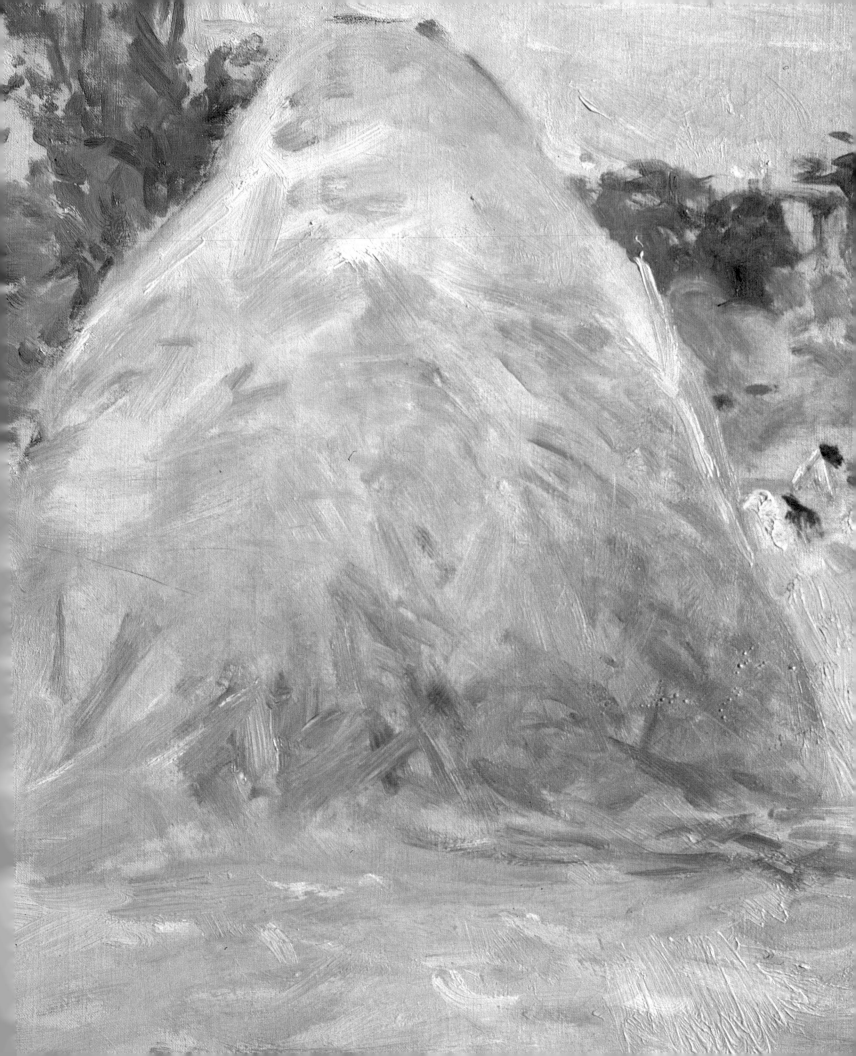

COLORPLATE 111

Julie with a Doll, 1884
Oil on canvas. 82 x 100 cm (32⁵⁄₁₆ x 39⅜ in.). Private collection.

COLORPLATE 111A

Julie with a Doll [detail]

by an optical reaction to the pink walls of her studio. When young, Morisot had once thought that Corot had "spoiled" one of his landscape sketches "by redoing it in the studio";[29] as in *Julie with a Doll*, she apparently always recognized the point at which her own work was complete, whether or not it fitted with commercial trends or even the taste of other painters whose work she admired. Certainly the vision she expresses in *Julie with a Doll* is much different from that of Mary Cassatt in *Little Girl in a Blue Armchair*, 1878 (see figure 69), and Renoir's in *Portrait of Julie Manet*, 1887 (figure 106), comparatively polished paintings of similar motifs.

However, in the late 1880s Morisot's paintings would become less spontaneous as she experimented with new media and as her working methods changed. She became friendlier with Renoir, whose drawings she admired and who, of all her contemporaries, shared most strongly her admiration for Boucher and the Rococo painters. She again tried her hand at sculpture and, in 1887, exhibited a white plaster bust she had made of her daughter (see figure 77). Although she had never shown any particular interest in the graphic arts, in 1888 and 1889 she made eight drypoints, including *Self-Portrait with Julie*, 1889 (figure 107), and in 1891 attempted color lithography, perhaps at Cas-

204

FIGURE 106

Pierre-Auguste Renoir, *Portrait of Julie Manet*, 1887
Oil on canvas. 64.8 x 53.3 cm (25½ x 21 in.). Private collection.

FIGURE 107

Self-Portrait with Julie, 1889
Drypoint. 18.2 x 13.6 cm (7 ³⁄₁₆ x 5 ³⁄₈ in.). National Gallery of Art,
Washington, D.C., Rosenwald Collection, 1953.

FIGURE 108

Two Girls at the Piano, 1888
Charcoal with red-chalk grid on paper. 53 x 40 cm
(20 ¾ x 15½ in.). Private collection, Chicago.

satt's encouragement.[30] Most important, drawing became a crucial element in the development of new ideas, and by 1887 Morisot used pastel, watercolor, charcoal, red chalk, and colored pencils to make numerous preparatory sketches for her paintings. Occasionally, as in her charcoal sketch for *The Piano*, 1888 (figure 108), she drew a red-chalk grid over these studies, presumably to enable her to transfer them directly onto canvas.[31]

Morisot's two large paintings of *The Cherry Tree* (colorplate 112 and figure 110), begun in 1891, were among her most ambitious projects and illustrate most clearly the results of her new working methods. With the exception of her painting *The Piano*, which occupied her for over a year,[32] Morisot made more preparatory sketches for the two versions of *The Cherry Tree* than for any other work (figure 109). The surfaces of her paintings no longer dissolved into a flurry of active brushstrokes, and the "pitched battle" of an earlier time virtually ceased, making way for a smoother, less differentiated paint application. Perhaps in homage to Boucher, her palette had become more vivid and acidic, but color was used primarily to emphasize the contours of form as described in her drawing. The depth of field was often shallow, somewhat like a stage set, suggesting that Morisot may, in fact, have intended a painting such as *The Cherry Tree* to be exhibited as a decorative panel. Although Morisot began working on the subject when she was at her summer house in Mézy, where she could paint outdoors, it was not until she returned to Paris in the fall of 1891 that she reworked it and started the second, smaller version (colorplate 112).

Degas particularly liked this version of *The Cherry Tree*,[33] but Renoir, who visited Morisot at Mézy, encouraged her to finish the first version (figure 110) so that it could be exhibited in Paris that fall.[34] However, although both versions have always been dated 1891, it is likely that Morisot was dissatisfied with them and perhaps continued to work on them well into the following year. Shortly before her death in 1895, she told her daughter how important *The Cherry Tree* had been to her;[35] thus, if she had finished work on the motif, it is likely that she would have included at least one version in her 1892 solo exhibition at Galerie Boussod and Valadon in Paris, and she did not do so.

Morisot may not have realized where her experiments would lead. Indeed, between 1888 and 1891 her vision changed more than it ever had before in her life as a mature artist. Her husband's death in 1892 deepened her already existing depression and dissatisfaction. She again copied a detail of a painting by Boucher, *Apollo Revealing His Divinity to the Shepherdess Issé* (figures 111 and 112), and

continued to experiment with sculpture, working as before with white plaster. In spite of her sadness, Morisot was painting more and no longer destroying a great deal of her work as in the past. She expressed these thoughts in her notebook: "I saw the pedestrians on the avenue so clearly and so simply—just as they would appear in Japanese prints. I was enchanted. I knew decidedly why I had been painting . . . badly and why I will never paint badly again"; then, somewhat sadly, she added, "I am fifty years old and at least once a year I have the same hope and the same joy."[36]

After her husband's death, Morisot moved to a small apartment. There, in her last paintings, she continued to explore themes that had dominated her work in the past. Hanging on the walls, in addition to her own paintings, were works by Degas, Monet, and Renoir, as well as Manet's *Woman with Fans (Portrait of Nina de Callias)*, 1873–74 (figure 113), which she hoped would hang one day in the Louvre, although she realized that this would not happen during her own lifetime.[37] The pictures hung alongside some Japanese prints that she had newly acquired from collector Tadamasa Hayashi (1853–1906) in exchange for her own painting *Paule Gobillard in a Ball Gown*, 1887.[38] One of these prints appears in her portrait of Julie called *Girl with a Greyhound*, 1893 (colorplate 113 and detail), in which the young girl's pose and the presence of the Japanese prints in the background are reminiscent of Manet's *Repose* (see figure 23), his portrait of Morisot painted twenty-three years earlier. Japanese prints seem to have affected Morisot's vision very little in comparison with their influence on the works of Cassatt and Henri de Toulouse-Lautrec (1864–1901). This becomes most apparent if one places Morisot's *Drawing for "The Cheval Glass,"* 1890 (figure 114), alongside Mary Cassatt's virtually identical subject, *The Coiffure*, 1891 (figure 115). Morisot's relation to the Japanese aesthetic appears to lie with her own ability never to overwork a painting and to place a stroke of color with exactly the shape and value needed to express her subject matter in the simplest of terms. For example, in *The Green Coat*, 1894 (figure 116), and *Girl with a Greyhound*, Morisot captures the presence of her subject matter in a manner evocative of a Japanese ink or wash drawing. With the exception of Julie's face, the painted areas are diffuse, becoming very thin and even nonexistent, thus making the bare canvas a vital element in Morisot's ability to create works that have both the spontaneity and freedom usually associated only with works on paper.

Morisot's death in 1895 at the age of fifty-four predated many of the triumphs of Impressionism. She died while Monet was still at work on his Rouen Cathedral

FIGURE 109

The Cherry Tree [BW 274], 1891
Oil on canvas. 55 x 33 cm (21¾ x 13 in.). Private collection.

FIGURE 110

The Cherry Tree [BW 275], 1891
Oil on canvas. 154 x 85 cm (60⅝ x 33⁷⁄₁₆ in.). Private collection.

COLORPLATE 112

The Cherry Tree, 1891–92
Oil on canvas. 136 x 89 cm (53⁹⁄₁₆ x 35⅟₁₆ in.). Private collection.

COLORPLATE 113

Girl with a Greyhound (Julie Manet), 1893
Oil on canvas. 73 x 80 cm (28¾ x 31½ in.). Musée Marmottan,
Paris.

COLORPLATE 113A

Girl with a Greyhound (Julie Manet) [detail]

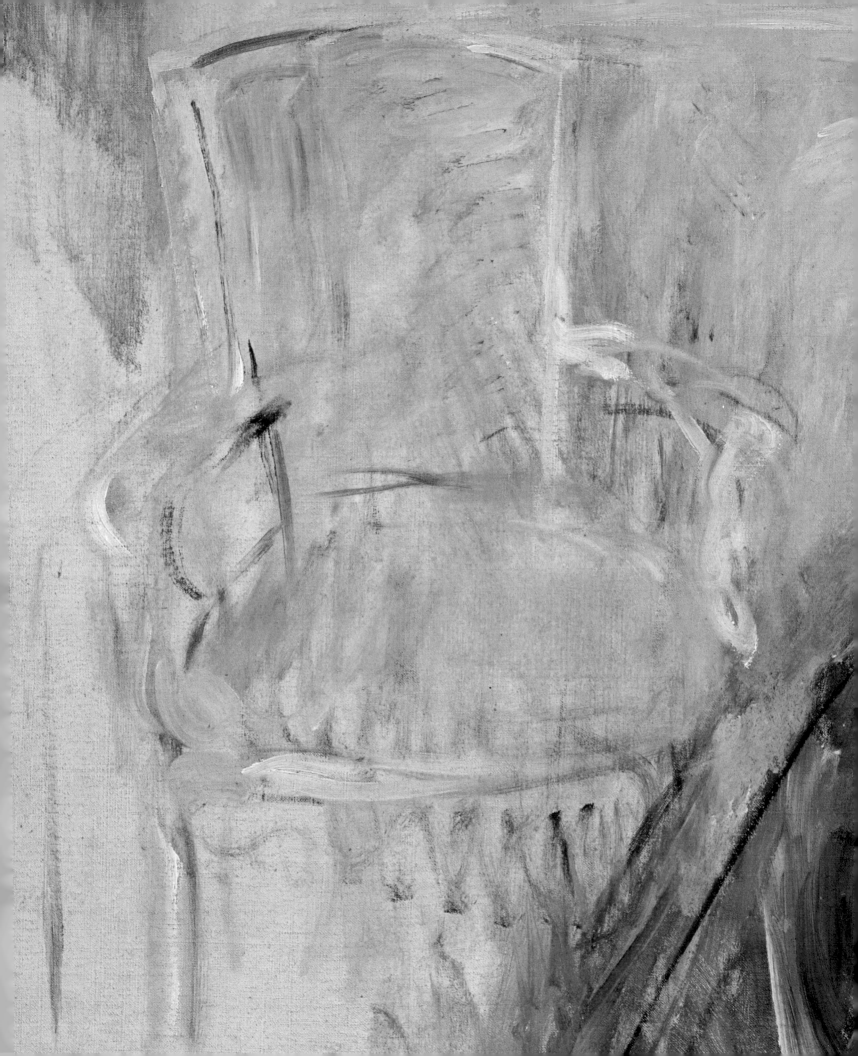

FIGURE 111

Detail of Boucher's "Apollo Revealing His Divinity to the Shepherdess Issé" [BW 320], 1892
Oil on canvas. 64 x 79 cm (25¼ x 31⅛ in.). A European collector.

FIGURE 112

François Boucher, *Apollo Revealing His Divinity to the Shepherdess Issé,* 1750
Oil on canvas. 129 x 157.5 cm (50¼ x 62 in.). Musée des Beaux-Arts, Tours.

FIGURE 113

Edouard Manet, *Woman with Fans (Portrait of Nina de Callias),* 1873–74
Oil on canvas. 113 x 166 cm (44½ x 65⅜ in.). Musée d'Orsay, Paris.

FIGURE 114

Drawing for "The Cheval Glass," 1890
Pencil on paper. 30 x 20 cm (11¾ x 7⅞ in.). Musée du Louvre, Cabinet des Dessins, Paris.

series—before he painted his first water lily; nor did she live to see Cézanne's first solo exhibition in 1895. Manet had at one time declared that Berthe Morisot would not have existed without him,[39] and it is possible that Morisot herself may have agreed with him. She had written to her sister Edma, "It looks as though I am coming to the end of my life without having achieved anything and only selling my work at bargain prices."[40] Yet it was in the paintings she executed after Manet's death in 1883 that she slowly developed her own vision and style, advancing far beyond what she had accomplished until that time. The Irish poet and novelist George Moore declared after Morisot's death that she was the only woman painter ever to create a style: "Her pictures are the only pictures painted by a woman

that could not be destroyed without leaving a blank, a hiatus in the history of art."[41]

Her influence on younger painters has remained unexplored. As much as *Girl with a Greyhound* recalls Morisot's affinity for Manet—and even Boucher—the sense of urgency and emphasis on Julie's sad expression seem to anticipate a mood found later in works by Edvard Munch (1863–1944). Yet there is no known record of who, excepting her Impressionist colleagues, saw Morisot's one-woman exhibition in 1892 or the memorial exhibition at the Galerie Durand-Ruel in 1896; nor is there a record of who attended her funeral. Although Munch was acquainted with the poet Mallarmé, whose tribute to Morisot appeared in the 1896 catalogue, it is not known if Munch ever saw the

FIGURE 115

Mary Cassatt, *The Coiffure*, 1891
Black crayon and graphite on paper. 38.3 x 27.7 cm (15⅛ x 10⅞ in.). National Gallery of Art, Washington, D.C., Rosenwald Collection, 1948.

FIGURE 116

The Green Coat [BW 409], 1894
Oil on canvas. 117 x 81 cm (46⅛ x 31⅞ in.). Private collection, Dallas.

213

FIGURE 117

Photograph of Berthe Morisot, 1894. Private collection.

his work and that of Berthe Morisot among the Impressionist artists.[42] Monet, who owned five of Morisot's works, often showed them to the painters who visited him at Giverny. After Morisot's death, Mary Cassatt wrote Julie Manet that the surviving members of the Impressionist group continued to rely on Morisot's name.[43] Paul Valéry, who married Morisot's niece Jeanne Gobillard, wrote an essay about Morisot in 1926 and dedicated it to Vuillard.[44] At the same time, Vuillard noted in his journal that he admired the freshness and "unfinished effect" of Morisot's sketches but that he was also "struck by the somewhat blunt conventionality of their point of departure."[45]

However, the other younger painters most familiar with Morisot's works were her daughter, Julie Manet, and her husband, Ernest Rouart (1874–1942); Julie's cousin Paule Gobillard (1869–1946); Renoir's pupil, Jeanne Baudot (1877–1957); and their friends Albert André (1869–1954), Jacques-Emile Blanche, Maurice Denis (1870–1943), Georges d'Espagnat (1870–1950), and André Dunoyer de Segonzac (1884–1974). Perhaps it was Morisot's own personality that contributed to her lack of recognition among the younger artists, for, as Valéry would later write: "[Berthe Morisot] could be unaffectedly and dangerously silent, and create without knowing it a baffling distance between herself and all who approached her, unless they were the first artists of her time."[46]

According to Théodore Duret (1838–1927), the chronicler of Impressionism, in Morisot's lifetime her position in society obscured her reputation as an artist, yet "she knew herself to be the equal of any other artist."[47] It was only after the French government's purchase of her painting *Young Woman in a Ball Gown* (see figure 45) in 1894 that Morisot, at the age of fifty-three (figure 117), felt she had achieved equal stature with her Impressionist colleagues. This event "derived importance in her eyes from the fact that it was a public recognition of her merit" and that henceforth it would be "impossible to regard her any longer as an amateur, as so many had persisted in doing."[48]

memorial exhibition—nor, for that matter, if Matisse, Toulouse-Lautrec, Edouard Vuillard (1868–1940), or Bonnard (who showed with Durand-Ruel the same year as Morisot's memorial exhibition) saw it, either.

In 1887 Pissarro reported that the younger painters Georges Seurat and Paul Signac (1863–1935) liked only

Notes

BW denotes catalogue numbers in Bataille-Wildenstein (Bataille, Marie-Louise, and Georges Wildenstein. *Berthe Morisot: Catalogue des peintures, pastels, et aquarelles.* Paris, 1961).

1 Denis Rouart, ed. *Correspondance de Berthe Morisot* (Paris, 1950), 68–69; Denis Rouart, ed. *The Correspondence of Berthe Morisot.* Translated by Betty W. Hubbard (New York, 1957; a second, small-format edition with identical pagination was published in London in 1959 by Lund Humphries), 73. Denis Rouart, ed. *The Correspondence of Berthe Morisot.* Translated by Betty W. Hubbard. Introduction and notes by Kathleen Adler and Tamar Garb (London, 1986), 84.

2 Odilon Redon, *A soi-même* (Paris, 1922); reprinted in Elizabeth Gilmore Holt, *From the Classicists to the Impressionists: Art and Architecture in the 19th Century* (Garden City, N.Y., 1966), 498.

3 Jacques-Emile Blanche, "Les Dames de la grande-rue, Berthe Morisot," in *Les Ecrits nouveaux* (Paris, 1920), 21. Unfortunately, it is impossible to determine which painting by Corot was owned by Morisot.

4 Rosamond Bernier, "Dans la lumière impressionniste," *L'Oeil* 53 (May 1959), 42.

5 Berthe Morisot, "Premier Carnet vert (1885–1886)," in *Berthe Morisot* (Paris, [1961]), 47.

6 Rouart, 1950, 66–67; 1959, 71; 1986, 82.

7 Rouart, 1950, 122; 1959, 124; 1986, 139.

8 Philippe Huisman, *Morisot: Enchantment,* trans. Diana Imber (New York, 1963), 54.

9 Paul Valéry, *Degas, Manet, Morisot,* trans. David Paul (New York, 1960), 120–21.

10 Valéry, 119.

11 Armand Fourreau, *Berthe Morisot* (Paris, 1925), 8.

12 Rouart, 1950, 133–34; 1959, 136; 1986, 152.

13 Rouart, 1950, 85–86; 1959, 89; 1986, 101.

14 Quoted in Fourreau, 21.

15 Fairfield Porter, *Art in Its Own Terms: Selected Criticism, 1936–1975* (New York, 1979), 156.

16 Curiously, the first works by Morisot on unprimed canvas are all Bougival scenes. Her decision to paint on the unprimed canvas may have been accidental, perhaps because she had run short of the usual materials. Works on unprimed canvas that were painted by Morisot in Paris do not appear until 1884, the last year she sojourned at Bougival. This suggests that she kept a large amount of the canvas at Bougival year-round and that when she stopped leasing the property she brought the remainder of the canvas to her Paris studio and continued to paint on it. Julie Manet notes that *Woman Hanging Out the Wash* (figure 101) was "painted on the reverse of a canvas" (Julie Manet, *Journal (1893–1899)* [Paris, 1979], 82) yet never verified if the back was primed. She may have worked on unprimed canvas as early as 1879, for when she was painting *In the Garden* (colorplate 106), her husband, Eugène Manet, did a painting from the same motif on the reverse, unprimed side of

another canvas. In 1879 Antonin Proust (1832–1905) recorded that Edouard Manet was obsessed with the idea of doing his portrait "on unprepared white canvas, in a single sitting" (Antonin Proust, *Edouard Manet Souvenirs* [Paris, 1913], 100). Morisot owned one such sketch by Manet, *Julie Manet at Fifteen Months,* painted by February 1881, which Manet completed in only an hour (Denis Rouart and Daniel Wildenstein, *Edouard Manet: Catalogue raisonné* [Lausanne and Paris, 1975], no. 298; 234, repr. 235).

17 Rouart, 1950, 14–15; 1959, 19; 1986, 24.

18 The following other works are painted on unprimed canvas: *Eugène Manet and His Daughter at Bougival,* 1881 (figure 103); *Woman Hanging Out the Wash,* 1881 (figure 101); *At Bougival,* 1882 (figure 102); *The Balcony* (BW 124), 1882; *The Story* (BW 138), 1883; *Sewing Lesson* (BW 145), 1884; *The Barrier at Bougival* (BW 152), 1884; *Young Woman Sewing in a Garden* (BW 158), 1884; *Reines-Marguerites* (BW 182), 1885; *Stream in the Bois de Boulogne* (possibly BW 202), 1886; and *Young Girl with a Dog* (BW 209), 1887.

19 *The Bath* was selectively varnished, meaning that varnish was applied on the heavily painted areas of the figure and not at all on the unpainted areas in the background. This may not have been done under Morisot's direction originally—in fact, it may have occurred after her death; when this painting was cleaned in 1980 it was again selectively varnished. The conservation department at the National Gallery of Art, Washington, D.C., also chose to varnish *The Little Servant* selectively when it was cleaned in 1985. As thread counts for Morisot's works on unprimed canvas are not available, it has been impossible to determine if, in fact, all were painted on the same material.

20 Letter to the author from Clément Rouart, Paris, 24 June 1986.

21 *Journal,* 85.

22 [Anthea Callen], *Techniques of the Great Masters of Art* (Secaucus, N.J., 1985), 234–37.

23 Berthe Morisot, entry of 2 May 1885, in "Carnet gris (1885–1887)"; reprinted in *Berthe Morisot* (Paris, 1961), 51.

24 Rouart, 1950, 72–73; 1959, 77; 1986, 89.

25 Rouart, 1950, 105; 1959, 107; 1986, 121.

26 Rouart, 1950, 87–88; 1959, 91; 1986, 104.

27 Rouart, 1950, 107–8; 1959, 110; 1986, 124.

28 Rouart, 1950, 39–40; 1959, 44; 1986, 52.

29 Rouart, 1950, 27–28; 1959, 32; 1986, 37.

30 Janine Bailly-Herzberg, "Les Estampes de Berthe Morisot," *Gazette des beaux-arts,* ser. 6, 93 (May–June 1979), 215–27.

31 Both *Study for "Young Girl Resting on Her Elbow,"* 1887, sanguine and charcoal on paper, private collection, and *Two Girls at the Piano,* 1888 (figure 108), have grids drawn over them.

32 Bataille-Wildenstein, 38.

33 *Journal*, 84.

34 Rouart, 1950, 160–61; 1959, 163; 1986, 183.

35 *Journal*, 84.

36 Berthe Morisot, "Premier Carnet noir (1890–1891)," in *Berthe Morisot* (Paris, 1961), 55.

37 Rouart, 1950, 120–21; 1959, 122; 1986, 137.

38 BW no. 210, 37.

39 George Moore, *Modern Painting* (London and New York, 1910), 236.

40 Huisman, 40.

41 Moore, 234.

42 John Rewald, ed., *Camille Pissarro: Letters to His Son Lucien* (Santa Barbara and Salt Lake City, 1981), 122.

43 Letter from Mary Cassatt to Julie Manet, undated and unpublished, private collection.

44 Paul Valéry, "Tante Berthe," in *Dessins, Crayons de Berthe Morisot*, exh. cat., Galerie L. Dru (Paris, 31 May–25 June 1926).

45 Edouard Vuillard, Journal, 1 June 1926, unpublished, Bibliothèque d'Institut de France, Paris.

46 Valéry, 183.

47 Théodore Duret, *Manet and the French Impressionists*, trans. J. E. Crawford Flitch (London, 1910), 175–76.

48 Duret, 176.

Checklist

In some cases the titles and dates of works differ from those used in previous publications. Such changes reflect new information found during the preparation of this exhibition catalogue. BW denotes catalogue numbers in Bataille-Wildenstein (Bataille, Marie-Louise, and Georges Wildenstein. *Berthe Morisot: Catalogue des peintures, pastels, et aquarelles.* Paris, 1961).

1 *Study* [BW 8], 1864
Signed lower left: *B. Morisot*
Oil on canvas
60.3 x 73 cm (23¾ x 28¾ in.)
Mr. and Mrs. Fred Schoneman

2 *Thatched Cottage in Normandy* [BW 10], 1865
Signed lower right: *Berthe Morisot*
Oil on canvas
46 x 55 cm (18⅛ x 21⅝ in.)
Private collection

3 *The Harbor at Lorient* [BW 17], 1869
Signed lower right on parapet: *B. Morisot*
Oil on canvas
43.5 x 73 cm (17⅛ x 28¾ in.)
National Gallery of Art, Washington, D.C., Ailsa Mellon Bruce Collection 1970.17.48

4 *Young Woman at a Window (The Artist's Sister at a Window)* [BW 18], 1869
Unsigned
Oil on canvas
54.8 x 46.3 cm (21⅝ x 18¼ in.)
National Gallery of Art, Washington, D.C., Ailsa Mellon Bruce Collection 1970.17.47

5 *Two Seated Women* [BW 19], c. 1869–75
Signed upper right: *Berthe Morisot*
Oil on canvas
52.1 x 81.3 cm (20½ x 32 in.)
National Gallery of Art, Washington, D.C., Gift of Mrs. Charles S. Carstairs 1952.9.2

6 *Boats at Dawn* [BW 418], c. 1869
Signed lower right: *Berthe Morisot*
Pastel on paper
19.7 x 26.7 cm (7¾ x 10½ in.)
Mr. and Mrs. Richard A. Hess

7 *Mme Morisot and Her Daughter Mme Pontillon (The Mother and Sister of the Artist)* [BW 20], 1869–70
Unsigned
Oil on canvas
101 x 81.8 cm (39½ x 32¼ in.)
National Gallery of Art, Washington, D.C., Chester Dale Collection 1963.10.186
[Exhibited at National Gallery of Art only]

8 *The Harbor at Cherbourg* [BW 614], 1871
Stamped lower right: *B.M.*
Watercolor and pencil on paper
15.6 x 20.3 cm (6¼ x 8 in.)
From the Collection of Mr. and Mrs. Paul Mellon, Upperville, Virginia

9 *The Harbor at Cherbourg* [BW 16], 1871
Signed lower right: *Berthe Morisot*
Oil on canvas
41.9 x 55.9 cm (16½ x 22 in.)
From the Collection of Mr. and Mrs. Paul Mellon, Upperville, Virginia

10 *At the Edge of the Forest*, 1871
Signed lower right: *Berthe Morisot*
Watercolor on paper
19.1 x 22 cm (7½ x 8⅝ in.)
From the Collection of Mr. and Mrs. Paul Mellon, Upperville, Virginia

11 *Woman and Child in a Meadow* [BW 615], 1871
Signed lower right: *Berthe Morisot*
Watercolor on paper
21 x 24 cm (8¼ x 9⁷⁄₁₆ in.)
Courtesy of Galerie Hopkins and Thomas, Paris

12 *View of Paris from the Trocadéro* [BW 23], c. 1871–72
Signed lower left: *Berthe Morisot*
Oil on canvas
46.1 x 81.5 cm (18¹⁄₁₆ x 32¹⁄₁₆ in.)
Collection of the Santa Barbara Museum of Art, California, Gift of Mrs. Hugh N. Kirkland

13 *On the Balcony* [BW 24], c. 1871–72
Signed lower right: *B Morisot*
Oil on canvas
60 x 50 cm (23⅝ x 19⅝ in.)
Private collection

14 **On the Balcony** [BW 618], c. 1871–72
Stamped lower right: *B.M.*
Watercolor on paper
20.5 x 16.4 cm (8⅛ x 6⅞ in.)
The Art Institute of Chicago, Gift of Mrs. Charles Netcher in Memory of Charles Netcher II
[Exhibited at Mount Holyoke College Art Museum only]

15 **Young Woman on a Bench (Edma Pontillon)** [BW 611], 1872
Signed lower left: *Berthe Morisot*
Watercolor on paper
24.9 x 15.1 cm (9¹³⁄₁₆ x 5¹⁵⁄₁₆ in.)
National Gallery of Art, Washington, D.C., Ailsa Mellon Bruce Collection 1970.17.159

16 **The Cradle** [BW 25], 1872
Unsigned
Oil on canvas
56 x 46 cm (22¹⁄₁₆ x 18⅛ in.)
Musée d'Orsay, Paris
[Exhibited at Kimbell Art Museum and Mount Holyoke College Art Museum only]

17 **Mme Pontillon and Her Daughter, Jeanne** [BW 621], 1871
Unsigned
Watercolor on paper
25.1 x 25.9 cm (9⅞ x 10¹³⁄₁₆ in.)
National Gallery of Art, Washington, D.C., Ailsa Mellon Bruce Collection 1970.17.160
A pencil drawing of a woman in a long dress seated on the ground at the edge of a bank of trees is on the verso of this sheet.

18 **Mme Gobillard and Her Daughter, Paule** [BW 635], 1871
Unsigned
Watercolor on paper
15 x 20 cm (5⅞ x 7⅞ in.)
Private collection

19 **Hide and Seek** [BW 27], 1873
Signed lower right: *Berthe Morisot*
Oil on canvas
45.1 x 54.9 cm (17¾ x 21⅝ in.)
Collection of Mrs. John Hay Whitney

20 **Reading** [BW 14], 1873
Signed lower right: *Berthe Morisot*
Oil on canvas
45.1 x 72.4 cm (17¾ x 28½ in.)
The Cleveland Museum of Art, Gift of the Hanna Fund
A *B* in black in the lower left corner remains visible from Morisot's first attempt to add her signature to this painting. Ultimately, she signed it in the lower right corner, using both red and black in the following decorative fashion: *B* (black); *erthe* (red); *M* (red); *orisot* (black).

21 **A Village (Maurecourt)** [BW 424], 1873
Signed lower right: *Berthe Morisot*
Pastel on paper
47 x 71.8 cm (18½ x 28¼ in.)
Private collection
[Exhibited at National Gallery of Art only]

22 **Corner of Paris, Seen from Passy** [BW 421], c. 1872–73
Signed lower left: *Berthe Morisot*
Pastel on paper
27 x 34.9 cm (10⅝ x 13¾ in.)
Private collection, New York

23 **Portrait of Mme Marie Hubbard** [BW 33], 1874
Unsigned
Oil on canvas
50.5 x 81 cm (19⅞ x 31⅞ in.)
The Ordrupgaard Collection, Copenhagen

24 **By the Seashore** [BW 627], 1874
Signed lower right: *Berthe Morisot*
Watercolor on paper
16 x 21.3 cm (6⁵⁄₁₆ x 8⅜ in.)
Private collection

25 **Laundresses Hanging Out the Wash** [BW 45], 1875
Signed lower left: *Berthe Morisot*
Oil on canvas
33 x 40.6 cm (13 x 16 in.)
National Gallery of Art, Washington, D.C., Collection of Mr. and Mrs. Paul Mellon 1985.64.28

26 **Harbor Scene, Isle of Wight** [BW 53], 1875
Unsigned
Oil on canvas
38 x 46 cm (14¹⁵⁄₁₆ x 18¼ in.)
Private collection

27 **Harbor Scene, Isle of Wight** [BW 54], 1875
Stamped lower left: *Berthe Morisot*
Oil on canvas
43 x 64 cm (16⅞ x 25¼ in.)
Collection of The Newark Museum

28 **Bow of a Yacht** [BW 630], 1875
Signed lower left: *Berthe Morisot*
Watercolor on paper
20.6 x 26.7 cm (8⅛ x 10½ in.)
Sterling and Francine Clark Art Institute, Williamstown, Massachusetts

29 **Figure of a Woman (Before the Theater)** [BW 59], 1875–76
Signed lower right: *Berthe Morisot*
Oil on canvas
57 x 31 cm (22½ x 12³⁄₁₆ in.)
Courtesy of Galerie Schröder und Leisewitz, Kunsthandel, Bremen, Federal Republic of Germany

30 **The Black Bodice** [BW 74], 1876
Unsigned
Oil on canvas
73 x 59.8 cm (28¾ x 23½ in.)
The National Gallery of Ireland, Dublin

31 **At the Water's Edge** [BW 640], 1879
Signed lower left: *B. Morisot*
Watercolor on paper
21 x 28 cm (8¼ x 11 in.)
From the Collection of Joan Whitney Payson
[Exhibited at Mount Holyoke College Art Museum only]

32 ***Luncheon in the Country*** [BW 642], 1879
Signed lower right: *B. Morisot*
Watercolor on paper
14 x 22 cm (5 1/2 x 8 11/16 in.)
Courtesy of Galerie Hopkins and Thomas, Paris

33 ***Cows*** [BW 649], 1880
Stamped lower left: *Berthe Morisot*
Watercolor on paper
20 x 26 cm (7 7/8 x 10 1/4 in.)
Mount Holyoke College Art Museum, South Hadley, Massachusetts, Museum Purchase: Gift of Alice Hench Fiske in memory of Paula Radway Utell and the Warbeke Art Museum Fund, 1985

34 ***Behind the Blinds*** [BW 82], 1878–79
Signed lower left: *Berthe Morisot*
Oil on canvas
73.5 x 59.5 cm (29 x 23 3/8 in.)
Mr. and Mrs. Moreton Binn

35 ***Woman at Her Toilette*** [BW 84], c. 1879
Signed lower left on frame of mirror: *Berthe Morisot*
Oil on canvas
60.3 x 80.4 cm (23 3/4 x 31 5/8 in.)
The Art Institute of Chicago, The Stickney Fund

36 ***The Lake in the Bois de Boulogne (Summer Day)*** [BW 79], 1879
Signed lower right on boat: *Berthe Morisot*
Oil on canvas
45.7 x 75.3 cm (18 x 29 5/8 in.)
The Trustees of the National Gallery, London

37 ***In the Garden (Women Gathering Flowers)*** [BW 80], 1879
Unsigned
Oil on canvas
61 x 73.5 cm (24 x 29 in.)
Nationalmuseum, Stockholm

38 ***Winter*** [BW 86], 1879–80
Signed lower right: *B. Morisot*
Oil on canvas
73.5 x 58.4 cm (29 x 23 in.)
Dallas Museum of Art, Gift of the Meadows Foundation Incorporated

39 ***Portrait of Marcel Gobillard (Little Boy in Gray)*** [BW 88], c. 1880
Signed lower right: *Berthe Morisot*
Oil on canvas
86 x 62 cm (33 7/8 x 24 7/16 in.)
Private collection, Geneva, Switzerland

40 ***In the Dining Room*** [BW 91], 1880
Unsigned
Oil on canvas
92 x 73 cm (36 1/4 x 28 3/4 in.)
Private collection

41 ***Nursing*** [BW 94], 1879
Stamped lower left: *Berthe Morisot*
Oil on canvas
50 x 61 cm (19 3/4 x 24 in.)
Private collection, Washington, D.C.

42 ***The Beach at Nice*** [BW 662], 1881–82
Stamped lower left: *B.M.*
Watercolor on paper
42 x 55 cm (16 1/2 x 21 5/8 in.)
Nationalmuseum, Stockholm

43 ***Pasie Sewing in the Garden at Bougival*** [BW 108], 1881–82
Unsigned
Oil on canvas
81 x 100 cm (31 7/8 x 39 3/8 in.)
Musée des Beaux-Arts, Pau

44 ***Tea*** [BW 125], 1882
Stamped lower right: *Berthe Morisot*
Oil on canvas
57.5 x 71.5 cm (22 5/8 x 28 1/8 in.)
Madelon Foundation, Vaduz

45 ***The Garden*** [BW 142], 1882 or 1883
Unsigned
Oil on canvas
99.1 x 127 cm (39 x 50 in.)
The Sara Lee Corporation
If the background here represents the garden of the Manets' rue de Villejust house, as usually claimed (*see Journal* p. 85), then the 1883 date is more likely. But if, as is also usually claimed (Bataille-Wildenstein, no. 142), this picture was exhibited in London in April 1883, it would need to be dated earlier.

46 ***Eugène Manet and His Daughter in the Garden*** [BW 137], 1883
Unsigned
Oil on canvas
60 x 73 cm (23 5/8 x 28 3/4 in.)
Private collection

47 ***Julie with Her Toy Boat (Child at Play)*** [BW 707], c. 1883
Unsigned
Watercolor on paper
23 x 16 cm (9 1/16 x 6 5/16 in.)
Private collection

48 ***In the Garden at Maurecourt*** [BW 154], c. 1883
Signed lower left: *Berthe Morisot*
Oil on canvas
54 x 65 cm (21 1/4 x 25 5/8 in.)
Lent by The Toledo Museum of Art; Gift of Edward Drummond Libbey

49 ***The Quay at Bougival*** [BW 135], 1883
Stamped lower right: *Berthe Morisot*
Oil on canvas
55.5 x 46 cm (21 7/8 x 18 1/8 in.)
Nasjonalgalleriet, Oslo

50 ***The Haystack*** [BW 133], 1883
Stamped lower left: *Berthe Morisot*
Oil on canvas
55.3 x 45.7 cm (21 3/4 x 18 in.)
Private collection, New York

51 *On the Veranda* [BW 160], 1884
Signed lower left on window ledge: *Berthe Morisot*
Oil on canvas
81 x 100 cm (31⅞ x 39⅜ in.)
Collection of John C. Whitehead

52 *Julie with a Doll* [BW 163], 1884
Unsigned
Oil on canvas
82 x 100 cm (32⁵⁄₁₆ x 39⅜ in.)
Private collection

53 *Little Girl with Her Doll (Julie Manet)* [BW 469], 1884
Signed lower left: *Berthe Morisot*
Pastel on paper
60 x 46 cm (23½ x 18⅛ in.)
Private collection
[Exhibited at Kimbell Art Museum only]

54 *By the Lake* [BW 147], 1884
Unsigned
Oil on canvas
65 x 54 cm (25⁹⁄₁₆ x 21¼ in.)
Private collection

55 *Self-Portrait* [BW 479], c. 1885
Stamped lower right: *Berthe Morisot*
Pastel on paper
47.5 x 37.5 cm (18¾ x 14¾ in.)
The Art Institute of Chicago, Helen Regenstein Collection
Pencil sketches of Julie as an infant, one heightened with pastel, are on the verso of this sheet.
[Exhibited at National Gallery of Art only]

56 *Self-Portrait with Julie* [BW 167], 1885
Unsigned
Oil on canvas
72 x 91 cm (28⅜ x 35¹³⁄₁₆ in.)
Private collection

57 *The Garden Chair* [BW 472], 1885
Stamped lower right: *Berthe Morisot*
Pastel on paper
40 x 50 cm (15¾ x 19¹¹⁄₁₆ in.)
Private collection

58 *The Garden Chair* [BW 181], 1885
Unsigned
Oil on canvas
61.3 x 75.6 cm (24⅛ x 29¾ in.)
Audrey Jones Beck

59 *Fan Decorated with Geese* [BW 702], c. 1884
Stamped lower left: *Berthe Morisot*
Watercolor on paper
47 cm (18½ in.) [diam.]
Mrs. Robert Cummings

60 *Woman Seated in the Bois de Boulogne* [BW 711], 1885
Signed lower left: *Berthe Morisot*
Watercolor on paper
19 x 20.8 cm (7½ x 8³⁄₁₆ in.)
Lent by The Metropolitan Museum of Art, New York; Harris Brisbane Dick Fund, 1948
[Exhibited at Kimbell Art Museum only]

61 *Forest of Compiègne* [BW 183], 1885
Stamped lower right: *Berthe Morisot*
Oil on canvas
54.2 x 64.8 cm (21⅜ x 25½ in.)
The Art Institute of Chicago, Bequest of Estelle McCormick
Listed as no. 135 in the catalogue of the memorial retrospective exhibition at Durand-Ruel, this picture was removed for some unknown reason and is not mentioned at all in the second edition of the catalogue.

62 *Detail from Boucher's "Venus at Vulcan's Forge"* [BW 143], 1884/1886
Stamped in blue lower right: *Berthe Morisot*
Oil on canvas
114 x 138 cm (44⅞ x 54⅜ in.)
Private collection, Paris

63 *The Bath (Girl Arranging Her Hair)* [BW 190], 1885–86
Signed on the edge of the table: *Berthe Morisot* (red)/*Berthe Morisot* (black)
Oil on canvas
91.1 x 72.3 cm (35⅞ x 28⁷⁄₁₆ in.)
Sterling and Francine Clark Art Institute, Williamstown, Massachusetts

64 *Getting Out of Bed* [BW 191], 1886
Signed lower right: *Berthe Morisot*
Oil on canvas
65 x 54 cm (25⅝ x 21¼ in.)
Collection Durand-Ruel, Paris

65 *The Little Servant (In the Dining Room)* [BW 194], 1885–86
Signed lower left: *Berthe Morisot*
Oil on canvas
61.3 x 50 cm (24⅛ x 19¾ in.)
National Gallery of Art, Washington, D.C., Chester Dale Collection 1963.10.185
[Exhibited at National Gallery of Art only]

66 *Gorey* [BW 745], 1886
Stamped lower left: *B.M.*
Watercolor on paper
17 x 24 cm (6¹¹⁄₁₆ x 9⁷⁄₁₆ in.)
Private collection

67 *Interior at Jersey* [BW 511], 1886
Unsigned
Pastel on paper
46 x 60 cm (18⅛ x 23⅝ in.)
Private collection

68 *Young Woman in White* [BW 506], 1886
Signed lower left: *Berthe Morisot*
Pastel on paper
41.5 x 53 cm (16⅜ x 20⅞ in.)
Collection of John C. Whitehead

69 *Young Woman Drying Herself* [BW 518], 1886–87
Unsigned
Pastel on paper
42 x 41 cm (16⁹⁄₁₆ x 16⅛ in.)
Courtesy of Galerie Hopkins and Thomas, Paris

70 *Nude from the Back,* 1886–87
Unsigned
Charcoal on paper
57 x 43 cm (22⁷⁄₁₆ x 16⁷⁄₈ in.)
Private collection, Paris

71 *View of Tours* [BW 523], 1887
Stamped lower left: *Berthe Morisot*
Pastel on paper
30 x 47 cm (11¾ x 18½ in.)
Private collection, Paris

72 *Portrait of Paule Gobillard,* c. 1887
Stamped lower right: *Berthe Morisot*
Colored pencil on paper
27.9 x 22.9 cm (11 x 9 in.) [sight]
The Reader's Digest Association, Inc.

73 *Swans* [BW 764], c. 1887
Unsigned
Watercolor on paper
19 x 26 cm (7½ x 10¼ in.)
Private collection

74 *The Lake, Bois de Boulogne,* c. 1887
Stamped lower right: *Berthe Morisot*
Watercolor on paper
29.5 x 22.2 cm (11⅝ x 8¾ in.)
The National Museum of Women in the Arts, Washington,
D.C., The Holladay Collection

75 *Little Girl Reading* [BW 219], 1888
Signed lower right: *Berthe Morisot*
Oil on canvas
74.3 x 92.7 cm (29¼ x 36½ in.)
Museum of Fine Arts, St. Petersburg, Florida. Gift of Friends
of Art in memory of Margaret Acheson Stuart

76 *Path in the Bois de Boulogne* [BW 780], c. 1888
Stamped lower right: *Berthe Morisot* and *B.M.*
Watercolor on paper
24 x 20 cm (19⁷⁄₁₆ x 7⅞ in.)
Private collection, Courtesy of Galerie Hopkins and Thomas, Paris

77 *Nice, View from Cimiez* [BW 769], 1888–89
Unsigned
Watercolor on paper
21 x 29 cm (8¼ x 11⅜ in.)
Private collection

78 *Villa Ratti,* 1888–89
Stamped lower right: *B.M.*
Pencil on paper
29 x 23 cm (11⅜ x 9¹⁄₁₆ in.)
Private collection

79 *Parakeet at a Window,* 1889
Stamped lower right: *B.M.*
Colored pencil on paper
19 x 21 cm (7½ x 8¼ in.)
Courtesy of Galerie Hopkins and Thomas, Paris

80 *Under the Orange Tree* [BW 237], 1889
Stamped lower right: *Berthe Morisot*
Oil on canvas
54 x 65 cm (21¼ x 25⁹⁄₁₆ in.)
Private collection, Courtesy of Galerie Hopkins and Thomas, Paris

81 *The Mandolin* [BW 238], 1889
Unsigned
Oil on canvas
55 x 57 cm (21⅝ x 22½ in.)
Private collection

82 *Fan Decorated with Vignettes* [BW 750], 1887
Unsigned
Watercolor on silk
50 cm (19⅝ in.) [diam.]
Private collection
The rightmost vignette is related to BW 166.

83 *View of the Bois de Boulogne* [BW 244], 1889
Signed lower left: *B. Morisot*
Oil on canvas
65.4 x 54.6 cm (25¾ x 21½ in.)
National Gallery of Art, Washington, D.C., Ailsa Mellon Bruce
Collection 1970.17.50

84 *View from the Terrace at Mézy* [BW 250], 1890
Stamped lower right: *Berthe Morisot*
Oil on canvas
53 x 65 cm (20⅞ x 25⁹⁄₁₆ in.)
Private collection, Washington, D.C.

85 *Path in the Garden at Mézy* [BW 570], 1891
Stamped lower right: *Berthe Morisot* and, underneath, *B.M.*
Pastel on paper
60.1 x 45.1 cm (23⅝ x 17¾ in.)
Private collection

86 *Sunflowers,* c. 1891
Stamped lower left: *B.M.*
Colored pencil on paper
27.3 x 19.1 cm (10¾ x 7½ in.)
Mr. and Mrs. Richard A. Hess

87 *Pears* [BW 577], 1891
Signed lower left: *Berthe Morisot*
Pastel on paper
42 x 48 cm (16½ x 18⅞ in.)
Private collection, Courtesy of Galerie Hopkins and Thomas, Paris

88 *The Little Flute Players (Julie Manet and Jeanne Gobillard)*
[BW 256], 1891
Unsigned
Oil on canvas
56 x 87 cm (22 x 34¼ in.)
Josefowitz Collection

89 *The Cherry Tree* [BW 276], 1891–92
Unsigned
Oil on canvas
136 x 89 cm (53⁹⁄₁₆ x 35¹⁄₁₆ in.)
Private collection

90 ***Study for "The Cherry Tree"*** [BW 573], 1891
Unsigned
Pastel on paper
45.7 x 48.9 cm (18 x 19¼ in.)
The Reader's Digest Association, Inc.

91 ***Girl Picking Cherries,*** 1891
Stamped lower right: *Berthe Morisot*
Red chalk on paper
74.3 x 50.8 cm (29¼ x 20 in.)
From the Collection of Mr. and Mrs. Paul Mellon, Upperville, Virginia

92 ***Young Woman Gathering Cherries,*** 1891
Unsigned
Red chalk on paper
55.8 x 43.1 cm (22 x 17 in.)
Collection of John C. Whitehead

93 ***Study for "The Haymaker,"*** 1891
Stamped lower right: *B.M.*
Pencil on paper
29 x 21.2 cm (11⅜ x 8⅜ in.)
M. and Mme Bernard Foray-Roux

94 ***Young Girl Writing*** [BW 267], 1891
Stamped lower right: *Berthe Morisot*
Oil on canvas
57.7 x 46 cm (22¹¹⁄₁₆ x 18⅛ in.)
Private collection, New York

95 ***Girls at a Window*** [BW 298], 1892
Stamped lower right: *Berthe Morisot*
Oil on canvas
65 x 49 cm (25⁹⁄₁₆ x 19¼ in.)
Courtesy of Galerie Hopkins and Thomas, Paris

96 ***Young Girl Reclining*** [BW 340], 1893
Stamped lower left: *Berthe Morisot*
Oil on canvas
65 x 81 cm (25⅝ x 31⅞ in.)
Private collection, New York

97 ***Girl with a Greyhound (Julie Manet)*** [BW 335], 1893
Unsigned
Oil on canvas
73 x 80 cm (28¾ x 31½ in.)
Musée Marmottan, Paris

98 ***Mallarmé's Sailboat*** [BW 345], 1893
Stamped lower left: *Berthe Morisot*
Oil on canvas
28.4 x 34.9 cm (11³⁄₁₆ x 13¾ in.)
Mr. and Mrs. Palmer Stearns

99 ***Julie Daydreaming*** [BW 374], 1894
Unsigned
Oil on canvas
70 x 60 cm (27½ x 23⅝ in.)
Private collection

100 ***Julie Playing the Violin*** [BW 354], 1894
Signed lower left: *Berthe Morisot*
Oil on canvas
65 x 54 cm (25⅝ x 20¼ in.)
Mr. Hermann Mayer

101 ***Portrait of Jeanne Pontillon*** [BW 338], 1894
Stamped lower right: *Berthe Morisot*
Oil on canvas
116 x 81 cm (45⅝ x 31⅞ in.)
Private collection, Switzerland

102 ***The Children of Gabriel Thomas*** [BW 367], 1894
Unsigned
Oil on canvas
100 x 80 cm (39⁵⁄₁₆ x 31½ in.)
Musée d'Orsay, Paris

103 ***The Coiffure*** [BW 361], 1894
Unsigned
Oil on canvas
55 x 46 cm (21⅝ x 18⅛ in.)
Museo Nacional de Bellas Artes, Buenos Aires

104 ***Seated Model*** [BW 830], 1894
Stamped lower right: *B.M.*
Watercolor and pencil on paper
23.1 x 16.8 cm (19⅛ x 6⅝ in.)
Philadelphia Museum of Art: The Louis E. Stern Collection

Index

Page numbers in *italics* refer to illustrations

Photograph Credits and Copyrights